Putting It Together

Putting It Together

How Stephen Sondheim and I Created *Sunday in the Park with George*

James Lapine

Farrar, Straus and Giroux | New York

Farrar, Straus and Giroux
120 Broadway, New York 10271

Illustration credits can be found on pages 387–390.

Library of Congress Cataloging-in-Publication Data
Names: Lapine, James, author.
Title: Putting it together : how Stephen Sondheim and I created "Sunday in the park
  with George" / James Lapine.
Description: First edition. | New York : Farrar, Straus and Giroux, 2021.
Identifiers: LCCN 2021008688 | ISBN 9780374200091 (hardcover)
Subjects: LCSH: Sondheim, Stephen. Sunday in the park with George. | Lapine, James.
  Sunday in the park with George. | Musicals—Production and direction—New York
  (State)—New York.
Classification: LCC ML410.S6872 L36 2021 | DDC 792.6/42—dc23
LC record available at https://lccn.loc.gov/2021008688

Designed by Gretchen Achilles

Our books may be purchased in bulk for promotional, educational, or business use.
Please contact your local bookseller or the Macmillan Corporate and Premium Sales Department
at 1-800-221-7945, extension 5442, or by email at MacmillanSpecialMarkets@macmillan.com.

www.fsgbooks.com
www.twitter.com/fsgbooks • www.facebook.com/fsgbooks

1   3   5   7   9   10   8   6   4   2

for Georges Seurat (1859–1891)

The art of making art
Is putting it together
Bit by bit . . .

—STEPHEN SONDHEIM

Contents

Prelude

I was sitting in the Hudson Theatre in 2017, watching a Broadway revival of *Sunday in the Park with George*, a musical for which Stephen Sondheim wrote the music and lyrics and I wrote the book. It was in fact the second Broadway revival of the show since its opening more than thirty-five years ago. Generally, when I watch any show of mine that I have not directed, my viewing is accompanied by an inner monologue critiquing the production: Why are they doing that? Don't they know this scene is about such and such? Did anyone read the stage directions? But this was opening night and I had already seen this production in previews. I was by and large pleased and found myself drinking a beer and sitting back to just watch the show with my critical switch in "off" mode.

After about twenty minutes or so, a voice came in my head: Who wrote this peculiar musical? Who were Sondheim and I in 1982, when we embarked on this project? And why are some people so passionately in love with *Sunday in the Park with George*, and others not so much? Was the show speaking to me this night, this moment, in a way that I had never before heard it? A reminder of my youthful creativity—the ability I had to access my imagination without the self-censorship and doubt that come with age? Or had I maybe just had one too many beers?

Writing *Sunday in the Park with George* changed my life, and I would venture to say it changed Sondheim's as well. It certainly was a different experience for him, after collaborating with Hal Prince on seven Broadway shows.

Working with Sondheim was a dream come true. On the other hand, my memories of directing the production remain complicated and occasionally painful. At least, that's the feeling I have carried with me all these years.

This book was born that night, as I sat in the Hudson Theatre. It revisits the two-year period from 1982 to 1984, when Sondheim and I came together to tell the story of a two-year artistic struggle one hundred years earlier: that of the French painter Georges Seurat as he created his masterpiece, *Un dimanche après-midi à l'Île de la Grande Jatte* (*A Sunday Afternoon on the Island of La Grande Jatte*, sometimes titled *A Sunday on La Grande Jatte—1884*).

I have interviewed some forty people who worked with us on the show. Actually, they were as much conversations as interviews, and I invited everyone I spoke with to please ask me questions as well. I was reminded that memory is uniquely personal and, as time passes, the facts of an event are often rewritten to reflect the teller and the stories he or she chooses to hold true. Sometimes emotional recall wins the day over fact. I am not the same person, the same writer, the same director I was then, and many of the people I spoke to are quick to make a similar point about themselves. Surprising to me was the one thing almost all of us shared: that creating this musical about making a work of art was a unique moment for all of us, and in some cases a defining one.

This book, then, is a mixed salad: one part memoir, one part oral history, one part "how a musical gets written and produced." For those of you who don't know the show, or don't remember it well, the text is reproduced at the back of the book.

Another reason I decided to write this: it would have been so helpful to me as both writer and director to have had a book like this to read in 1982, before I embarked on my first Broadway show.

JL

Dramatis Personae

(For reference, listed in alphabetical order. **Boldface** *indicates individuals who have been interviewed and are quoted in the book.)*

AUTHORS

Lapine, James..Book and direction
Sondheim, Stephen..Music and lyrics

PRODUCERS

Azenberg, Emanuel..Producer and General Manager
Bishop, André..Artistic Director (Playwrights Horizons)
Jacobs, Bernard*...President of the Shubert Organization
Schoenfeld, Gerald*..Chairman of the Shubert Organization
Smith, Philip*..General Manager of the Shubert Organization; now Chairman
Weitzman, Ira...Program Director (Playwrights Horizons)

CAST

Baranski, Christine..Clarissa [later renamed Yvonne] (Playwrights Horizons)
Bryne, Barbara...Old Lady; Blair Daniels, an art critic

D'Arcy, Mary..Celeste #2; Elaine

Ferland, Danielle..Louise, the daughter of Jules and Yvonne

Grammer, Kelsey..Young Man; Soldier; Alex Savage (Playwrights Horizons)

Ivey, Dana..Yvonne, Jules's wife; Naomi Eisen, a composer

Kimbrough, Charles..Jules, another artist; Bob Greenberg, the museum director

Mastrantonio, Mary Elizabeth..........................Celeste #2 (Playwrights Horizons)

Opel, Nancy...Frieda, a cook; Betty, an artist

Parry, William..Boatman; Charles Redmond

Patinkin, Mandy...George

Peters, Bernadette..Dot; Marie, George's grandmother

Spiner, Brent..Franz, a servant; Dennis, a technician

Vaughan, Melanie...Celeste #1; Waitress

Westenberg, Robert..Soldier; Alex, an artist

Byers, Ralph...Jules (Playwrights Horizons)

Gershenson, Sue Anne......................................Woman with baby carriage; Photographer

Groenendaal, Cris...Louis, a baker; Billy Webster, Harriet's friend

Jellison, John..Man with bicycle; Museum Assistant

Kane, Bradley...Boy (Playwrights Horizons)

Knudson, Kurt*..Mr. Lee Randolph, the museum's publicist

Marcum, Kevin...Louis, a baker; later Jules (Playwrights Horizons)

Mathews, Carmen*...Old Lady (Playwrights Horizons)

Moore, Judith*...Nurse; Harriet Pawling

DESIGN TEAM

Ferren, Bran...Special Effects

Hould-Ward, Ann...Costume Design
Lehrer, Scott..Sound Design (Playwrights
                                           Horizons)
Morse, Tom...Sound Design
Nelson, Richard*..Lighting Design
Straiges, Tony...Scenic Design
Zipprodt, Patricia*...Costume Design

MUSIC TEAM

Ford, Paul...Piano
Gemignani, Paul..Musical Director
Sperling, Ted..Synthesizer
Starobin, Michael...Orchestrator

DIRECTION

Murray, Johnna...Associate to James Lapine
Zinn, Randolyn...Movement Director

STAGE MANAGEMENT

Blackwell, Charles*...Production Stage Manager
Orner, Fredric H. ....Stage Manager
Robertson, Loretta..Stage Manager

CASTING

Lyons, John...Casting Director

MISCELLANEOUS

Breglio, John...Mr. Sondheim's lawyer
Douglas, Sarah..Associate of Flora Roberts,
                                           Mr. Sondheim's agent
Graham, Stephen...Producer
Grody, Kathryn...Wife of Mandy Patinkin
Lane, George...Mr. Lapine's agent
Nathan, Fred*..Press Representative
Verlizzo, Frank..Artwork

*Deceased

From Ohio to Sondheim

Mansfield, Ohio

1961

I am an accident of the theater.

The first Broadway show I saw was Bye Bye Birdie. *The lyricist of that show, Lee Adams, happens to have come from my hometown, Mansfield, Ohio. I was eleven and it was my first visit to New York City. We traveled on an overnight train and stayed at the Hotel Astor in Times Square, in a room that overlooked the smoking Camel sign. Pretty heady stuff. The day after we arrived, we went to a matinee of the show. Mind you, we didn't know Lee Adams or his family, but as far as we were concerned, after Johnny Appleseed (who had lived briefly in our town), he was the most famous person to have emerged from Mansfield.*

After the show, I stood amid a large crowd at the stage door to get a souvenir program signed for my cousin Janis. I'd promised. There was a great rush toward Dick Van Dyke when he emerged from the theater. In what I would characterize now as a bit of New York City moxie, I wormed my way through the assembled throng and got to the long railing that separated fans from stars. Worried that I would miss my chance, as Mr. Van Dyke finally moved along and came closer to our section, I stepped on the bottom of the railing and shoved the souvenir program in his direction. Contact was made, but not quite how I had intended. I struck him in the nose, causing a minor paper cut on that famous proboscis. He stared at me for a mo-

ment, grabbed the program from my hands, hastily signed it, then shoved it back and quickly moved away as he dabbed his nose. The people around me were not happy, but my cousin Janis was ecstatic when I brought that autograph back to Mansfield.

As much as I enjoyed the show, I didn't return home with any dreams of a life in the theater. (That trip did, however, make me fall in love with New York City, and luckily enough, a couple of years thereafter, my father took a job in New York and we moved to nearby Connecticut.)

My only foray onstage in Mansfield was playing Jack, of beanstalk fame, with the children's summer theater group in the local park. Mind you, I had no memory of this until I had written Into the Woods and someone from Mansfield sent me this clipping:

PRINCIPALS IN DRAMA—Barbara Miefert, as the Rainy Day Pixie in the cast of "Jack and the Giant," presented by the Mansfield Children's Theatre in South Park last night and again tonight, has an audience as she steps from an attic trunk. Left is Tom Huffman, the Giant, with Jean Lisle, who played the part of Jack's mother in the Thursday night show, and Jamie Lapine, who has the other title role, at right. John Miefert, the stage manager, checks his property list as he stands behind the trunk. (Photo by Ed Byers)

In high school I also performed in Neil Simon's Come Blow Your Horn and Meredith Willson's The Music Man. My talents as an actor were limited, though I enjoyed the camaraderie that came with putting on a show. That pretty much was the sum total of my experiences in the theater until I was twenty-eight years old.

I majored in history at college. My junior year I became friends with a fellow student, Phillip Blumberg, who was passionate about the theater. He was from the Bronx and he knew a great deal about the downtown avant-garde scene in New York. The first "experimental" show he took me to was titled Commune, by The Performance Group. As I recall, the show had something to do with communal life and the Charles Manson murders. It was performed in a loft and we had to take our *shoes off before entering. The seating was on the floor and the actors interacted with the audience—a new experience for me. What I remember most about the evening was that at the end of the play, the actors took all the shoes that we the audience had taken off at the entryway and dumped them in the middle of the performance space, making us sift through this smelly pile of shoes so we could go home.*

In my senior year, I took a photography course and fell in love with the camera. As it was the Vietnam era and I was in no mood to be drafted, I decided to go to graduate school to study photography and design. After that, I moved to New York City with the intention of being a fine-art photographer, my idols being Robert Frank, Garry Winogrand, and Lee Friedlander. To support myself, I worked as a waiter, a page at NBC, and an assistant at the Architectural League of New York, while landing the occasional photojournalist or graphic design gig.

New Haven

1975

Phillip Blumberg, my friend from college, was in the graduate program at the Yale School of Drama, and through his introduction I was able to get a freelance job designing the magazine yale/theatre, *which was edited by the graduate students in dramaturgy. I lived in New York—and prided myself on being a downtown guy, taking up residence in SoHo and then Tribeca well before those neighborhoods became gentrified and hip. My exposure to the theater mostly revolved around the world of Richard Foreman, Robert Wilson, Meredith Monk, and other noncommercial and avant-garde practitioners of the day.*

Robert Brustein, the dean of the school, liked my work on the magazine and the following year offered me a full-time position designing posters and advertising materials for the Yale Repertory Theatre. To fill out the job, I taught an advertising design course to the students studying theater administration. Living and working in New Haven became an immersive experience in the theater.

During the month of January, Brustein had instituted a period in which everyone involved in the school—students and teachers alike—would engage in an area of theater that was outside their particular arena of study or expertise. Playwrights built sets, designers acted, actors wrote plays, etc. My students were aware that my tastes tilted more toward nontraditional theater and encouraged me to direct some-

thing. I had fantasized about directing a film one day, knowing that the director Stanley Kubrick began his career as a photographer for Look magazine and the director Robert Benton was once the art director for Esquire. I figured this might be an opportunity to try my hand at working with actors, so I agreed to do so if they could find me a suitable project to tackle. One of the students found an abstract poem/play by Gertrude Stein called Photograph, which was five acts long and only three pages in length. This seemed like a good choice, as it gave me free rein to use photographic images to fill out the storytelling, such as it was. We assembled a group of non-actors and presented the play as a kind of "theme and variations," repeating the text in a half dozen or so different visual scenarios. One of the images I used as inspiration was one of my favorite Seurat paintings, A Sunday Afternoon on the Island of La Grande Jatte. The program was a small paper bag with a photo of Stein on it. Inside were a series of "baseball cards" with images related to the production; information about the cast; and the entire text of the play in case anyone wanted to follow along. Also, shelled peanuts if anyone got hungry. (A nod to Jimmy Carter.)

The production got a lovely review in the New Haven Register. Jennifer Hershey, the student who produced the show, suggested we do it in New York City. She found a theater in a loft in SoHo, and the owner agreed to present the work if we could provide the financing. A close friend of mine, Roberta Bernstein, who was writing her doctoral dissertation at Columbia on the artist Jasper Johns, informed me that Johns was a great fan of Gertrude Stein. At her suggestion, I wrote him a letter about the project and told him we were looking for funding. Lo and behold,

Scene from Photograph inspired by the Seurat painting. Our production was mounted on a shoestring. To suggest pointillism, our designer, the artist Maureen Connor, made these costumes from free paint-sample charts she collected from hardware stores; she also made bibs and aprons in which were sewn colored crayons and chalk.

through the Foundation for Contemporary Arts, an organization Johns had founded with John Cage and Robert Rauschenberg, I was given twenty-five hundred dollars to mount the play.

The production was truly from the "Mickey and Judy" playbook: "Hey, my uncle has a barn. Let's put on a show!" We actually cast it by putting up "actors wanted" signs around SoHo. Our company included my yoga teacher from Yale, a dancer friend, the cashier from SoHo Natural Foods, and a ten-year-old girl who was the daughter of a friend.

Another friend of mine who worked in the art world asked how she might be of some help. I casually mentioned that it would be nice if we could get someone in to review the show. With no idea of the protocol involved in such matters, she simply picked up the phone and called the chief critic of The New York Times, *Richard Eder, and sweet-talked him into coming. As I recall, he attended the show with his young son and we were rewarded with a rave review. Only two years after landing the design position at Yale, I somehow won an Obie Award for directing. Go figure.*

Next

1977

Shortly after my New York directing debut, Mary Silverman and Lyn Austin of the Music-Theater Group approached me about creating a new piece for them. I had been fascinated with a Jungian case history of a ten-year-old girl who had a series of dreams that foreshadowed her death. Jung used this study to bolster his theory of the collective unconscious—ancestral memory. That first incarnation, called Twelve Dreams, *was more of a performance-art piece than a play, but it whetted my appetite to write. I had caught the theater bug and wondered if it would be possible to actually make a living in that world. By this point I had left Yale and was teaching design at the Fashion Institute of Technology. It was a job I was truly unqualified for, but the pay was far better than at Yale and it allowed me to move back to New York City.*

Around this time, my friend the playwright Wendy Wasserstein had suggested to Edward Kleban, the lyricist of A Chorus Line, *that he meet with me to discuss a project he was developing. I was contacted by his agent, Flora Roberts, and went to meet with her. Flora was a plump woman of a certain age with a gravelly voice and a warm demeanor. I would learn later that she had once been a nightclub singer and was now one of the most important agents in the theater. It seems that Kleban had a series of songs that had been inspired by works of art, and was looking to put* together a musical revue he called Gallery. He had approached Mike Nichols to work on the project, but Nichols wasn't interested. Nichols's associate Luis Sanjurjo, whom I had met socially, had suggested me because he'd read of my Gertrude Stein piece. Flora was scoping out my interest and at the same time letting me know this was not an offer. I said I understood and shortly thereafter met Kleban.

Ed was an eccentric fellow. He had no idea what to do with these songs, which he had been writing for twelve years. I listened to them and free-associated a series of drawings—a storyboard, really—to try to give them some kind of context. We met a couple more times, and then, one odd afternoon when I showed up for a meeting, Ed decided to take me apartment hunting instead of working. Eventually, Flora Roberts summoned me back to her office and told me that Ed didn't want to continue with me. I was paid a thousand dollars for "consulting services" and that was that.

1978

I was given a monthlong summer residency at the Millay Colony, an artist's retreat on the grounds of the poet Edna St. Vincent Millay's home in Austerlitz, New York. Five of us were housed and fed and, on the occasional night, regaled with poetry recitations by Millay's wonderful eighty-four-year-old sister, Norma.

With commerce in mind, I decided to see if I could write a play that would provide me some income. I called it Table Settings. The action revolved around a dining table and chairs and involved three generations of a neurotic and tortured Jewish family. It didn't have much of a plot—it was a one-act made up of impressionistic short scenes and monologues. Think Neil Simon, only very stoned and very off-Broadway. André Bishop, who was running the nonprofit theater Playwrights Horizons—housed in a funky former porn house on Forty-second Street west of Ninth Avenue—gave the play a workshop production in its ninety-seat upstairs theater. After a mixed-positive review from Mr. Eder, a young fledgling producer, Joan Stein, approached me about mounting the show commercially. Around the same time, the aforementioned Luis Sanjurjo saw the show and shared the script with Stephen Graham, who was working for Mike Nichols's partner, Lewis Allen. Stephen had studied briefly at the Yale School of Drama when I was working there, so I knew of him. I introduced Luis and Stephen to Joan Stein and they immediately hit it off. They optioned the play and shortly thereafter produced it on a commercial *contract, renting the main stage of Playwrights Horizons.* As it happened, the same day* Table Settings *opened in 1979 I was fired from my teaching job at the Fashion Institute. Fortunately, the play was generally well received and provided me a very modest living for a year and a half. Theater was suddenly looking like a viable career opportunity.*

STEPHEN GRAHAM

LAPINE: What was your impression of me when we met about *Table Settings*? We really didn't know each other.

GRAHAM: You didn't seem very much like a director.

LAPINE: By that you mean—

GRAHAM: You seemed like a regular person.

LAPINE: What's a director usually like?

GRAHAM: Well, when I thought of a director, I thought of someone like the director in the 1930s version of *A Star Is Born*, or one of those intense British directors from the National Theatre, or Mike Nichols, who was very razzle-dazzle.

LAPINE: Yeah, I didn't fit into any of those categories. We had a lot of fun doing *Table Settings*. Did we talk about another project right away?

GRAHAM: Not immediately. I think we both went off to other projects.

After Table Settings *I got to know the composer-lyricist William Finn at Playwrights Horizons, as I had designed the album cover for his show* In Trousers. *When Finn saw* Table Settings, *he thought it was directed like a musical and approached me about directing his next piece. Under André Bishop's guidance, we were given the opportunity to work together on a show that came to be known as* March of the Falsettos. *We were given the upstairs theater for four weeks' rehearsal, and*

---

* The union Actors' Equity has basically two kinds of contracts for its members: nonprofit and commercial. The nonprofit contract is for a limited run by a sanctioned institutional theater and its weekly salary is based on the number of seats that the theater has. A commercial show is independently financed and has a minimum contract salary set for actors, again based on the theater's capacity and whether it is a Broadway or an off-Broadway venture, but actors and their agents can negotiate for higher salaries and terms of employment. It is the job of the producing team to raise money for the production, book a theater, and negotiate fees for the creative team with the intent to make a profit for their investors and themselves.

with a few songs already written, Bill and I created the show and opened it to the public. It was enthusiastically received and followed Table Settings *in a commercial run in the downstairs theater. Gail Merrifield Papp, who was head of play development at the Public Theater (and also the wife of its founder, Joseph Papp), came to see the show and set up a meeting for me to meet with Joe. He asked me if I had anything I would like to do at the Public Theater and I gave him a recent draft of* Twelve Dreams, *which he produced later that year. I think by this point I knew that I was not going back to being a graphic designer.*

GRAHAM: A year or two later you came to me with the Nathanael West story.

LAPINE: *A Cool Million.* I thought it might be a musical.

GRAHAM: I remember you gave me the book. I read it and thought, Oh, it's interesting.

LAPINE: I went out to L.A. to meet Randy Newman about writing the music for it. He read it and said it was too dark for him, which is pretty funny coming from Randy Newman.

GRAHAM: That is pretty funny. You mentioned Joni Mitchell as somebody that you would like to work with in theory, but I didn't have Joni Mitchell's phone number.

LAPINE: No, we never got to Joni. Like that was ever going to happen. So, you were talking with Lewis Allen about the project. He was the one who suggested Stephen Sondheim and called him to see if he wanted to meet about the show. Unbeknownst to us, Sondheim had seen some of my work and wanted to meet me.

Stephen Sondheim

The Introduction:
June 12, 1982

Stephen Sondheim was already a legend in the theater when I met him. He had been a protégé of Oscar Hammerstein, whom he had known since he was ten. By the age of twenty-seven he had written the lyrics for West Side Story, *and soon thereafter the lyrics for* Gypsy. *By the time of our first meeting, Sondheim's Broadway credits also included* A Funny Thing Happened on the Way to the Forum, Anyone Can Whistle, Do I Hear a Waltz?, Company, Follies, A Little Night Music, Pacific Overtures, Sweeney Todd, *and* Merrily We Roll Along. *He'd won five Tony Awards.*

I made my way to Sondheim's on a sunny Saturday afternoon in the middle of a huge antinuclear march that seemed to have taken over the city. Many streets were closed and the sidewalks were teeming with people. Getting to his Turtle Bay townhouse on time proved to be something of a challenge, and not wanting to be late, I sprinted half the way there. Breathless and nervous, I rang the doorbell. After a few moments Sondheim opened the door and ushered me in as we exchanged hellos. The entryway led almost directly to a long, dark living room; the one small window at the back of the room was stained glass and let in very little light. The walls were lined with fascinating antique puzzles and games. Two couches faced each other, separated by a large oblong table where small candles burned.

(opposite)
Stephen Sondheim

LAPINE: Do you remember the first day we met?

SONDHEIM: In person, no—I know the first day I was exposed to your work.

LAPINE: Was that *Table Settings* or *Twelve Dreams*?

SONDHEIM: I think it was *Twelve Dreams*. That was certainly the play that made me want to work with you.

LAPINE: So we were introduced by—

SONDHEIM: Lewis Allen.

LAPINE: Right. Now, at this point in time I had written and directed two plays, and directed one musical: *March of the Falsettos*. I was about to direct my first Shakespeare that summer. I didn't know that much about musical theater, but I certainly knew you were a person of renown. I'm embarrassed to say it even now—before we met I'd only seen one show of yours: *Sweeney Todd*. I loved it so much I saw it three times.

SONDHEIM: I must tell you, I never thought of myself as a person of renown.

LAPINE: Well, that's probably one of the reasons why we got along so well. I arrived at the appointed hour—5:00 p.m.—and you opened the door and we came into this room where we are now chatting. After a few niceties were exchanged, you lit a joint and passed it to me. You didn't ask if I wanted any. You must have known from my play *Table Settings* that I liked marijuana, so—

SONDHEIM: I just figured that anybody of your generation smoked dope all the time, which was true.

LAPINE: I loved that you did that. I was actually very nervous coming to meet you; the minute I came in here, you put me right at ease. And somehow the dope put us both on the same plane. We discussed *A Cool Million*. We were in such different places in our lives. I was almost twenty years younger than you. I had experienced a lot of good fortune in my few off-Broadway theatrical outings and you were coming off *Merrily We Roll Along*, which had closed on Broadway prematurely a few months prior. You were in a pretty dark place.

SONDHEIM: Well, yes. That was a bad time. The reception of *Merrily* really shook me, because there was so much anger and, I think, hatred toward the show in so-called Broadway circles. They just resented Hal Prince and me so much—our partnership and success—they couldn't wait to shoot us down. I thought, I don't want to be in this profession; it's just too hostile and mean-spirited. So, yes, I was really thinking, What else can I do? I thought, I'd love to invent games, video games; and that was what I really wanted to do. But then I saw *Twelve Dreams* . . .

LAPINE: Really? I didn't know that. What I do remember was we must have chatted for at least a couple of hours. We didn't move. And it was exhilarating.

SONDHEIM: Well, one of the things we talked about was how I'm very ill read. I don't read very much, but I had read *A Cool Million* a long time ago.

LAPINE: Yes, you mentioned that and said you would reread it and get back to me.

SONDHEIM: And when I read it—I had forgotten the story is basically the same as *Candide*, a musical I had already worked on.

LAPINE: Right. One thing I remember very clearly about that day: About an hour into our conversation the doorbell rang. You got up and went to the door. I heard you raise your voice louder and louder and finally you slammed the door shut. I'm sitting in the other room thinking, What the hell is going on out there? You came back fuming. I asked if everything was okay and you told me it was a complete stranger who wanted to meet you. I guess this was not the first time this had happened. I was thinking to myself, Whoa, that's crazy.

SONDHEIM: Yes. It didn't happen that often, but it happened enough times.

LAPINE: I'll tell you just how naïve I was then. I remember you were talking about Broadway, and how you never had a very long-running show; and I think we discussed some shows that were currently having long runs—we talked a lot about what shows we liked and didn't like. I naïvely said to you: "Well, I'm sure if you wanted to dream up an idea that would lend itself to becoming a long-running show, you could do that." You narrowed your eyes and looked at me and sharply replied: "I would *never* do that!" I was so embarrassed.

SONDHEIM: No, you shouldn't have been embarrassed.

LAPINE: Well, in retrospect it's kind of funny—and really, I thought that was so fantastic when you said, "I'd never do that." You were right, of course. It's not how you think. Many years later you once said to me, "I always believe my shows are going to be successful." I was taken aback and asked why. You answered, "Their subjects are always so interesting to me, I assume they would be interesting to others as well."

SONDHEIM: You reminded me that how we got to know each other was by comparing our tastes, both in movies and plays. We found that we pretty much agreed on most things.

LAPINE: I brought up that I had recently seen Buñuel's *Exterminating Angel*. You brought up your affection for his *Discreet Charm of the Bourgeoisie*, which I was not familiar with.

Our conversation flowed freely. Eventually Sondheim said he had an engagement that evening and that he would get back to me after looking at A Cool Million. *I went out into the night a very happy fellow—and a very high one. I don't remember telling anyone about my Sondheim meeting other than Stephen Graham and Lewis Allen. Part of me thought nothing would come of it—my method of mitigating possible disappointment and rejection.*

Sondheim got back to me after a week or so and said he was not interested in doing A Cool Million *but would be happy to discuss the possibility of another project. I brought up Buñuel's* Discreet Charm . . . *and said that I would love to see it with him. I asked Stephen Graham if he would arrange a screening, which he did at his apartment two weeks later.*

STEPHEN GRAHAM

GRAHAM: I had not met Sondheim prior to screening the movie.

LAPINE: Did you have any impression of him?

GRAHAM: I was kind of in awe. Like with Mike Nichols, he was one of those people in whose company you think, Oh, I hope I don't say something really stupid.

LAPINE: Did we discuss the movie after we saw it?

GRAHAM: I honestly don't remember much. It was over thirty years ago. I don't think there was any indication after we watched the movie that this was something you two were going to pursue.

That summer I was directing A Midsummer Night's Dream *at the Delacorte Theater in Central Park. This had originally been scheduled for the following season, in the small Martinson Hall space at the Public Theater, but at the last minute another project fell through for the park and Joe Papp asked me to do* Midsummer *there. I had never directed a Shakespeare play—in fact, I had never really directed a play other than the two I had written. I was ill prepared to tackle this, but there was no way you said no to Joe Papp. Steve and I agreed to pick up our conversation in August, after* Midsummer *opened.*

STEPHEN SONDHEIM

LAPINE: When we first met, I was about to direct *A Midsummer Night's Dream.*

SONDHEIM: Yes, in the park, with William Hurt. It was a magical production.

LAPINE: Well, you're kind—

SONDHEIM: I'm not kind. What you did with the set—making it look like an extension of the park. All the tricks and surprises—come on. It was great.

LAPINE: Well, I got panned in *The New York Times.*

SONDHEIM: Oh. Well, I knew I was right. *(laughter)*

LAPINE: That was a first for me. It's funny, because I went home after reading that review, and I thought, Oh, Stephen Sondheim's never going to work with me now. I thought, Why would he?

SONDHEIM: Gee, thanks. You had a lot of faith in my character.

LAPINE: No. I think I lost faith in myself after that project. The day after the review came out, the phone rings at my place as I'm licking my wounds. It was you, inviting me to come over to look at *your* bad reviews.

SONDHEIM: Yes. I'm so used to it. I got terrible reviews.

LAPINE: I didn't know that. I somehow thought you had always gotten raves.

SONDHEIM: On everything? I was dismissed, ignored. The first time I ever got a good review I was forty years old, on my sixth show, *Company*. It's the first time I ever got a rave—well, it was not in *The New York Times*, because they panned it; but I got some good reviews outside the *Times*.

LAPINE: It kind of made me love you—that you called the day that my review came out. It also taught me what it means to be a good colleague.

SONDHEIM: The work is the work.

LAPINE: Yes. That's a hard one to learn: to put criticism into perspective. And by the way, you did actually show me your bad reviews.

SONDHEIM: Yes, I kept scrapbooks.

LAPINE: I was shocked when I read some of them. I couldn't believe it. But of course, you've gotten the last laugh.

September 8, 1982

STEPHEN SONDHEIM

SONDHEIM: For our next meeting, you came over and brought a number of images for us to look at.

LAPINE: It was in the late afternoon one weekend. I was excited you wanted to continue our conversation.

SONDHEIM: I thought, This guy is so avant-garde. The way you find a musical idea is, you pick a book up; you read the book; you say, that would make a good musical; you get a producer; he buys it; and then you write it. The idea of coming in with a lot of disparate photographs and throwing them on the floor and saying, "Does any of this strike your fancy?"—I thought, I'm the wrong generation for this guy; I'm just the wrong generation. I'm so traditional.

LAPINE: I like what you wrote in your book *Look, I Made a Hat*. You said that your mind went to movies and plays for adaptation, and I talked more about ideas and images; but that's what made ours an interesting collaboration.

SONDHEIM: Yes. But it also has to do with, again, the generation difference. The idea of taking images and gradually forming them into a work— that was completely new to me. I'm sure you weren't the only person

Georges Seurat, *A Sunday Afternoon on the Island of La Grande Jatte*, or *A Sunday on La Grande Jatte—1884*, 1884–1886 (The Art Institute of Chicago / Art Resource, NY)

doing it, because your whole generation did that kind of what we call nontraditional work, which is images and concatenations of things.

LAPINE: You're forgetting that you did mention when we first met that you liked the idea of "theme and variation."

SONDHEIM: Oh, yes, because I'd always wanted to do a theme-and-variation show.

LAPINE: As you may remember, the first thing I did in the theater was the Gertrude Stein piece, which was essentially a theme-and-variation work. I told you about it and you showed me this French book on the *Mona Lisa*—

SONDHEIM: Oh, yes, yes. It was a magazine called *Bizarre*.

LAPINE: So that's one of the reasons I brought the images to show you; thinking, Well, maybe we'll connect to something visually. We looked at the random images and we kind of chatted about each one. The last image I showed you was Seurat's *Sunday Afternoon on the Island of La Grande Jatte*. I brought a postcard of it, and we started riffing on it. You immediately said, "Oh, it looks like a stage set," and then we just started going on from there.

SONDHEIM: Why are fifty people not looking at each other?

LAPINE: I pointed out how the proportions were out of whack, the child in the center of the image, the man in the foreground, and what's the monkey doing there? This painting was one of the images that I used in the Gertrude Stein piece.

SONDHEIM: Right. That's why you brought it.

LAPINE: You were intrigued.

SONDHEIM: And as we were talking, you said the magical thing. You said, "The main character is missing." I said, "Who?" And you said, "The artist." Boing! All the lights went on. It's Mrs. Lovett getting the idea of killing everybody. I just thought, Yes, yes, that's it. That was the beginning of the race—a great moment.

LAPINE: The key thing for me was that our time together was fun—our ideas bouncing off one another. Remembering that *Sweeney* was the only show of yours I was really familiar with, before I left on this visit you gave me cassettes and scripts of all your shows. I left your house that night with another great buzz.

A Blank Page:
September 15, 1982

I went off and just started writing. I didn't know where I was heading; I did no research on the painting or on Seurat—I just wrote down whatever sprang into my head as I studied the image. The one thing I was sure of was that the act would end with a re-creation of the painting—a tableau vivant. *I wrote five pages or so and a week later I returned to Sondheim's to share what I had written. Remember, there was no fax machine, no Internet, no way to transmit documents. This time when I arrived at midday, I discovered there was a certain amount of activity in the house and that Steve had a small staff. It had a very different vibe than in the late afternoons when we had met prior and the place was empty.*

STEPHEN SONDHEIM

LAPINE: The next time we met I was ushered upstairs. I walked into your
    impressive study and found you reclining on your daybed.

SONDHEIM: As always, yes.

LAPINE: There was a chair opposite you and I sat. After some small talk,
    I nervously gave you the first five pages that I had written, and I sat
    there as you read them, wondering, What is he going to make of this?

You read them very slowly; and when you finished you said, "I'm going to read them again," and you did. I just sat there staring at you nervously. You finished the last page and then went back to one of the beginning pages and said, "I think there should be a song here." You pointed to the space after the lines: "More boats, more trees . . ." I'd never written a musical. I didn't know how this worked.

SONDHEIM: Well, you'd been around a musical. You knew about Bill Finn's *March of the Falsettos*.

LAPINE: Yes, but that was not a real book musical. *March of the Falsettos* was just a series of songs. We didn't even have an outline when I came into that project.

SONDHEIM: Fair enough.

LAPINE: So, you pointed out this place for a song and I asked why. You responded, "You know, this is really arty and I think you're going to need an opening number that puts the audience at ease; and I think this is a good place for one." And that's where the song "Sunday in the Park with George" ended up.

SONDHEIM: And then you went off and wrote a monologue for that song.

LAPINE: Yes. I think you asked me to jot down some ideas for what Dot might be thinking. I went off and wrote that and brought it in the next week.

5

```
                              NURSE
              What Madame?

                              LADY
                          (points off-stage)
              That!

                              DOT
              They're making way for the exposition.

                              LADY
              What exposition?

                              NURSE
              The International Exposition. They're
              going to build a tower.

                              LADY
              Another exposition ...

                              NURSE
              They say it's going to be the tallest
              structure in the world.

                              LADY
              More foreigners. I'm sick of foreigners.

                              GEORGE
              More boats.

      More boats appear.

              More trees.

      More trees descend.

                              DOT
              I'm getting tired, and the sun is
              too strong today.

                              GEORGE
              Almost finished.

                              DOT
              I'd rather be in the studio George.

                              GEORGE
              I know.

                              LADY
              They are out early today.

                              NURSE
              It's Sunday Madame.
```

[handwritten annotations: "opening arps", "Look across water", "posing? Sunday?"]

SONDHEIM: "A dribble of sweat." I thought, Dribble—I can't do dribble. I changed it to trickle. But that monologue was the song. I thought, That's a great idea for a song. Just a lady posing in the sun; and she's just feeling a little piece of sweat going down her back.

LAPINE: It did start it off for us, yes. Though it took a long time before I heard that song.

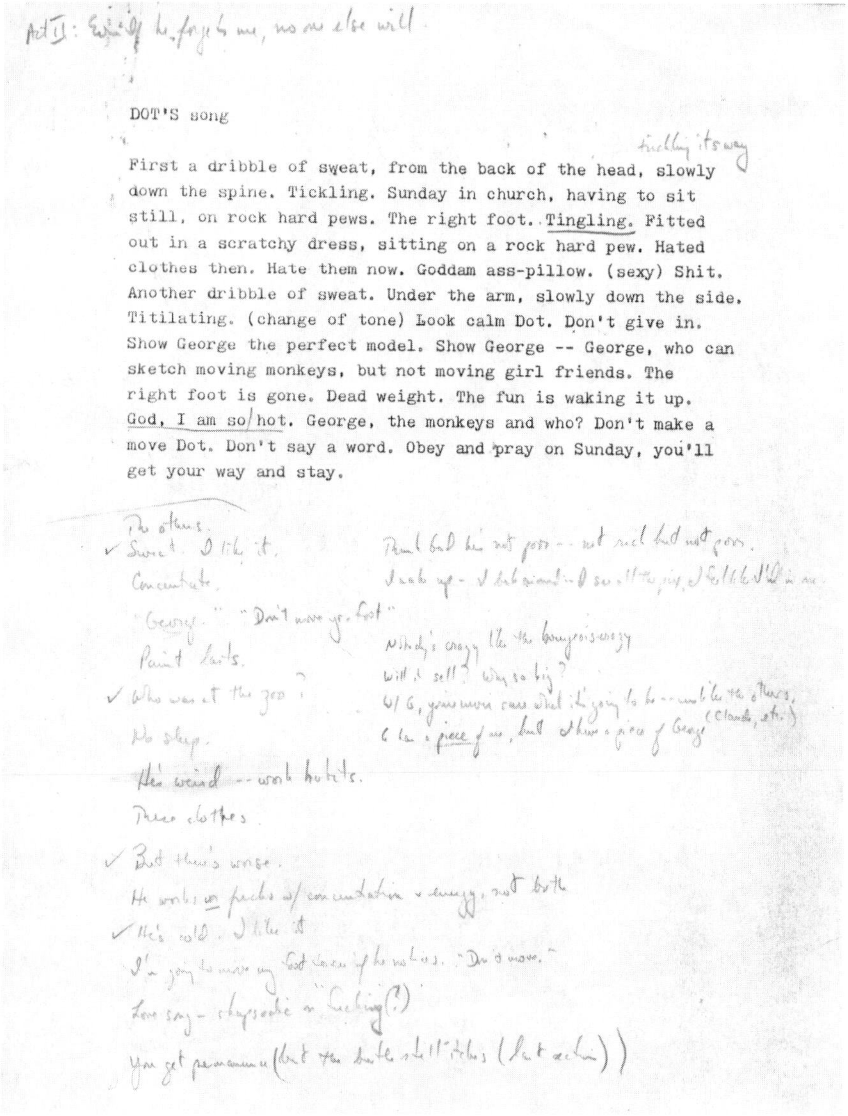

Act II: Even if he forgets me, no one else will.

DOT'S song

First a dribble of sweat, from the back of the head, slowly *tickling its way*
down the spine. Tickling. Sunday in church, having to sit
still, on rock hard pews. The right foot. Tingling. Fitted
out in a scratchy dress, sitting on a rock hard pew. Hated
clothes then. Hate them now. Goddam ass-pillow. (sexy) Shit.
Another dribble of sweat. Under the arm, slowly down the side.
Titilating. (change of tone) Look calm Dot. Don't give in.
Show George the perfect model. Show George -- George, who can
sketch moving monkeys, but not moving girl friends. The
right foot is gone. Dead weight. The fun is waking it up.
God, I am so/hot. George, the monkeys and who? Don't make a
move Dot. Don't say a word. Obey and pray on Sunday, you'll
get your way and stay.

[handwritten marginal notes, largely illegible]

We decided to meet once a week, and we did so from September 22 until October 29. I would write a few more pages each week, working in order. I still didn't do an outline. However, I did begin to do research on the painting and discovered a myriad of drawings and croquetons—a term Seurat coined for the plein air painted studies he did on cigar-box tops. These sketches became the setting of each scene as Seurat began to build his painting.

STEPHEN SONDHEIM

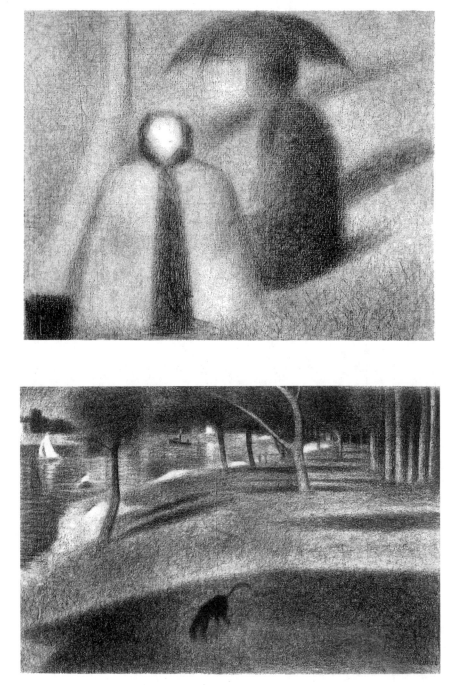

(top) Georges Seurat, *La nourrice (Nurse)*, study for *La Grande Jatte*, 1884–1885. Conté crayon on paper

(right) Georges Seurat, *Landscape with dog*: study for *La Grande Jatte*, 1884

A white stage. White floor, slightly raked and extended in
perspective. The proscenium arch continues across the bottom
as well, creating a complete frame around the stage.
An arpeggiated CHORD.
(The following might be accompanied by an overture.)

Enter GEORGE, an artist, mid-twenties. Tall, dark beard,
angular, wearing a soft felt hat with a very narrow brim
crushed down at the neck, and a short jacket. He looks
rather serious. He stands for a moment with a large drawing
pad and box of chalks under arm, staring out into the audience.
He steps forward, turns around and examines the white playing
area. He goes to the side where a rope is hanging. He unties
it and lowers from the fly space at the rear of the stage,
a backdrop of blue sky. He then goes to the stage left wing
and pulls a sliding floor unit, which when in place fills
a large area of the stage, creating a grassy-green expanse.
From the stage right wing he pulls another floor unit, which
abutting the green area, creates an expanse of water. He
then unties another rope and lowers from the fly space many
trees which spread through the playing area. GEORGE then
steps downstage center and turns to examine the stage. He
studies it for a moment. He goes to the side wall and touches
a button. The lighting bumps, giving the impression of an
early morning sunrise on the island of "La Grande Jatte" --
harsh shadows and streaming golden light through the trees.
GEORGE goes to the wings and escorts DOT towards the audience.
She is also in her twenties, wearing a traditional 19th century
outfit: large straw hat, full length dress with bustle, etc.
When he gets her downstage left, he turns her profile, then
places himself further downstage. She turns to him.

                    GEORGE
                  (annoyed)
        No. I want you to look out at the
        water.

                    DOT
        I feel foolish.

                    GEORGE
        Why?

                    DOT
                  (indicating bustle)
        I hate this thing.

                    GEORGE
        Then why wear it?

                    DOT

        Why wear it? Everyone is wearing them!

LAPINE: Our next meeting was around lunchtime one day. Luis, your majordomo, brought me up a plate of food on a gorgeous tray with fine china, silver place settings, and a linen napkin. You never ate lunch.

SONDHEIM: Yes, right. Luis was very elegant. He did everything for me. He cooked. He cut my hair. He tailored my clothes.

LAPINE: It's a moment that inspired me later in life to do the adaptation of Moss Hart's *Act One*. The moment when Hart came to meet with George S. Kaufman at his home—

SONDHEIM: Yes, that must have been a similar thing. Kaufman lived very elegantly.

LAPINE: When I read that book, there were a lot of similarities.

SONDHEIM: Sure, I see it now. Which reminds me. One of the first things I remember was that you sketched out the relationships of the people.

LAPINE: Right. Did I bring that in first?

SONDHEIM: I think I saw that when I came down to your loft for a visit.

LAPINE: Do you remember coming to my place? I was panicked that you wanted to see where I lived.

SONDHEIM: Sure. Yes, it wasn't poverty row, but it was, as they say, minimal. You served cheese.

LAPINE: I was nervous about you visiting. It was a small, dark, funky loft in the Financial District. I think I asked Luis to get someone to help me clean it before you came.

SONDHEIM: I wish you hadn't cleaned it.

LAPINE: I know. You wanted to see it before it was tidied up. It was like

Anne Frank's hiding place—an attic over an art supply building on three-block-long Ann Street. You had to go up some back stairs to get to it.

SONDHEIM: I remember the room. But mostly what I remember is that transparent piece of paper on your desk. That's so vivid in my head right now. You put a piece of tracing paper over the reproduction of the painting and you had little arrows going: mother, question mark; lover; and you had already started to orchestrate the characters based on who the six or seven main characters in the painting were. You were making a structure out of a visual.

LAPINE: We talked at great length about the characters, about where the story might be headed and what the dramatic situations might be, immersing ourselves in the world of these people. You asked a lot of questions and took copious notes. I kept wondering when I was going to hear a song, but I never pressed you on it. We talked a lot—

SONDHEIM: About all the songs—

LAPINE: —particularly "Sunday in the Park with George." If memory serves me correctly, you came up with that title. We went to see a Royal Shakespeare production of *All's Well That Ends Well* on Broadway and we were talking about titles before the show started. I suggested *By George*, which you promptly informed me was already taken—a play that was a compilation of the writings of George Bernard Shaw. You then suggested *Sunday in the Park with George*, which I immediately liked.

SONDHEIM: And I was working on that song.

LAPINE: Eventually, you'd read me three or four couplets for the opening number. You'd ask, "Would Dot say this?" or "Would she say this?" And then we'd talk about it. And when I answered which one I preferred you'd ask me to tell you why that was the one I liked. We talked about her use of language, how she spoke, her station in life, and what she'd be thinking about; and then you'd flip a page and go, "Now, would she then say—" and show me another set of couplets. It was like a quiz. You eventually did that on many of the songs. You kept saying, "I don't want to write the wrong song."

One of many of Sondheim's lyric sketches for the song "Sunday in the Park with George"

SONDHEIM: I was about to say, that's the point. It's not a waste to write a bad song. It's a waste of time to write a wrong song. That's why I do so much talking before writing, because I want to be sure that it's going to be worth the effort; because I'm a slow writer, and I don't want to spend three weeks on a song, and then it's a good song but it doesn't belong in the show.

PUTTING IT TOGETHER

LAPINE: Yes. Well, the hard part for me was that they were always four great couplets. They were all clever and funny. I enjoyed being put on the spot to choose what I thought the character would say.

SONDHEIM: It's the only way I can get into the playwright's mind—by law-yerly asking, "Why did she say this? Wouldn't she say 'dog' instead of 'cat'?" Then you would say, "No; you see, she thinks dogs are this and cats are that . . ." And that's how I get to know the people, by asking the playwright. It's like casting. I'm the actor. I have to know what you intend before I can do the scene.

LAPINE: I wish you had dated all your songs and notes. It would have been fun to know exactly what came when. From my end, I basically wrote my scenes in order. At some point I must have figured out a structure for the first act, though in those days I probably didn't write it down—I could keep it in my head. So, in the beginning you didn't know where I was going, either, until I brought in my next set of pages.

SONDHEIM: We would discuss where you were headed.

LAPINE: Yes, I'm sure we talked about that. Sometimes I wouldn't know. I'd come over here to share what I had been writing, and I'd leave thinking to myself: Is he ever going to write a song? But after a while, I just told myself that if you didn't write the songs, I would at least have a play!

SONDHEIM: Oh, I was.

LAPINE: That's the thing; I was never sure what you were doing. I should also mention that ever since you gave me those cassettes I was constantly listening to your work. It made me *very* nervous. I thought, Holy fuck, these songs are amazing. I am so out of my league here.

SONDHEIM: Oh, really?

LAPINE: Yes.

SONDHEIM: Well, you were a virgin. Come on. It's scary the first time.

LAPINE: I wasn't really scared. I was intimidated because of my lack of knowledge. I think maybe we hit it off because I *didn't* know your work.

SONDHEIM: Oh, could be.

LAPINE: I wasn't like the guy hunting down your address and ringing your doorbell trying to meet you. I wasn't a fan, and probably that was kind of refreshing for you in some ways.

SONDHEIM: Oh, yes, sure. You came at it with no opinion, no previous opinion about, Gee, I liked *Company* but I didn't like *Follies*. Most collaborators I would have worked with would have had opinions on the shows.

LAPINE: I think it was just wildly brave of you to have decided to work with me.

SONDHEIM: But I'd seen your work. I don't know that I would have written with you if you had written something I didn't admire.

LAPINE: It took so long for you to write that first song. In the back of my head I began thinking, Maybe this isn't going to work out. It's like a relationship. It's like you're dating someone you like but on some level it's not clicking, something's not right.

SONDHEIM: The way your diffidence is built into you, my procrastination is built into me. Everything you wrote, every conversation we had when we would schmooze about what's going to happen in this scene, was engaging—my only concern, always, was that I didn't think the show needed songs. I thought, Why don't you just do it as a play, because that's what you've got.

LAPINE: Yes, you said that on more than one occasion.

SONDHEIM: It was so rich, the whole thing. I said, the thing is—and it's not being modest—songs could tear apart this delicate texture.

LAPINE: It was so *not* delicate to me.

SONDHEIM: You are—and this will make you blush, but you are—a poet. Songs—music—can be very intrusive. That's what worried me.

LAPINE: And that's probably why I would tell myself if you never wrote anything, I would at least have a play. I thought you had one foot out the door, which in retrospect is kind of funny, because in my life at that time I always had one foot out the door. I had real commitment issues, and here I was with somebody whose foot seemed further out the door than mine.

SONDHEIM: Oh, my gosh. I never detected any of that.

LAPINE: Well, we didn't know each other. And I never said anything. More to the point, I was used to working with Bill Finn, who wrote songs quickly and often played them half-finished for us to discuss.

SONDHEIM: I always looked forward to everything you wrote. Not only did I enjoy your company, but also I thought everything you were showing me was fun and good and alive and stimulating, and I wanted to write it. There was no reason to have second thoughts, you know. And you did not write a lot of stuff that is not in the show. You knew what you wanted.

LAPINE: The only thing I definitely knew I wanted was that they were going to end up in the pose of the painting at the end of the first act. It was nice to know your ending.

SONDHEIM: I always try to figure out with a lyric what the last line's going to be before I go on. Where's it going to get to? Because as Oscar Hammerstein taught me, if I treat a song as a play, you want to know what the curtain's going to be. That means, what's the last line—not necessarily a punch line. It could be a refrain line, but you say, it's going to get there. That's what you knew about the making of the painting.

LAPINE: One of the great surprises of researching this book was looking at the boxes of your material. The great preparation you took before writing a song is why it's such a great score. All this time when I thought you were not writing, you were working; you were preparing. That doesn't come across in your book *Finishing the Hat*, either. It's really interesting to point out that you spend a lot of time just making notes. When you say you don't want to write the "wrong" song, I think what you are saying is that you have to understand why there *is* a song—what its purpose will be in the storytelling and how it serves that overall dramatic arc.

SONDHEIM: I guess it comes from my training under Oscar: always think character and story, and then you think about the song.

LAPINE: Yes. This was all new to me. I really didn't tell anyone we were working together, so I didn't have anyone with whom to discuss this process I was going through. This was my way of sparing myself embarrassment if it didn't happen.

SONDHEIM: I had just the reverse reaction. I used to carry the postcard of the painting in my pocket. I remember when my friend Cynthia O'Neal asked me if I was working on anything—I said, "I'm working with this guy named James Lapine," and she asked, "What's the show about?" I said, "You want to see the cast; you want to see the set?" Then I would pull out the postcard of the painting.

LAPINE: If only I had known. I wouldn't have worried you were going to leave me at the altar.

SONDHEIM: I couldn't wait for people to know that we were doing this.

First Reading

During this period, I had a commission from Playwrights Horizons and I was thinking I could use Sunday *to fulfill that commitment. I'd almost finished the first act and thought maybe we could do an informal reading, so Steve and I could hear the book. I figured that might be helpful in moving him along with the score. But first I checked back in with Stephen Graham to let him know where we were with the project.*

STEPHEN GRAHAM

LAPINE: Why didn't you stay involved when we moved on to the *Sunday* idea?

GRAHAM: Well, this is an index of my acuity as a theatrical producer. To be perfectly honest, you were being very inclusive and gentlemanly, and I was a complete dunderhead. I should have thought, These two guys are geniuses; shut up and do whatever they do. But instead, I thought I knew everything. I thought *Sunday* was a bad idea and it would be too cerebral. My idea of a musical was *West Side Story*. I was kind of a reactionary—one of those guys who think, you know, Sondheim's lyrics were so great in *Gypsy* and *West Side Story*. Why couldn't he just carry on writing lyrics with Jule Styne? So I bowed out.

André Bishop, me,
Ira Weitzman, and
William Finn

Stephen Graham did move on to produce other projects, but he is best known for founding the New York Theatre Workshop, one of the most influential off-Broadway theaters of the last couple of decades. He then went back to school and received his doctorate in English literature from Columbia University; his dissertation was on George Eliot. He is now a professor at Bard College.

After we parted company on Sunday, I went ahead and approached André Bishop, who not only was the artistic director at Playwrights Horizons but had become a close friend after he produced Table Settings and March of the Falsettos. (In 1991, he left Playwrights to become the artistic director of Lincoln Center Theater, where he has had an extraordinarily successful run and guided innumerable Tony Award–winning productions.)

ANDRÉ BISHOP

BISHOP: One day you came into my office to discuss your commission, and in your slightly mysterious way, you said, "Well, I think I know what I want to do: a musical." I said fine, because we were interested in musi-

PUTTING IT TOGETHER

cals. Then you said, in this coy way, "Well, how would you like it if I did a musical with Stephen Sondheim?" Even then Sondheim was a god to people like me, so of course I said yes! Shortly thereafter, I came down to your place on Ann Street with all my original cast albums, because you—if I may say this—didn't really have a firm grasp of the American musical. I don't think I ever got those recordings back, by the way.

Ira Weitzman was the director of musical theater projects at Playwrights Horizons and was instrumental in launching William Finn's career. We worked together on March of the Falsettos *before Ira moved on to Lincoln Center with André and became head of their musical theater program.*

IRA WEITZMAN

WEITZMAN: André told me that what you proposed for your commission was this secretive collaboration with Sondheim. We were not allowed to speak of it. We were told to call it Project X. Honestly, it seems ridiculous now! Having grown up on Sondheim, I was very excited. Well, to use his phrase, "I was excited and scared."

November 1, 1982

For a reading of the first act, André had rented a theater down the street from Playwrights Horizons and had a piano brought in. There was no audience other than André, Steve, Ira, and John Lyons, the casting director at the theater.

Johnna Murray, who had been my stage manager on March of the Falsettos *and* A Midsummer Night's Dream, *also joined us to deal with the actors and read stage directions. A small group who'd never laid eyes on the script read multiple roles: Daniel Gerroll, Pamela Reed, George Hearn, and Patricia Elliott among them. The piece was still in its skeletal form, but the afternoon proved useful for getting a sense of the structure of the book.*

STEPHEN SONDHEIM

LAPINE: I was a nervous wreck at that first reading.

SONDHEIM: I'd done four notes or something like that.

LAPINE: Yes. You got up on the stage and played your opening arpeggios. I don't remember when you wrote them, actually, or if I had heard those chords before then. I do remember that I told André we were just going to read the first act—but I think I failed to mention that there were no songs. After you were done playing, you returned to your seat. André looked at me and I whispered, "That's all the music you're going to hear."

ANDRÉ BISHOP

BISHOP: I thought Sondheim was approachable. When we got together to discuss the project I was very, very nervous. I was shy then, and had some strange instinct that I had to prove my worth to him and wasn't quite sure how to do that. I was trying to figure out what the show would sound like, so I kept referencing every vaguely famous nineteenth-century French composer. I remember talking about that and getting myself more and more deeply in the mud.

I don't have much of a recollection of how that reading went, other than to say that I think it intrigued everyone. Steve and I chatted briefly about the reading afterward, but we didn't have a meeting before I took off for Europe a week later. One reason for my travel was to go to Paris and visit La Grande Jatte.

It turned out to be difficult to find the island. I took the Métro to La Défense—the huge and very modern business area outside of Paris—and walked from there to the Île de la Grande Jatte. As I crossed the bridge, a light rain began to fall. I didn't even realize I had reached the island because all I saw were high-rise buildings everywhere; nothing suggested that it had once been a rural park.

In my broken French, I asked a number of people if there was a park anywhere. The first few people said no; then someone suggested that I might be looking for the tip of the island, and pointed me in that direction. Dispirited and wet, I walked several blocks, and coming around the corner of a tall apartment building, I stopped dead in my tracks. There was an open slip of land at the end of the island and there, at the edge of the water, stood a few people under umbrellas and holding fishing poles, summoning the figures in the paintings. The moment also suggested an ending for our show. I immediately pulled out my camera and took some photos. When I got back to my hotel room, I sent Sondheim a telegram letting him know that I had touched sacred ground.

SUNDAY IN THE PARK WITH GEORGE (I-1)

(DOT)

The First Song:
November 28, 1982

STEPHEN SONDHEIM

LAPINE: When I returned from Paris, I came in for our weekly meeting and
   you announced that you had the first song ready to play—the title song.
   You moved to the piano bench and asked me to come sit next to you and
   turn the pages. This is going to sound odd, but I'd never been in such
   close proximity to you. Do you know what I mean? Suddenly we were
   sitting shoulder to shoulder.

SONDHEIM: It was a collaboration.

LAPINE: Yes. It was kind of an emotional moment for me. I was so grateful
   to hear a song.

SONDHEIM: Also, I was sharing my creative juices with you for the first
   time, the way you had done.

LAPINE: You were nervous.

SONDHEIM: I was nervous, as I always am with a collaborator. You had done
   it to me, and you had been nervous; and of course I had to do it to you.

LAPINE: So we sat down. I had never heard you sing. You attacked the keys.

It was like, OOMPH—like a strong wind blowing me away from the piano.

SONDHEIM: I'm overemphatic when I audition for people.

LAPINE: Nerves. And that's a really difficult song to sing. It has that long stretch at the end where you had to belt out that litany in one breath. Plus I was supposed to turn the pages for you and I don't read music, so it was a little overwhelming. Frankly, I didn't know what to make of the song when you finished.

SONDHEIM: That's interesting.

LAPINE: I was watching you, listening to you, trying to imagine it being sung in a woman's voice; and you said, "It's not in this key, it's in that key, but I've got to sing it in this key," or whatever. And when you finished, I did what you essentially did to me when I gave you my first pages: you read them over a few times. I asked you to sing it again. Actually, I think you wanted to.

SONDHEIM: Yes. I was going to say, I always want to go again when I do a song for a collaborator because the first time I'm too nervous.

LAPINE: Yes, but I think I was a disappointment to you as a listener because I'm not effusive; I don't think I gave you the support that you deserved and were accustomed to.

SONDHEIM: No, it's not that. What I was used to was a person like Arthur Laurents [*West Side Story, Gypsy, Anyone Can Whistle*], who loved or hated it with equal passion, whatever I came up with.

LAPINE: You said Hal Prince was a great enthusiast.

SONDHEIM: Oh, Hal, also—his career is based on that energetic enthusiasm he has for whatever he's working on. Hugh Wheeler—the guy who wrote *Sweeney Todd* and *Night Music*—was a cool customer, too. I never got a response from him. So you were the second collaborator like that. I thought, All right. I recognized right away that the diffidence was part of you, not your attitude toward the song. I got that.

LAPINE: What were some of your other collaborators like? George Furth [*Company, Merrily We Roll Along*]?

SONDHEIM: George was unique. When I met George, he was, I guess, forty years old. He had never owned a phonograph. He never listened to music, ever. He was not interested in music in any way, shape, or form. So, he just wrote dialogue. And that's one of the reasons that the songs in *Company* don't grow out of the scenes. His dialogue is completely unmusical, because that's not him. Arthur Laurents was *very* musical. Writing with him was not unlike writing with you. He'd write the scene and we'd talk about what would be music and I would start to write. And he would say, that sounds right, or that sounds wrong.

LAPINE: Jim Goldman [*Follies*]?

SONDHEIM: He had been a cello player as a young man, and he was also very musical. In *Follies* the music came out of the dialogue, except for the pastiche numbers.

LAPINE: And did they write the way we wrote—did they bring in a scene for you to read and discuss?

SONDHEIM: Yes. The only exception was John Weidman [*Pacific Overtures, Road Show*] and our show *Assassins*, where he just went off and wrote the entire book before giving it to me!

LAPINE: Amazing. Anyway, back to our first song. I really got used to you singing the songs, and I could really hear when you performed them how they were meant to be interpreted. It was very helpful not only as the librettist, but especially as the director.

SONDHEIM: I can sing on pitch, but when I'm nervous and trying to play the piano at the same time and give it some force, I lean on the acting and not on the melody. Also, I rarely put the melody line in the accompaniment. So that means there's no way for you to get to know what the tune is. Otherwise I have to practice playing the song with the tune, which is just too much trouble; so I just ask everybody to wait until they can hear it sung by an actor.

Meeting Seurat: December 11, 1982

Steve and I traveled to the Art Institute of Chicago for an up-close-and-personal look at the painting. We had made plans to meet with the museum staff, who gave us a lecture on the work and showed us X-ray photographs that had been taken of the canvas, revealing the many revisions Seurat had made to his masterpiece over the two years it took him to complete it. We could see the variety of paint strokes that made up the "dots." We were really able to get a sense of Seurat's obsessional nature: the exactitude of his work and the precision of every brushstroke on the canvas. I had seen the painting years before, but now it had a much greater emotional impact. It was a thrilling afternoon.

At one point I asked the curators what the object was behind the two main figures who are standing on the right side of the image. Simultaneously, one said, "It's a waffle stove," as the other said, "It's a baby carriage." It was good to know that there were things even the experts couldn't agree on when it came to this painting.

As we continued to read about Seurat, it was unnerving to learn that many of the character traits that we had intuited from the painting turned out to be accurate. I suppose, just given the complexity of the painting, it wasn't a leap to make Seurat an obsessive and a recluse. It was curious that I had denoted one of the figures in the painting to be his mother before I learned that he'd actually had an unusually close relationship with her, and that they had eaten dinner together every night. It

was also a breakthrough to learn that he'd had a child with his mistress, Madeleine Knobloch, but had never told his mother about the relationship or the baby. It wasn't until after his death that she learned of the birth and death of her grandchild. These particulars gave me the freedom to imagine that perhaps Seurat had had another mistress before or after Knobloch, and perhaps another child as well.

1983

As we welcomed in the New Year, the writing began to pick up steam. We continued to meet regularly. The songs "Yoo Hoo" and "No Life" were routined into the first scene, and Steve tackled the music for the second scene, in which George paints as Dot applies her makeup for their night out at the Follies. Seurat's painting of Made-leine Knobloch, Young Woman Powdering Herself, *inspired the moment. In his book* Look, I Made a Hat, *Sondheim wrote:*

> If there is any song in the score that exemplifies the change in my
> writing when I began my collaboration with James Lapine, it would

"Color and Light"

be "Color and Light." The flow between spoken and sung monologue, the elliptical heightened language, the stream-of-consciousness fantasies, the abrupt climactic use of unaccompanied dialogue, these are all musical extensions of hallmarks in Lapine's playwriting . . . In response, I organized this song, and much of the score, more through rhythm and language than rhyme.

STEPHEN SONDHEIM

LAPINE: I think "Color and Light" is one of the most remarkable numbers in the show. A great marriage of dialogue and song. I felt as if we were in total sync.

SONDHEIM: That's the kind of thing I love doing anyway—a combination of music and lyrics. The dialogue was so poetic it felt like a spoken lyric; you avoided Latin-root words and contractions to give it the feel of nineteenth-century speech patterns.

LAPINE: The painting sequence told you everything you needed to know about George.

SONDHEIM: Oh, yes. And Dot echoing it with her syncopated powder puff and all that. Man, that's really fun.

LAPINE: I learned so much from watching you create that song—how dialogue serves the music and vice versa. Those months of just talking about character, talking about the painting, developing these two main characters paid off beautifully. You seemed confident in what you were writing and the work came faster. After hearing the song, I was very psyched to do a workshop. I remember you being worried that the score would not be remotely finished. I said, well, we'd listen to whatever we had.

SONDHEIM: Again, that is such an attitude of your generation. For me, you finish it and then you present it. You don't say, well, we'll worry about it later.

LAPINE: But in the past you had to audition your shows for backers, right?

SONDHEIM: Yes, but the shows were finished. Then they were rejected, but they were finished.

LAPINE: I liked that quote in *Look, I Made a Hat* on your collaboration with Hal: "[His] function was to keep the truck moving, mine to see that it didn't fall off the cliff." In our collaboration, I felt as if I was the engine of our show, organizing the readings and organizing the workshop . . .

SONDHEIM: You've been that with every show we've written. You produce. You are one of those writers—you not only write and direct, you produce your shows. You do all the pushing, all the nudging. You do all of that.

Sondheim
Goes
Off-Broadway

Workshop

Preparations were made for a workshop in June. Workshops were not common at this time. The best-known example of a show developed in workshop was A Chorus Line *at the Public Theater, but that was literally "written on the actors"—based on their own experiences. Our workshop would be a very different venture. Because of the nature of the musical, I asked for sets and costumes so we could see the world of the show and the progression of Seurat's work on the painting. I also floated the idea that subscribers to Playwrights be invited to attend "in-progress" presentations.*

ANDRÉ BISHOP AND IRA WEITZMAN

LAPINE: I had proposed a seven-week workshop. Three weeks of rehearsal, one week of tech, and three weeks of performances—with costumes and sets, no less! Where did you get the money for that?

BISHOP: We were able to raise some money from mostly—this is going to sound like something out of *The Producers*—wealthy widows. One was Mimsi Harbach, who had been married to the son of the great operetta librettist and lyricist Otto Harbach. Another, Rhoda Herrick, just recently died.

LAPINE: Do you recall the budget?

BISHOP: No. I'm sure it would be laughable today. Maybe something like eighty thousand dollars, which was enormous for us.

(opposite) The building at 416 West Forty-second Street that became Playwrights Horizons in 1977

WEITZMAN: I wrote letters to funding sources and various foundations, including, I think, Exxon. Remember when Exxon had a big arts endowment? It was a little bit controversial when word got out that we were doing this, because the nonprofit theaters then were very, very separate and distinct from the commercial theater, not like today. Now there's almost no telling the difference between one and the other. Steve Sondheim was perceived as a commercial artist. Not that he wrote commercially, but his venues were the commercial theater.

BISHOP: We planned on having two benefit performances to help pay for the production. I remember Mrs. Oscar Hammerstein gave us some money because she and Steve were quite close. On the other hand, Mrs. Richard Rodgers was really a lot of trouble. Her husband had worked with Sondheim on *Do I Hear a Waltz?* She didn't like the idea of *Sunday.* She was, at that point, head of the New York State Council on the Arts. She didn't like the idea that we were doing this musical that she thought was commercial. I think her disfavor was really motivated more by her feelings about Steve than Playwrights Horizons. She really went to great lengths to see if Playwrights Horizons' funding from the Council on the Arts could be stopped because she felt we were selling out to Broadway interests. If only she could see what is going on today with these nonprofit theaters. Anyway, she was very powerful, and it was worrisome because a lot of our funding came from the New York State Council on the Arts.

LAPINE: Did you talk to her daughter Mary Rodgers?

BISHOP: I did talk to Mary, but Mary had a complicated relationship with her mother. My memory is that Mary did try to help, but I don't know to what degree. So I wrote Mrs. Rodgers a letter pointing out that we were one of the few off-Broadway or nonprofit theaters doing new American musicals. I said something like, "We haven't gone commercial, and if you think this musical that is barely half-written, about a pointillist painter, is commercial, you've got to be nuts!" I was really angry. Then I stated that we'd done this musical and that musical and worked with these writers and those writers in the musical theater. "Instead of cutting off our funding, what I think you should do is get down on your knees and kiss my feet."

LAPINE: Whoa.

BISHOP: Yes, this was untypical of me, but it was maddening what she was doing. I got a letter back, in the days when people wrote letters, that simply said, "Dear André, Point taken. Sincerely, Dorothy Rodgers." And she stopped making trouble.

As I continued laying the groundwork for our workshop, Sondheim and I kept up our weekly meetings. Act One had pretty much been mapped out, so we began to discuss the second act, which I had begun to outline. Now that we had established the foundation of our story, I could not just intuit the writing. We had to know where we were going.

STEPHEN SONDHEIM

SONDHEIM: We always thought of it as these two acts, right? Act One takes place making the painting, and Act Two is what happens with the painting in the subsequent hundred years.

LAPINE: Actually, at first, I toyed with there being three acts.

SONDHEIM: Oh, I don't remember that.

LAPINE: I imagined that our first act was the birth of the painting, 1884 to 1886. The middle act was going to be the life of the painting from 1886 to 1986. It would involve a scene with Seurat painting *Les Poseuses* (*The Models*), with the Celestes posing nude with Dot.

I wanted to deal with the death of Seurat; how the painting languished unsold in an attic before it was bought and brought to America; the time the painting almost went up in flames at the Museum of Modern Art in New York in 1958, the only time the painting was lent to another museum; etc. The third act would be the painting today. That's when we'd meet our contemporary George.

SONDHEIM: But see, I thought the *Les Poseuses* section was going to be the beginning of the second act.

LAPINE: It was indeed the beginning of a sketch for the second act, but it became clear that my idea of doing three acts was far too ambitious.

(right) Georges Seurat,
Model Facing Front,
study for *Les Poseuses,*
1886–1887

(below) The painting
being protected from the
fire at MoMA, 1958

BLINDED, firemen grope their way through smoke into gallery. Seurat drawing on wall escaped damage.

MASKED with handkerchiefs as protection, museum employes carry Seurat art to nearby buildings.

FIREMEN DRAPE TARPAULIN OVER SEURAT'S "GRANDE JATTE," INSIDE GLASS CASE TOO HEAVY TO MOVE

Casting

It was time to begin choosing actors for the upcoming workshop. I had the idea of Bernadette Peters for the role of Dot. Bernadette was a native of Queens, New York; she began her career at the age of three and a half on a television show called Juvenile Jury, *and has been working ever since. When she came to our attention for the role of Dot, she already had a formidable résumé that included starring in* George M!, Dames at Sea, *and* Mack and Mabel, *among other shows. She'd also appeared in many films, including one of my favorites,* Pennies from Heaven. *We reached out to her agent and sent her a script. Steve followed up with a phone call to her in California, where she lived.*

STEPHEN SONDHEIM

LAPINE: Somehow the draft I sent her had included the scene reenacting the painting of *Les Poseuses*.

SONDHEIM: Yes, she'd read the scene and her first remark to me was, "I don't do nude." That was the exact sentence. I thought, Well, okay, but how was the show, Mrs. Lincoln?

BERNADETTE PETERS

LAPINE: Did you know Steve Sondheim?

PETERS: No. I got the script and was told you were doing a workshop. At the time I was in San Francisco, at the Fairmont Hotel. I spoke to Steve on the phone.

LAPINE: Did I ever tell you why I thought of you for the role?

PETERS: No.

LAPINE: I saw you on the Academy Awards that year. You were performing the number "What'll I Do" on the show. I watched you and I thought, That's Dot. That's the woman I'm writing about.

PETERS: That's wonderful. I remember talking to you on the phone at the hotel, too. I was very interested in doing the workshop.

LAPINE: Were you a fan of Sondheim? Had you seen many of his shows?

PETERS: No. I had seen *Side by Side by Sondheim* in London. I just couldn't stop humming and singing the songs.

LAPINE: Well, you were in *Gypsy* as a child.

PETERS: Honestly, I wasn't that familiar with the shows as much as the songs. I remember telling you when we spoke, "Do you know who should be George? Mandy Patinkin." You said, "Well, funny you should say that . . ."

LAPINE: You said, "It's the guy who's in the *Evita* commercials." I don't think you had actually seen him in *Evita*. You looked at him like I looked at you. I said I thought Mandy was perfect, too, except Mandy was a tenor. Steve was writing for a baritone.

PETERS: Well, Steve had to switch the music for both of our voices. He originally thought of Dot as a soprano, I think.

When I met Mandy Patinkin, he had recently won a Tony Award for his memorable portrayal of Che Guevara in Evita, *and had just completed shooting the film* Yentl *opposite Barbra Streisand. Mandy was raised in Chicago and studied at Juilliard.*

MANDY PATINKIN

PATINKIN: In '78, while I was doing *Evita*, I was at a party at Hal Prince's house, and there was a back room that had a baby grand piano. I didn't want to hang out with the crowd, so I went into the room and sat on the couch next to a lady. I didn't know who the lady was at first, and we started talking. It turned out it was Angela Lansbury, and it was an extraordinary conversation. And, as I'm talking to her, I realize it's the wrong guy sitting there—it should have been my late father. How he loved this woman. The first time I visited New York—my bar mitzvah gift—my dad took me to see her in *Mame*. And as I'm having this thought about my dad, a guy walks in the room and Angela stands up and says, "Mandy, I'd like you to meet Stephen Sondheim." And at that moment, I did not have it together in my head that he was the guy who wrote *West Side Story*, but a click went off, because my roommate Ted Chapin had shown me this album he had of a Sondheim benefit concert where Sondheim's name was spelled out with Scrabble tiles. "Well, you're the guy on the Scrabble album, aren't you?" and Steve said, "Yeah." I said, "You performed that amazing song 'Anyone Can Whistle' on that recording, right?" and he said, "Yeah." And then I asked, "Could you play that for us now?" So he sat down at the piano for just Angela and me, and sang "Anyone Can Whistle." That's the first time I met Stephen Sondheim.

LAPINE: Do you remember when we met?

PATINKIN: Was it when you came over to my apartment to talk to me about a workshop of *Sunday*?

LAPINE: Yes, I came over to meet you, and you had your infant son Isaac in your arms the entire time. You had just gotten back from shooting *Yentl*.

PATINKIN: Yes, he was born during that shoot.

LAPINE: It was really hard for us to connect, because you had the baby to deal with, and you were also exhausted. I didn't know if you had read the material or not.

PATINKIN: I'd read it. It was only the first act. And I remember you said to me, "Stephen and I wanted to do a work of art based on a work of art." I said, "Oh, that sounds pretty pretentious."

LAPINE: That's funny. I don't remember that.

PATINKIN: And then, after this whole wonderful meeting—I think you were just ready to leave—you kind of threw in the fact that I had to audition for Steve. "What?" I said, stunned. You responded, "Yeah, you have to. Don't worry about it, it's just a formality." I mean, I thought you were offering it to me. I had recently won a Tony Award for *Evita*. I was a very nervous fellow and not a good auditioner, and I thought to myself: Tony Award? I thought that was supposed to make things easier for me. That's not the game here, I guess.

LAPINE: Did I really say *audition*? I probably said, "You have to sing for Steve."

PATINKIN: "You have to sing for Steve," but the way I interpreted it was—

LAPINE: Audition?

PATINKIN: *(laughing)* It was an audition, James.

LAPINE: Steve thought of the character of Seurat as being a bass baritone, and he wanted to hear what it sounded like in a tenor's voice. It's funny you say it was a wonderful meeting we had, because I don't remember it that way at all.

PATINKIN: How do you remember our first meeting?

LAPINE: I was deeply intimidated by you.

PATINKIN: *(laughing)* Oh, my God. We're so nuts!

LAPINE: I remember feeling—nothing bad professionally, like I didn't want to do it with you, but I just didn't feel—

PATINKIN: Safe?

LAPINE: Yeah, that's one way to put it. You sometimes talked about your guy friends as "buddies." I didn't feel like I would ever be your buddy. You know what I mean? I didn't feel we connected.

PATINKIN: I was very frightened back then, and it scared other people how frightened I was. I was more frightened of myself, and people interpreted that as dangerous territory. I came to learn that over time.

LAPINE: Of course, we were all frightened in some way.

PATINKIN: Yeah.

LAPINE: Anyway, I guess you eventually sang for Steve.

PATINKIN: Steve called me first. I told him, "Listen, I'm not very good at auditioning." He just said, "Don't worry about it. The only person who doesn't have to audition for me anymore is Angela, because I've worked with her so many times." And I'm thinking, Angela, Angela, Angela. This woman keeps coming into my life. So I said, "Yeah, yeah. Okay, okay." So then Paul Gemignani, whom I knew when he was the musical director of *Evita*, met with me and we worked on the only song Stephen had written for the character yet: "Color and Light." And Gemignani is playing with keys and everything, and I don't know what's happening. I had some comfort with him, but he wasn't assuring me that the part was mine. "Steve's going to run you through some stuff," he said. I don't remember whether you were in the room . . .

LAPINE: I must have been.

PATINKIN: And then Sondheim comes in and I run what I worked on with Gemignani and then that was that. The next thing I knew, it was okay.

LAPINE: Yeah. Well, the other reason Steve might have done that is because he probably wanted to get your voice in his head for further writing.

Auditions

In 1979, when I was doing the workshop of my play Table Settings *at Playwrights Horizons, John Lyons was an intern there and ran the sound on that show. André promoted him to be the theater's casting director, which he did for six years before forming his own casting office and eventually branching out to casting films. He went on to become a film producer and later president of production at Focus Features. He is now again producing independently.*

JOHN LYONS

LAPINE: How did you go from intern to running sound to assistant stage manager to casting director?

LYONS: You know, I had no idea how to be a casting director. Like so many things at Playwrights Horizons at the time, it was completely by the seat of our pants. André had good instincts about people and kept moving us up the ladder. We used to post casting notices and our phone number on the bulletin board at Equity and in ads in *Backstage*. When 564-1237 rang, I answered and said, "Casting."

LAPINE: Yes, those were the days when you could suddenly be doing a job you had absolutely no training to do. Sort of like me writing and directing plays.

LYONS: How lucky were we? It was a little improvisatory. I think people roughly knew what their jobs were, but we were kind of making it up as we went along. When we heard Sondheim was coming to Forty-second Street, it was like, What the hell? It became clear that this was a completely different level of theater and we were all going to have to raise our game.

LAPINE: And when you met Steve for the first time?

LYONS: He was always, I would have to say, incredibly generous to all of us. I remember one of the things he said that was very liberating: "I don't really care how well the actors sing. First and foremost, I want them to be able to act." By then, I felt I had a pretty good handle on the musical elements because of my own musical background. Also, we had recently done *March of the Falsettos*.

LAPINE: Well, Steve often says that about actors, and it took me some time to learn to ignore it. If an actor is not the world's best singer, they at least have to be musical. They have to have confidence as a singer. That was a lesson I learned the hard way.

LYONS: Paul Gemignani was very helpful. He made sure the bases were covered.

Paul Gemignani was to be the musical director on our workshop. Forty-five at the time, Paul was already something of a Broadway legend. He had worked with Sondheim since Follies, *when his mentor, the musical director Hal Hastings, moved him up from being the percussionist to conductor. Paul was originally a jazz percussionist before a chance meeting with Hastings when they both happened to be in Chicago. Hastings took a shine to him and got him a job as assistant conductor on one of his road shows. He eventually brought him to New York to play* Follies, *his first Broadway show. After* Follies *Paul went on to conduct Sondheim's* A Little Night Music, Sweeney Todd, *and* Merrily We Roll Along, *as well as dozens of some of the best musicals that have graced Broadway. He is an imposing and sometimes opinionated man, but it didn't take long for his sensitive and generous soul to emerge. Paul joined John Lyons and me in the audition room.*

PAUL GEMIGNANI

LAPINE: We would be doing auditions together and I'd like somebody, but they didn't sing very well. You would jump up on the stage with that person and work with them. Sometimes you would say, "You're auditioning the wrong song." Or you would tell the accompanist to take the song they were singing down a step. Then another step. You would analyze where a song sat best in a person's voice and you'd discover that many actors could sing better than they were presenting themselves.

GEMIGNANI: I actually went through professional conducting training, and part of that is voice training, meaning I had to be able to sing. I had to learn all about the voice and how it works. Most of the young conductors today come up from the keyboard.

JOHN LYONS

LAPINE: If I remember correctly, Steve came to callbacks, but not initial auditions.

LYONS: Sounds right. There were a lot of wonderful actors who we had worked with but we didn't know how well they sang. Christine Baranski—we used to call her the first lady of Playwrights Horizons— had never sung for us.

I'd had the pleasure of working with Christine Baranski on A Midsummer Night's Dream *in Central Park, where she stole the show in the role of Helena. After* Sunday, *Christine went on to win a Tony Award for Tom Stoppard's* The Real Thing, *and has had a distinguished career in film and television.*

CHRISTINE BARANSKI

LAPINE: So, your audition for Sondheim was . . . ?

BARANSKI: Beyond intimidating. I did not, at that point, really study singing. I'd gone to the Juilliard School for four years and was never taught anything about the musical theater, never did a scene from the musical theater. In fact I was very, very shy about singing.

LAPINE: Do you remember what you sang for Steve?

BARANSKI: I said that I wanted to sing *Carmen*. He said, *Carmen Jones*? And I said, no, *Carmen*. Bizet's *Carmen*. I actually think I sang the "Habanera" because—this is so funny—when I started singing, I learned that I had a really good range, but only when I sang in an operatic voice. Then I didn't feel vulnerable. A nun had humiliated me in sixth or seventh grade. She'd made everybody stand and sing to get a music grade, and I sang a religious song, "Immaculate Mary, Thy Praises We Sing." I was so nervous my voice was shaking, and she imitated me and then told me to sit down. I think a lot of people have an experience like that early in life, where they sing and feel so vulnerable. She did that thing that left such a scar. But anyway, you cast me; and I didn't have a song that required a lot of singing. It was "No Life," which I could kind of manage. You had trained musical theater people in that production, but I was not one of them. My contribution to *Sunday in the Park* was my acting.

When I am auditioning actors, I like to push them out of their comfort zone a little bit. I want to throw curveballs to see if they are willing to play that way. I might ask them to improvise something or reinterpret the song they chose to sing. If it's a ballad, I might have the pianist play it as a cheesy up-tempo number—something like that. I've had actors who would not go there, who were not comfortable working that way, so we both knew we would not be a good match. I really like to work with people who enjoy improvisation—who allow me to try things and give me choices or stimulate my thinking. I want to create a workspace where I don't have to feel afraid of making mistakes, and I want to be surrounded by people who feel similarly. It's one of the reasons I love working with children. They always just jump in fearlessly to anything you ask of them. They usually are in the theater because they want to have fun.

We had an open call for girls to play the role of Louise, the little girl in the painting. We were lucky to find eleven-year-old Danielle Ferland.

DANIELLE FERLAND

LAPINE: Let's see, you were just a schoolkid from Stratford, Connecticut, with no professional experience and with parents who were in no way involved in the arts. How did you end up auditioning?

FERLAND: I had a teacher at a dancing school who would take some of the children into New York to meet agents. She told my parents that she thought I had talent and would they be interested? My parents looked at me and said, "If you want to do this, we will do it."

LAPINE: Do you now, as a parent, appreciate what they did for you?

FERLAND: Of course, and I tell them that all the time. At the time, they had friends who told them they were out of their minds. We lived an hour and a half from the city. The fact that they were game, not knowing anything about what goes into committing to a professional theater production—and having two other kids—in retrospect, it is kind of amazing they let me do it.

LAPINE: But were you passionate about acting?

FERLAND: I didn't know. I knew I enjoyed singing in the house and I enjoyed this one particular teacher and the summer program she taught.

LAPINE: Do you remember your audition?

FERLAND: Vividly. It was on a Saturday, and when we walked into Playwrights Horizons, there were a shit ton of kids waiting in the lobby. We had driven in because there were no trains. My dad took one look and muttered, "Jesus Christ." He was hoping to get out of there in ten minutes. It was his day off.

LAPINE: Were you nervous when you finally came into the audition room?

FERLAND: No! I didn't know enough to be nervous.

LAPINE: You didn't appear nervous. I instantly liked you because you had a strength about you. And you weren't trying to be "cute," like most of the other girls.

FERLAND: I sang "Where Is Love?" from *Oliver!* When I finished, I remember you coming onto the stage and saying, "I want to work with you and I want you to be very natural." You had me sing "Take Me Out to the Ball Game" several different ways. "Be funny. Be sassy. Be angry." You directed me. And then you had me sit on the edge of the stage and sing "Where Is Love?" again. And you said, "I want you to *really* ask yourself that question, and sing as though you're speaking to someone who's right in front of you. Don't perform it." You worked with me very intimately.

LAPINE: I loved that you weren't groomed to come into the room and get a job. I sensed you were just coming in to have an adventure.

FERLAND: That's how I felt! Ignorance truly is bliss. Like when you don't know anything and you're shooting from the hip. I just had so much fun.

LAPINE: I love working with kids. But I don't love stage parents.

FERLAND: And my parents weren't that.

LAPINE: I told them to let it be your experience. Don't ask Danielle what happened at rehearsal when she gets home. If she wants to bring it up and talk about it, great. I wanted you to learn from the experience and not feel tethered when you walked in that rehearsal room. I gave you the same kind of professional respect I gave all the actors.

Paul Gemignani had discovered Mary Elizabeth Mastrantonio a few years earlier, when he was casting the road company of Sweeney Todd *in Chicago. He helped her get her first gig in New York City, understudying Maria in a revival of* West Side Story. *He asked her to audition for* Sunday.

MARY ELIZABETH MASTRANTONIO

MASTRANTONIO: By the time I auditioned for you, I had done a few musicals. I'd also done a production of *Amadeus*. And I was just returning from Hollywood, where I'd made the film *Scarface*. I was nervous because I hadn't sung in a long time.

LAPINE: You sang beautifully.

MASTRANTONIO: After I did my song, you asked me to sing "Happy Birthday" like an eighty-year-old woman. I mean, I was twenty-five at the time! Yeah, that was a little intimidating because I'd just never done that type of thing before. I hadn't read the script. I figured out that you wanted me to understudy Bernadette, and she played an old woman in the second act.

Nancy Opel was just out of Juilliard when she was cast as Patti LuPone's cover in Evita, *playing the title role on the Wednesday matinees.*

NANCY OPEL

OPEL: My first audition for you was at Playwrights Horizons, and you, Gemignani, John Lyons, and Steve were there. When I got out of school, I wanted to work with Hal Prince and I wanted to work with Stephen Sondheim, and bingo, my first show was with Hal Prince and there I was standing in front of Stephen Sondheim.

LAPINE: Do you remember what you sang?

OPEL: Absolutely. "Will He Like Me?" from *She Loves Me*. I got about a third of the way through the song and Steve said, "Thank you." It was a knife in the heart. He didn't like what I did? Okay, that's all right, I recovered. Then you had us do improvs. That was also a first for me.

LAPINE: And that was your auditioning experience?

OPEL: No, I was called back and was coached on the song "Sunday in the Park with George." After I learned it, I sang it for everyone. It was not something that you would normally belt—high Fs and Gs—but I did my best. After, Steve said, "Oh, man, that's really high, isn't it?"

LAPINE: We were hearing it sung for the first time.

OPEL: He said, "Well, let's take it down a little bit," so then, suddenly, it felt like I was singing in Chita Rivera's key. It was crazy. But very exciting.

Brent Spiner, a very talented actor, was in the cast of Table Settings. *I asked Brent to come in and audition for the workshop. Mind you, we occasionally clashed when we did* Table Settings, *but he turned in a terrific performance, and since that production turned out to be a success, and I had directed a couple of more productions since then, I figured working here together would be different. (Shortly after doing* Sunday, *Brent went on to play Data on the hugely successful and long-running television series* Star Trek: The Next Generation.*)*

BRENT SPINER

LAPINE: So, when we worked on *Table Settings*, it was pretty clear that you weren't so fond of me. And also, not so supportive, I might add.

SPINER: Yes. You were new to the game. You didn't have a vocabulary to talk to actors.

LAPINE: True. I was kind of surprised you wanted to audition for *Sunday*.

SPINER: Well, you asked me to, and I'm always loath to say no if somebody asks me to do something. And, you know, obviously—

LAPINE: Sondheim, yes. When you were working on *Table Settings*, did you think it was going to be successful?

SPINER: No. I couldn't have been more surprised at the time when it became a hit.

LAPINE: Were you surprised that I was working with Sondheim?

SPINER: Yes.

LAPINE: Did you read the script before you accepted?

SPINER: No, but I had a callback and you had me learn some of the number where George is painting: "Red, red, orange." And that song kind of said to me: "Oh, this is interesting. This is going to be a unique musical." I kind of knew I was not going to be playing that part, but I was game to be part of the workshop.

Once we had made a commitment to do the workshop, I spent less time meeting with Steve and more time preparing for the production. He continued writing, and whenever there was a new piece of music, I would go to his house to hear it. Steve was also attending callbacks for actors, so we would see each other then as well. The casting process took over two months, and during that time I also continued writing the second act.

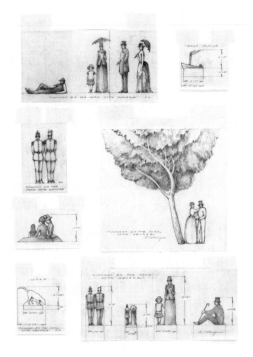

Set rendering by Tony Straiges

The Design Team

Sets

One of the most exciting elements of Sunday *was the design component. This was the area where I felt most confident and at home. I assembled a design team and began meetings to discuss the workshop.*

The play offered a unique opportunity to work backward from an image—an image filled with challenging visual contradictions. How do you suggest pointillism in a theater where the audience sits at variable distance from the stage? How do you create the depth and perspective and varying scale of the figures? How do you show Seurat's two-year process, from his first sketch to the finished painting?

When I went to work at the Yale School of Drama, my first job was to design a poster for Alvin Epstein's magnificent production of A Midsummer Night's Dream. *The set designer, Tony Straiges, and I became fast friends. Tony grew up in Minersville, Pennsylvania, the son of a coal miner. He had experienced as unlikely a path into the theater as I had. He had no college degree when he began working—in the world of puppetry. He ended up as a graduate student at the Yale School of Drama. Tony had designed six Broadway shows prior to* Sunday in the Park.

Tony Straiges

TONY STRAIGES

LAPINE: Do you remember when I brought up the subject of your designing *Sunday in the Park*?

STRAIGES: Yes. We were having lunch with our friend Lynda Lee Burks in a Brooklyn Heights diner and you said you were going to do this musical based on Seurat's painting.

LAPINE: Were you familiar with the painting?

STRAIGES: No, I wasn't. In fact, the first time you talked about it, I asked you who Seurat was. So you told me a little about him and the painting, and eventually I asked who was doing the music and you said Stephen Sondheim. I said, "Come on. Who's *really* doing the music?" I was flabbergasted.

LAPINE: Yeah, I got that a lot. What was the first Broadway show you designed?

STRAIGES: It was *Timbuktu!*

LAPINE: Funny, because I did the terrible poster and artwork for that show. You got me that job.

STRAIGES: I forgot that.

LAPINE: So, we began discussing what the design for *Sunday* might be.

STRAIGES: We talked about the nature of the painting, and how we could re-create it with real people. You talked about people popping up or magically appearing; mixing two-dimensional images with real people. We had the idea of flat cutouts of people and animals coming through the floor.

LAPINE: I think a lot of the visual ideas were in the script.

STRAIGES: Yes, but figuring how to do them was a challenge, particularly at Playwrights Horizons.

LAPINE: When did you and Steve meet?

STRAIGES: I started by making a white model and we brought it over to show him.

LAPINE: I wanted him to be involved in every aspect of the show from the get-go. To know what things were going to look like.

STRAIGES: The day we brought it over, I think we put it on a coffee table and we all sat on the ground to look at it. I was really nervous as the three of us stared inside the little box.

LAPINE: I have this image of the cat jumping up on the table where the model was.

STRAIGES: Steve immediately grabbed the cat's tail and yanked it off the table.

LAPINE: He didn't hurt the cat. He was worried for your model.

STRAIGES: No, I know. Cats like boxes.

LAPINE: Sondheim, who likes to say that he is not a very visual person, enjoyed discussing the mechanics of the set. How we were going to pull off certain visual tricks. The Playwrights Horizons space offered many challenges. There was no stage right and very limited space on stage left. How were we going to get a canvas this size on and off the stage?

STRAIGES: There was no way to fly it in, either, so we got the theater to break through the stage-left wall.

LAPINE: I believe we had to take the space from their lobby area, too. They built a new wall and created a shallower lobby.

STRAIGES: Right. And then we were able to slide in the canvases.

Costumes

André Bishop knew the legendary costume designer Patricia Zipprodt and suggested her for Sunday. *Pat had designed dozens of Broadway shows, including* Cabaret *and* Fiddler on the Roof; *innumerable ballets and operas; and one of my favorite movies,* The Graduate. *She was intrigued but didn't feel she had the time to devote herself fully to the workshop. She suggested that perhaps she and her assistant, Ann Hould-Ward, could do the project together. Sadly, Patricia passed away in 1999, but I spoke with Ann about the experience.*

ANN HOULD-WARD

LAPINE: You and Patricia costumed that entire workshop production?

HOULD-WARD: We did.

LAPINE: I'm assuming it wasn't all designed and then built. You must have had to pull most of the costumes from various collections.

(left) Patricia Zipprodt

(right) Ann Hould-Ward

HOULD-WARD: Most of it was pulled at that point in time.

LAPINE: What about Bernadette?

HOULD-WARD: We had our version of what came to be called the "iron dress"—the dress she wore in the first scene and stepped out of for the title song. That was a big challenge. And then she had a regular version of the dress in another scene, which required a bustle that had to turn around to indicate that she was pregnant. I should add, at first we tried to do what you had written—that her belly inflated to pregnant proportions in front of George! We had a special-effects person who worked for nothing trying to rig that, using life vests from an airplane. Do you remember the first time we tried it onstage? It made this enormous sound.

LAPINE: Who could forget that moment? It sounded like the world's loudest fart.

HOULD-WARD: That's right, and you were like, No, we're going to cut that.

LAPINE: I wouldn't stop working on an idea like that today.

HOULD-WARD: We could do it now. Easily.

LAPINE: You and I were in the same boat back then. I was collaborating with Sondheim and you were working with Zipprodt. We were the novices working with the masters.

HOULD-WARD: Patricia was so kind. And also, despite having done so many great shows, she never lost her excitement. She took pride in the million things she'd designed in the past, whereas I was really young and eager and just starting out. I think she saw a reflection of herself in me. We also just liked to have fun together.

LAPINE: How did you and Patricia work? Who did the sketches?

HOULD-WARD: We both did. She drew Bernadette's clothes except for that end-of-the-act dress; and I drew the rest of the show.

LAPINE: That must have been exciting.

HOULD-WARD: I was scared I would let everybody down. I was "excited and scared," as the song from *Into the Woods* goes. I always loved that song, because I knew exactly what that emotion was. I still had a lot to learn. I'll never forget a meeting we had at Steve's house. Patricia and I were discussing how we were going to try and make that "iron dress" and accomplish what you wrote. I was mostly listening and finally I got up the courage to say, "Well, you know, it's just a really difficult thing to do." Steve looked at me and said, "Well, you have four measures of music; do you think if you had eight it could work?" I stammered, "Oh, I guess," because what could I say? He obviously didn't get what I was really trying to explain—that this was an impossible task to accomplish, particularly with no budget. So . . . we did get a little extra music!

LAPINE: That's very funny. But you solved it!

HOULD-WARD: We did solve it. We built a structure in the dress that could stand on its own. Poor Bernadette had to bend her knees until the frame within the dress hit the ground; then she had to unclasp the front, which was essentially a door on hinges, slip out of the dress without tipping it over, and close it! She was a good sport.

LAPINE: There were a lot of challenges in the script for the designers. Did you have an integral relationship with Tony Straiges?

HOULD-WARD: I remember going out to Tony's house for the first time to look at the set. He lived in the top floor of a small apartment house in Brooklyn Heights. There were model pieces in the stove. The stove wasn't used for food. It was used for storage. There were paintbrushes everywhere, no living space. He was living in a design studio.

LAPINE: Well, Tony was like Seurat. He put such incredible detail and care into his work. And he was kind of a recluse in his way. They had a lot in common.

HOULD-WARD: Yes. I just remember how beautiful that model was. He is such a quiet man. His art spoke for him. He cares passionately about his work.

LAPINE: Well, he was there every night painting the set after rehearsal was over.

HOULD-WARD: I loved how it looked in that little ninety-seat theater, too. It was like being in a king's theater in a castle.

LAPINE: He created a jewel box.

HOULD-WARD: There was such an amazing perspective because of the narrowness and depth of the space. I think it was most exquisite in that space.

Richard Nelson

Lighting

Richard Nelson (not to be confused with the playwright of the same name) was a seasoned lighting designer who worked on Broadway, doing both plays and musicals as well as designing in the dance world with the likes of Merce Cunningham, Twyla Tharp, Martha Graham, and Paul Taylor. He was a terrific collaborator, at all times smart and engaged. One of his many memorable lighting moments came at the end of the number "Color and Light," when he engulfed the character of George and his canvas in a sea of pixelated light, building the effect perfectly in sync with Sondheim's passionate music. Sadly, we lost Richard to a brain tumor in 1996, at the age of fifty-seven. Ironically, Tony Straiges and I were working with him at the time. We were in the midst of tech for a new play, Golden Child *by David Henry Hwang, at the Public Theater. At one point, I looked over and saw that Richard had fallen asleep at his tech table. He passed away several days later. I loved that he wanted to work to the very end of his life.*

The Musical Team

PAUL GEMIGNANI

LAPINE: So you had recently worked with Steve on *Merrily We Roll Along*. What was that experience like?

GEMIGNANI: You have to understand, I don't know about it from a writer's standpoint. Of course it was disappointing to everyone that the production didn't have a life. But I don't ever think about whether a project is bad or good. I believe in what is in front of me and I try and make that work, no matter what, and that's what I was doing during *Merrily*. I thought the score was sensational. My job as a musical director is to service the composer and writer the best I can. I don't expect anybody to go, "Oh, the violins really sound great." It's about being involved in the creative process that helps the writer and the composer do their thing, and they're going to get the kudos. Also, people rarely remember who the director is on a show, particularly as time passes. They mostly remember who the composer was.

LAPINE: Of course. It's a musical, so that's as it should be. When did you hear about *Sunday*?

GEMIGNANI: Sondheim called me over to hear some music and told me what the show was about. I was thrilled. I thought it was an incredible idea.

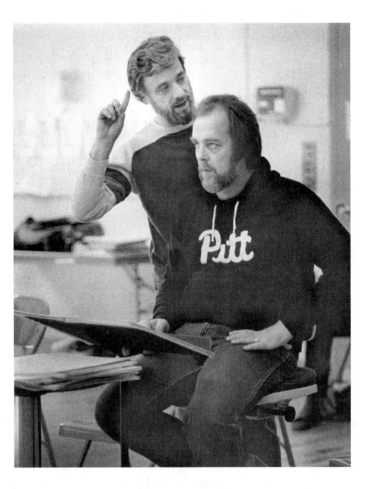

Paul Gemignani

LAPINE: Were you surprised that he was working with an inexperienced collaborator and was going off-Broadway to work on the show?

GEMIGNANI: Not really. First of all, because I was not initially a theater person—meaning I didn't grow up in that world—going down to Playwrights Horizons didn't faze me. I'd worked in nightclubs all my life. Conducting shows eight times a week is like putting nails in the shoe. But working on a new piece, that's what's really interesting. You also had to make things up, really quickly, especially with the way Steve writes, and that was the exciting part. Most directors don't involve you unless you involve yourself. *You* always involved everybody working on the show, because you cared about our ideas. You may have told us to

PUTTING IT TOGETHER

fuck off sometimes, but we felt *involved*. So I enjoyed those times more than anything.

LAPINE: I was a little nervous not being a Broadway guy and not being musically trained.

GEMIGNANI: Yeah, but you had good instincts.

LAPINE: It only made sense for me to listen to the people around me. We were all in a room together. Everybody's expertise was different from mine. I'm always curious to know what the people around me think. Didn't you express your opinions in the other shows you did?

GEMIGNANI: I did, but nobody ever listened. You made everybody feel on the same level and that we were all doing the show together. Most A-list directors want to be the king. The only other person who was as good that way was Michael Bennett. When you are in a creative job, people are so afraid to say what they think. Because of the people who trained me, that was never an issue. I was very comfortable with you. I was more uncomfortable with other, shall we say *conventional* directors, because when with them, if one of us said something, we often either got "Who asked you to talk?" or "That's the dumbest idea I ever heard in my life."

But I must say that the shows we did together were tough. We did not do easy shows together, James. That made them so fulfilling. Knowing that you could be wrong but still feel free enough to express an opinion.

LAPINE: There's sort of no right or wrong. It's just helping me as a writer and director articulate a vision.

GEMIGNANI: It was a little more daunting having you as the writer *and* the director. It's easier for me to say to the director that something doesn't make sense when I'm not also sitting in front of the writer.

I asked Michael Starobin, twenty-seven at the time, to join our team. Michael had been the musical director and orchestrator on March of the Falsettos, *and he was someone who I found to be smart, game, and always fun to have in the room. Though Gemignani didn't know him, he agreed to let him be the second rehearsal pianist as well as play the synthesizer for the presentations.*

Michael Starobin

MICHAEL STAROBIN

LAPINE: Did you know Steve's work at all?

STAROBIN: Not very well. I was familiar with *Company*, and in fact in between *March of the Falsettos* and working on *Sunday*, I orchestrated and
music-directed a production Playwrights Horizons did of *Company* out
in their theater in Queens. It had just a four-piece rhythm section. Sondheim came out to see it and was not pleased at all with what I had done.
When, much later in the *Sunday* process, I reminded him that I had
worked on that show, he sort of blanched and then laughed.

LAPINE: So your contribution to the workshop was . . .

STAROBIN: Certainly not my piano playing. I was like the worst rehearsal
pianist. What I did know about was the MIDI synthesizer, which had
been invented right around that time. It brought a number of advances
in what you could do in replicating orchestral music, and that was my
contribution when we began our presentations. I was able to do the
synth work and also I brought in a friend to play trumpet for the calls at
the end of the show.

LAPINE: So you really didn't come on as orchestrator until the next round.

STAROBIN: Right. It was kind of amazing that Sondheim turned from his
other collaborators to go with people of much less experience, much
younger, completely out of the Broadway tradition. I mean, neither of us

really knew what was traditional, let alone the mechanics of a musical or how you structure a piece.

LAPINE: Well, we did do *March of the Falsettos*.

STAROBIN: Yes, but that was certainly not in the Broadway tradition. You know, I think everyone in the music department was nervous because they knew I had done all of their jobs for you. I had music-directed for you. I had copied the show. I was the only person in the music department who was your guy.

Second Reading: May 9, 1983

We decided to do a reading of the latest script prior to going into rehearsals. At this point we had a number of new songs to hear, as well as a rough draft of the second act. Our song ideas seemed to come in different ways. The aforementioned first song—the title song—emerged from Steve's instinct that we needed a lighthearted opening number. The next song, "Yoo Hoo," came from the original stage direction:

> *(There is laughter from the back of the stage. The trees rise. A backdrop lifts revealing a large likeness of Seurat's framed painting* Bathers at Asnières. *[Could be cutouts in perspective; could be actors; song or dance?] In front of the image stand a man and woman studying it.)*

After some discussion, Steve and I decided that we wanted to create a tableau vivant of Seurat's first major painting early in the show. We figured the technique would pay off in a big way at the end of Act One. Because we could not pre-set the piece on our tiny stage at Playwrights Horizons, we used a wagon to wheel it in from the wings as the boys in the painting sang "Yoo Hoo."

Asnières refers to an island across from La Grande Jatte, so the idea was that the young subjects in the painting were yelling across the river to the inhabitants of "our" island. At the end of the song, the boys froze into the tableau as the characters

(opposite top) Georges Seurat, *Seated Boy with Straw Hat,* study for *Bathers at Asnières,* 1883–1884

(opposite bottom) Georges Seurat, *L'écho* (*Echo*), study for *Bathers at Asnières,* 1883–1884

of Jules and Clarissa—an artist mentor of George's and his wife—come upon the painting at an exhibition. (Mind you, they'd come not to praise the painting but to bury it.) Steve took elements of the dialogue I'd written and made them into the song "No Life."

"Color and Light" was another song written around existing dialogue. I found it interesting how organically the songs grew from the book and I began to understand why Steve had waited for me to complete the entire first act before he began to compose.

The other sequence we completed—at least in part—was called "Gossip." Dramatically, what we knew about Seurat came largely from other people's impressions of him—and this was an opportunity for the habitués of the park to gossip about the enigmatic George and his mistress, Dot.

William Parry was cast to play the Boatman. He had come to our attention through Ira Weitzman, and had a varied résumé featuring many downtown shows at La MaMa and the Public Theater, including some seven productions with Hair director Tom O'Horgan.

PUTTING IT TOGETHER

The Boatman in the foreground with Franz and Frieda. Georges Seurat, detail from *A Sunday Afternoon on the Island of La Grande Jatte*, 1884–1886 (The Art Institute of Chicago / Art Resource, NY)

WILLIAM PARRY

PARRY: Okay, here's the absolute truth of it. I got cast in *Sunday*, and we did that preliminary reading of what was the first act a couple of weeks before the first rehearsal. After it was over, I went to the phone booth on the corner and called my agent. She asked, "So how did it go?" I said, "It was great. I just sat and listened to this really interesting piece, and Stephen Sondheim sang through what he has of the score. But I really have no idea what I would be doing in this. I don't think there's much to bite into . . ." and she said, "Stop right there. You are doing this project." And I said, "Well, I—" She said, "No, no, no. There's no 'Well, I—' You are going to do this project. There is no telling what it will become. There is no telling what you will end up doing in it. You've got to trust it. You've got to be there." I've been with her for forty-seven years, and she never gave me a bit of advice that was better than that. It really changed my professional life and more.

First Day of Rehearsal: May 31, 1983

Rehearsals for the workshop were held at 890 Broadway studios, a beautiful complex of spacious rehearsal rooms owned by Michael Bennett. This was my first real inkling that my circumstances had changed.

The first day usually begins with a meet-and-greet with the cast and producers; the designers generally present renderings of the set and costumes; and then there is a read-through of the script with the composer and/or lyricist playing and singing the score. I find this one of the most stressful days for everyone. The actors are often meeting one another for the first time, and then they must sit down and read the script aloud. Often, some adopt a kind of mumble, just to signal to the others that they are not "performing." It's an excruciating exercise.

Since the reading three weeks prior, Steve had added to the score a reprise for the song "Gossip": the "Day Off" sequence, a series of short songs sung by George's subjects as he draws them; and most important, he finished the finale of the first act, "Sunday." When he sang the finale song at the piano, we all knew we had a stunning ending to the first act. (We didn't really realize how truly glorious it would be until we heard the company sing it for the first time days later.) I had written very detailed stage directions indicating exactly how I wanted the tableau vivant of the painting to come together under George's exact direction. The reprise of the simple arpeggios that accompany George's litany "Order. Design. Tension. Balance. Harmony," which we heard at the beginning of the show, made for a seamless transition to the anthemic song "Sunday" and the completion of the finished painting/ tableau.

MANDY PATINKIN

LAPINE: You had never met Bernadette before that first rehearsal, and neither had I.

PATINKIN: I was just a fan. I remember she walked in the room and my heart just went crazy from the moment I set eyes on her.

BERNADETTE PETERS

LAPINE: I didn't meet you until the first day of rehearsal. I remember exactly how you looked, and when you came in you were so confident and warm. It put everyone at ease. Do you remember the crazy thing that happened that first day?

PETERS: No.

LAPINE: Someone came into the room from the 890 offices, called us over, and whispered, "There's an emergency call for you. Your father is sick." You rolled your eyes and said, "No. He's not." It turned out you had a stalker. Your manager Tom Hammond was there and he went off to handle it.

PETERS: Oh, yeah. I remember that stalker.

DANIELLE FERLAND

LAPINE: Were you nervous meeting Sondheim at the first rehearsal?

FERLAND: I remember him being like a looming figure. I had heard he was, like, really famous, and when we finally met him I felt that he should have been more dressed up. I remember that because my mom said it.

He had on, like, chinos, and they were all ripped at the bottom. And I remember him singing some of the score. He was sitting at the piano and playing through stuff and singing with his eyes closed. And that was kind of odd. Also kind of cool.

During the first couple of days of rehearsal, we taught the music and did various improvisational exercises. When I lived in SoHo, my place was near the Byrd Hoffman Studio, which was Robert Wilson's workspace and also an arty hangout for those of us in the neighborhood. I would drop in there on occasion and check out the goings-on, which were often various improvisational events. This came in very handy when I did the Gertrude Stein piece, which was largely improvised. As a director without that much experience under my belt, I thought part of my job was to bring a roomful of people with different backgrounds and training together. Improvisational exercises seemed like one way to do it.

5.30.83

PROMENADE EXERCISES

Musical-chairs: when the music stops, assume a pose

Changing partners: when the music stops, one partner remains behind -- the other advances to the partner frozen ahead

Half the strollers pick their pose from another stroller

Conditions:

Too hot

Too cool

Too tired

Impending rain

Boredom

Flirtation

Don't wish to be with your partner

Sexy

Poses:

Establish parasol positions for women; top hat positions for men.

Pick your best angle/profile.

Fight to be in the front of the picture.

My notes on exercises

PUTTING IT TOGETHER

WILLIAM PARRY

PARRY: You were having us do acting exercises. Theater games. For example, one day you had Bernadette seated and we were to promenade past her, choosing an attitude to play that reflected how we felt our characters might feel toward her. I really liked all that stuff. I was sort of *home*. I thought, This is terrific. I like doing this. It was surprising to me that there were a number of people in the room that *really* didn't like it—that thought it was just so sophomoric. I had spent so much time working with the likes of Tom O'Horgan, putting worlds together. It felt very natural to me.

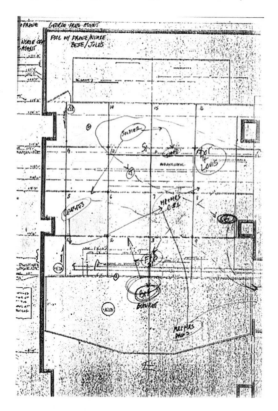

Blocking sheet

BERNADETTE PETERS

PETERS: I felt the first few days of rehearsal were different from what I was used to because you wanted to play games and do exercises. I guess other directors sort of do that, too, but I had never worked with one. I guess it brings a cast together so that everybody feels they're contributing and important. After a couple of days, then it was, "Let's concentrate on this scene. Let's rehearse that." I think we all began to feel more comfortable when we got down to work.

Because of my graphic design background, I sketched out my staging ideas on sheets of grid paper. The grid was like a chessboard and I marked out who moved where and when. The stage managers taped out the floor exactly like my grid so I could easily replicate my intended blocking with the actors. Of course, these blocking sheets were often just a place to begin, but it took a certain pressure off me to have a plan when I walked into rehearsal every day. For March of the Falsettos, *the only other musical I had directed, this method had worked well. Of course, in retrospect, I realize it must have made the cast also feel like chess pieces at times, which, in some ways, they were.*

Although I have been unable to track down our stage manager, Fred Orner, for this book, I did speak with the assistant stage manager, Loretta Robertson, who had worked on several off-Broadway shows prior to Sunday. *This was our first time working together. Her dream had been to stage-manage on Broadway—but after accomplishing that with* Sunday, *she came to realize that this wasn't the career path for her. She left the business to become a physical therapist.*

LORETTA ROBERTSON

ROBERTSON: It was a shift for me to work with you, because you were much more laid-back than the other directors I had stage-managed for. The directors I had worked with were very direct: "We're going to do this. We're going to do it this way." Even Des McAnuff, who was considered experimental, was still like, "No, it's got to be this way."

LAPINE: Well, I think we were "discovering" the show. It was very skeletal when we started. It got built in that workshop. Sure, sometimes I didn't know where I was going, but I always knew where I was going to end up: in that painting. Clearly, I didn't really have the directing craft down to explain their "motivation" to the actors when it came to giving them blocking. On the other hand, Sondheim had enough craft for all of us.

ROBERTSON: I had no expectations for the show because it was a workshop. I think, because Sondheim was associated with the project, some of the cast thought, We're going to get our ticket straight to Broadway. Of course, most of the actors didn't get to read a script before they accepted the gig, and it was a surprise to some that their roles were relatively small.

Carmen Mathews, who played George's mother, was the oldest member of our company, at seventy-two. The actor Remak Ramsay was cast in the role of Jules, playing a painter of note who was a mentor to Seurat. Ramsay was forty-six at the time, and the second-oldest member of our company. He had worked several times at Playwrights Horizons, notably in A. R. Gurney's plays, and I thought him a fine actor. He was invited to participate in this book but didn't respond.

NANCY OPEL

OPEL: We were doing an improvisation exercise where we were sitting on the floor as if we were in the park having a picnic, and Remak Ramsay was not happy doing these improvs. In a certain way, being young and inexperienced, I was rolling with everything. It didn't occur to me to not roll with everything; I was like, Hey, this is fun and this is cool. But Remak did not think it was cool. He just seemed angry, you know. I was kind of scared of him.

STEPHEN SONDHEIM

LAPINE: Remember Remak Ramsay? He was our Jules, until he wasn't. He didn't show up for rehearsal one day. I think it was at the end of our first week. He had written you a letter, quitting.

SONDHEIM: Oh, I'd forgotten this.

LAPINE: His letter said something to the effect of, "Why are you working with this guy, James Lapine? He doesn't know what he's doing. I quit."

You called me up to tell me you got this letter, but you spared me the details. All you said was that you wrote him back and his hands were probably singed from holding that piece of paper.

Remak Ramsay's leaving the show was not the only discouraging news I received after the first week of rehearsal. I came home exhausted one night to find a three-page letter from Ed Kleban. It began by describing a lunch he'd had with a "colleague" who had read Sunday *and told him that elements of it were evocative of Kleban's musical* Gallery, *which I had briefly worked on with him. He went on from there in such detail that it seemed he must actually have read* Sunday *himself. Kleban wrote that I had a moral and legal obligation not to appropriate his work, and copied the letter to his attorneys. My head was swimming. I put the letter back in the envelope, didn't speak of it to anyone, and crawled into bed.*

After a few days I decided I'd better deal with Kleban, so I wrote him a short note simply reminding him of my production of Photograph, *explaining how I used the* Sunday *painting as inspiration for a segment in that show, and how it had been the reason Wendy Wasserstein had introduced us in the first place. I invited him to see our presentation and said I thought it would put his apprehensions to rest.*

During the three-week rehearsal period at 890 Broadway, Steve and I would speak almost daily. I would fill him in on my work, generally putting a positive spin on everything, and he would fill me in on his progress—no doubt putting a positive spin on everything, too. Eventually, I casually mentioned the letter from Kleban. It was then that I discovered that Ed's agent, Flora Roberts, was also Steve's agent. Steve didn't seem particularly concerned, so the subject was dropped.

Work on the material was moving apace in the rehearsal hall. My anxiety level was suddenly ratcheted up when the "Broadway" column in The New York Times *announced:*

What is going to be the hottest ticket in town this summer? The obvious answer is "Cats." But not during the three-week period from July 9 to 30. That is when "Sunday in the Park with George" . . . will make a fleeting appearance at Playwrights Horizons. [According to Sondheim:] "This is not a way station to Broadway . . . It is a work in progress. We want to take a look at it and let it determine its own future course."

Any hope I naïvely had for an under-the-radar workshop experience was imme-diately dispelled.

BERNADETTE PETERS

PETERS: When I first worked with Steve on the music, he was very spe-cific, but he would also give you very good reasons for his notes. If you asked a question, like, "How about if I did that this way, or didn't hold that note?" he would actually take what you said into account and think about it. Then he'd go, "No. That doesn't work because . . ." As we know now, he's thought it out every which way beforehand and there's a spe-cific reason for his choices. He also writes for the character, so he would explain to you why the character wouldn't do that. He would say, "I wrote this song because James gave me this monologue." "Color and Light," for example. He would tell me how the song came to be. Why he wrote it. The rehearsal process was exciting because you never knew what material was going to come in next.

LAPINE: I learned so much from you and Mandy. You guys walked into that rehearsal room prepared and ready to work and you were consummate professionals. Both of you had so much more experience than I did. I would rehearse something a couple of times and be ready to move on, but you were like, "No, no, no." You both wanted to rehearse a scene or a moment until it was absolutely perfect. The questions were always flying. You were both always very focused during rehearsals, and you definitely raised my game. There was no small talk.

MANDY PATINKIN

PATINKIN: When we began rehearsals, it was a little frustrating for me, as I didn't have much to sing. When I officially got the job, you asked me, "Do you draw? Do you paint?" And I said no. "Well, you might want to go to the Art Students League and take some classes." I went there several times and started learning to draw, and I loved it. You can't give me a better gift than a task. I also had to figure out, how do you hold the brushes and how do you switch them? And make sure I was doing the right paint stroke in the right area in the right color at the right time. There was no acting involved. It was, sing the words and get the right color on the dot.

LAPINE: Had you done a workshop before?

PATINKIN: No. It was completely new territory for me, in terms of the way of working.

MARY ELIZABETH MASTRANTONIO

MASTRANTONIO: I remember being so gobsmacked by the talent in the room and the confidence of the actors. And it was very much like a play with music. I just watched people. Christine Baranski—she was so confident in her attack of her character, grasping this woman she was playing. I thought, Man, I will have to grow into that. And Nancy Opel just started using this accent, and the Boatman, and the Little Girl—that little girl! I was like, Oh, my God. This kid's amazing! I looked at the material and the lyrics and thought, I can't horse around. I mean, I had to concentrate. You were giving notes and explaining something to the company about a concept you had and yours truly raises her hand and says, "Excuse me, James? I don't really understand what that means." I don't think the person next to me did, either.

LAPINE: I could get a little intellectual sometimes, trying to explain what I had written and how I envisioned the show. I knew how I wanted the show to look and feel; I just didn't always have the craft to articulate that to others.

MASTRANTONIO: And I didn't have the craft to be able to ask you a question. I came through music, so you and I were basically in the same boat. You don't even know what you don't know. When Gemignani was creating the finale "Sunday," he would point to an actor and say, "Okay, you sing that, that, that, that, and that. Now swap it over. No. Now, you sing that, that, that, and that. Mary Elizabeth, Melanie [Vaughan], you sing that and that. Now everybody sings "Sunday." You can't notate something like that, so mostly we all just remembered it. And then, was it . . . Michael?

LAPINE: Starobin?

MASTRANTONIO: Yes. He would go home and write it all out because we probably could never remember it the next day. It was so exciting. That finale remains the most beautiful moment on a stage, I think, ever.

The show began to take shape, but I could sense a growing unease among many in the cast.

Melanie Vaughan, a spectacular soprano, was a veteran of four Broadway shows and had worked with Hal Prince and George Abbott. Paul Gemignani had worked with her, and had brought her in to audition. We cast her as one of the Celestes—the two shopgirls who are hunting for men in the park on their day off. For some reason I named them Celeste #1 and Celeste #2.

MELANIE VAUGHAN

VAUGHAN: I had done readings and things like that but had never done a workshop like *Sunday*. It was a very frustrating experience in many ways. In my prior experiences the director always said, "Do it this way. Do it that way. I want this. I want that." And, if you tell me what you want, I can probably find a way to do it in a believable fashion. But working with you was not the normal experience for me. I mean, Harold Prince—I've heard him give line readings. Like, full-on *line readings*. He would act it out.

LAPINE: And actors didn't take exception to that?

VAUGHAN: Nobody seemed to mind it. Well, it *was* Harold Prince. When you would say, "Well, what do you think?" my reaction would be: You're supposed to tell *me* what to do. The show was very arty and you were very arty. Also—I talked about this with other people in the company—the script was very sparse. At the time, it was very frustrating.

Nancy Opel and Brent Spiner played Bette (later renamed Frieda) and Franz, housekeeper and chauffeur to Jules and Clarissa (later renamed Yvonne).

NANCY OPEL AND BRENT SPINER

OPEL: You know, when you're a kid, you're coming out of academic train-ing where they sort of tell you what to do. And coming into *Evita*, which was my first professional job out of school, they just gave me a promptbook and told me what to do. And there you were, starting us with improvs. We got scared because we didn't know what was coming next.

LAPINE: To me, that's a gift to actors: to give them the freedom to try things out. I wanted you to feel you were part of making something and put-ting your stamp on it.

SPINER: Nancy and I really became the biggest pains in your ass. I remem-ber saying to you, "I don't have a character. Where is my character?" And you said, "You're not a character, you're a *color*." And I said, "Oh, well, would you mind telling me what color?"

LAPINE: Oh, God, it's so painful to hear this now, but I get it. I mean, the thing is, it was a show born from an image. I could be very clear on writing a character. I certainly knew who Dot and George were. Jules,

Yvonne, and George's mother were clearly drawn characters. But I hadn't figured out who some of the ancillary characters were yet. You were lost . . . what can I say? I couldn't really argue with you on that front because at that point you were a "color" in the overall portrait I was creating. And you and Nancy helped me when you came up with the idea of the German accents and then Steve's song helped bring these two characters into focus. We were writing it on the two of you. The characters did emerge. Today, I will tell actors that I don't have a grasp of a character or an answer to a particular question. But what I do promise them is that I *will* eventually have that answer. And, you know, now that I have a track record and some awards on my shelf, I find I have the confidence of most actors I cast when they walk in the door. Today, I can have a more intelligent and constructive conversation with actors. Today, I wouldn't say, "No, don't do that." I would explain why their choice doesn't feel right for the play. Sometimes, it's more a process of elimination to begin to understand what you do intend. I can live a lot in my head. You were not wrong in feeling what you felt. My orientation in those days was mostly visual first. I had to sketch it all out before I could fill in the details and nuances. My writing was like that, too. It began with a sketch.

IRA WEITZMAN

WEITZMAN: I think it was a company of people who had given themselves over to this process without having the full information that an actor needs to fulfill their characters. So, they had to invest a lot of faith in the material. There were tensions. Absolutely, there were tensions.

LAPINE: Did people talk to you?

WEITZMAN: No, not directly as a complaint, but I'm a close observer of any company that I'm involved in, because that is the true way for me to help when problems arise, which is really what I do. I can troubleshoot situations. If I dare say, I think it was probably an extremely difficult and risky challenge to both write and direct a new musical, particularly one with the ambition of *Sunday in the Park with George*.

CHRISTINE BARANSKI

BARANSKI: I think there are directors who are more actor-friendly. They get inside the actor's process, or they talk in terms of how to get the result. And then there are directors who just tell the actor, "This is the result I want." A lot of American actors aren't comfortable with that. I would argue that a lot of English directors, certainly in the past, were totally result-oriented, and it didn't bother the English actors. "Oh, that's what you want?" And they'd figure out how to do it. But American actors are used to a director massaging them into a performance or it coming from the inside out.

Obviously I began to sense after the first couple of weeks that I wasn't the most popular guy in the room. There was definitely a disconnect with some of the actors. I think being a writer-director—and a new one at that—I was still learning how to divide the two roles. I didn't know how to just be the director, though I knew exactly what I liked and what I didn't like.

MELANIE VAUGHAN

VAUGHAN: One day you were giving notes to Brent Spiner, Nancy Opel, and myself. We were just sitting there like a wall—total deadpan, just staring back at you. There was no response to anything you were saying. All three of us did that. I apologize. That was really kind of mean.

LAPINE: What were you angry about?

VAUGHAN: We were frustrated because we didn't know what to do, so we figured we'd take it out on you because you were supposed to *tell us* what to do.

LAPINE: Why didn't one of you say, "You know, James, we just don't really know what we're doing. We're really frustrated"?

VAUGHAN: I would do that now. At the time, I wouldn't do that because you were the director. You were the power person in the room.

LAPINE: But you *were* clearly communicating to me that you were unhappy.

VAUGHAN: I'm sure we were, yeah. At that time, I was a person who hid a lot. And I was so afraid that if I did something poorly or wrong, people would say, "That's awful. Get rid of her right now. Fire her. She's no good." And that colored my reactions to everything. And sometimes my response was to become aggressive, you know, or to become angry. That's just who I was at the time. I hope to God I've changed for the better over the years. And, as I look back on that experience, I realize actually that [your style] was one of the better things that could have happened to me, in the sense that I learned to not wait for somebody to tell me what to do.

MANDY PATINKIN

PATINKIN: I would draw all day in rehearsal. I would sit there drawing the Boatman, drawing my mother, and drawing the Celestes. Then you would have me walk to a place on the stage, just stand for a second, and say, "I have to finish the hat," turn around, and walk away. It was frustrating.

Mandy Patinkin and
William Parry

WILLIAM PARRY

PARRY: I thought you were going to fire me. Early on, you came and talked to me, and you said, "It's interesting that the Boatman is down front and you're only seeing half of him; he's in total profile. I think maybe he has a patch on his other eye." And I said, "Yeah, okay." You went on, "And maybe he has a limp. There's something with his leg being so straight in the painting." You had a lot of really good ideas. This was all great stuff, so I said, "Yeah, this is great. Thanks. I'll work on this." So I'm putting this in the hopper, starting to work on it, wearing the patch. I'm about four days into wearing that patch, and when I put it on I could feel myself—because I had lost my stereoscopic vision—getting quiet, and being more reserved, and it was starting to bother me a little bit. I was getting, like, a little pain in my head, which could've been psychosomatic. And one day you said to me, "Bill, I don't know what you're doing. I mean, this character is a rough man and a workingman, and I'm just seeing you as so small and held back." The feeling that I got from you was, "Maybe I've made a mistake here. Maybe you are miscast." And I'm thinking, Shit, because now I really want to be in the show.

LAPINE: So what did you do differently after that conversation?

PARRY: I did a sea change. Every day at lunch, I would go out to Union Square Park and hang out there. Always alone. And that was when Union Square Park was a pretty dicey place. There were a lot of homeless people. And I just watched them. I'd lie down on the grass. I mean, it sounds so silly, but it really helped.

When I first started directing, I wanted things exactly as I saw and heard them in my head. Smart actors don't want to feel hemmed in to a preconceived notion of how to play a character with no room to move. (Of course, I have rarely heard an actor complain about a lyric or how it was set to music, or about the music itself, and when they did, it usually had to do with where the music sat in their voice.)

When I direct now, I still do what I did when I directed Sunday*—I don't give any substantial direction right off the bat. I just let the actors dive into the role without too much guidance. Some people hate that and some people are really happy to* *come into the room with their own ideas. The difference is that now I let the actors know how I work and why I work that way: that I learn a lot by seeing where the actors' instincts take them. Also, I want them to get a sense of one another. After a couple of days, I firmly take the reins: this is what I'm looking for; this is who this character is; and this is what the scene is about. And if I haven't yet formulated a game plan for a scene or an actor's arc, I make that clear. When I was directing Sunday, I was working instinctually. I think what I've learned is to be better at articulating my vision for a project. To let the acting company know what's going on inside my head, which doesn't necessarily mean that I won't change my mind about things—but at least we will all have a common point of view from which to begin the work. All of that said, I also have come to realize that some people will like working with me, and some won't. And that it goes both ways.*

"The Day Off"

STEPHEN SONDHEIM

SONDHEIM: Once we were in rehearsal, I wrote what came to be called "The Dog Song," which originated from a stage direction of yours in the script. Initially we listed it as the introduction to "The Day Off" sequence.

LAPINE: Yes, "The Day Off" was conceived as a series of songs for our secondary characters. "The Dog Song" was intended to be a moment of humor for George—sketching the two dogs that are in the painting—he inhabits them as he sings in their quirky voices.

SONDHEIM: There was a machine called a vocoder that I think we discovered when we went together to see Laurie Anderson perform at BAM. It's a sausage-shaped microphone that transforms your voice into a chipmunk or an old lady, or whatever sound you like. It's a magical thing. So I went with Paul Gemignani to one of the shops in the Forties, near Broadway. We looked at them and we thought Mandy could conceal one in his sketch pad. When we approached him with the idea, he scoffed, "I don't need a vocoder. I'll give you whatever voice you want." He auditioned three wonderful and separate dogs for us and we chose the ones we wanted.

(opposite) Mandy Patinkin

LAPINE: He was grateful to have a new song. In fact, this was the first solo song we gave his character.

Taking this idea of George projecting what was going on in the minds of the people he sketched, the next songs that followed comprised the rest of "The Day Off" number. Each sketch began with George singing along with his subjects for the first two lines to let the audience understand the conceit. During the four weeks in the rehearsal hall, Sondheim delivered "The Boatman's Song"; a song for Franz and Bette, which was simply known as "The Day Off—Pt. IV"; and "Soldiers and Girls" for the Soldier and Celestes. (There were a few different song versions in this spot. One was entitled "The One on the Left," which was wonderfully clever but too long, and it never made it into the show.) Then Steve delivered "Beautiful," the deeply touching penultimate song in the first act, for George as he sketched his mother. It was an amazing output in such a short amount of time.

Johnna Murray, who had been stage manager on March of the Falsettos, *had become my assistant director.*

JOHNNA MURRAY

MURRAY: It was fascinating, because there was no email, no fax machine, no computers, no Internet! So, in fact, I had the great honor of seeing the new material before anybody else, and I mean in both directions. The most notable difference was that you would just give your latest pages to me and say *go*, and I would get there to Sondheim's, and then I would generally have to wait for some time to get Steve's work for you. He never seemed to think it was finished. I said, "Well, I don't think anyone expects it to be finished; I think they want to know how the new song fits in with the piece. The actors want to learn some of the melody. Whatever you have, I'm sure, would be fine." That was obviously not fine with him. He wanted it to be just right, which is a wonderful quality, and why he is Stephen Sondheim.

Playwrights Horizons: June 21, 1983

We moved to Playwrights Horizons for a six-day tech, having sketched out all of the blocking of Act One. Walking into the theater and seeing a fully realized set was a bit of a shock to everyone. Somehow, safely in the 890 studios, this "workshop" venture had remained an interesting experiment. Now, we were really putting on a show. The reality was staring us in the face. And yet it was a great comfort for me to be back on Forty-second Street, where I was surrounded by my friends and associates at the theater. (One of Playwrights' new interns for the music department was the young composer Jeanine Tesori.)

ANDRÉ BISHOP

BISHOP: I talked to you about the show and offered some suggestions, but I wasn't as involved as I would have liked to be. I used to flagellate myself about that; what a missed opportunity to not have been more involved with you and Steve. Secondly, I was so busy raising money and you were not rehearsing in the building, so there wasn't the normal kind of day-to-day contact we were used to. Honestly, I didn't know what shape the material was going to take. Neither did anyone, really. Besides, I've never been one of those artistic directors who carry around yellow pads and give endless notes. I think the key is to work with artists you believe in and then, to some degree, just trust them. I trusted you and Steve to come through with something wonderful.

We dove into tech, transferring our staging from the rehearsal hall to the set, all the while reviewing the new material and book changes. One day, Steve came into rehearsal and saw something he didn't like.

STEPHEN SONDHEIM

LAPINE: I don't think we've ever had a disagreement or a fight.

SONDHEIM: No, but there was one ugly moment.

LAPINE: The moment where—I don't remember what it was about, something I was trying out?

SONDHEIM: I'll tell you exactly what it was. I wandered in during the rehearsal. One of the most moving things about the show is when they all come back at the end. You had the sketch pad on the floor. It had to do with the fact that the sketch pad—either George picked it up or they gave it to him, I can't remember what it was. You were rehearsing and I said something like, I thought it was too sentimental or too *something*— right in the middle of you working. That was the only bad moment I think we've ever had.

LAPINE: I don't remember what I said or did.

SONDHEIM: It was the look on your face. All I know is, when I went home I wanted to shoot myself. I thought: You don't do that, ever, to anybody.

LAPINE: You were very apologetic. I was probably upset that whatever transpired was in front of the company. Mom and Dad were having a disagreement in front of the children. It's why I don't like anyone watching me rehearse. It's very nerve-racking having someone watching you when you're trying to create something.

SONDHEIM: On my very first show, *West Side Story*, Jerry Robbins [the director and choreographer] was rehearsing. I went into the rehearsal room. He immediately turned to me and said, "Get out." He didn't say it that way, but it was the look on his face—and I couldn't understand why. *That* was why. He was *making*. You don't want to be making something in front of somebody else.

LAPINE: Well, I always cared very much about your opinions, and I still feel that way now. If I'm directing someone else's work, I want them to come in *after* I've got it the way I want it, so they can say "That's great" or "That's not good."

SONDHEIM: That's the whole point. You're the first person I worked with who I would play an unfinished song for, because you insisted.

LAPINE: That's right.

SONDHEIM: I had never played an unfinished song for anybody for the same reason. You want to finish your product, and then present it. If it's not finished, then somebody will say, "Well, *blank, blank*"; and I will say, "Well, I'm going to do that."

LAPINE: When we were working together, discussing ideas about the show, we did a lot of prefacing our remarks by saying, "This may be the dumbest idea . . ." And sometimes it *was* a dumb idea, but often dumb ideas can lead to smart ones. You have to trust your collaborator and yourself, and not self-censor.

SONDHEIM: It all had to do with your "Let's try this"—a semi-improvisational thing that you do. It's something I wasn't used to, but it's part of the same process, which is, Just let me get the feel of it. It was the way you worked, so I worked that way, too.

First Performance: July 6, 1983

STEPHEN SONDHEIM

LAPINE: We were sitting together the very first time we had an audience. André came out and made this long speech letting the audience know that this was an ongoing workshop, the show was not finished—

SONDHEIM: We only had one act—

LAPINE: Actors might be holding scripts . . . there were so many provisos about what was going to go wrong, it was almost like a comedy routine! The show began, and there's the moment toward the beginning when the tree flies out as George is erasing it on his sketch pad. The audience burst into laughter. You grabbed my arm so hard I almost jumped out of my seat. You whispered, "They got it, they got it!" You were so excited that the moment landed.

SONDHEIM: I did the same thing the first preview of *Sweeney Todd*, when Mrs. Lovett gets the idea for killing everybody. *Bing!* And the entire audience—they didn't know what the plot was, and there was this great GASP. I grabbed Hugh Wheeler the same way. It's great when you prepare something for an audience and they get it the first time. It's a great moment.

LAPINE: I was bruised, Steve.

SONDHEIM: I'm sorry.

LAPINE: No, no, no. It was funny, because if somebody fucked up a line or a lyric, you'd do the same thing.

SONDHEIM: Oh, that, too. Yes, I guess I do that.

LAPINE: It was fun. The actors used to joke about hearing you in the audience, because you would sometimes—

SONDHEIM: My laughter.

LAPINE: Laughter, or an involuntary grunt.

SONDHEIM: Oh, really? I usually try not to grunt. That's something Arthur Laurents always did, but he did it so that everybody would know. So I try to avoid that.

LAPINE: Here we were in this small theater. We have our four-piece band: Paul Gemignani conducting and doing percussion, Tom Fay playing piano, Michael Starobin on the synthesizer, and Phil Granger on flügelhorn and trumpet. The audience was so thrilled to be there. I mean, this was a new thing, getting to see a show in process, sitting with the creators. André or Ira continued to make a speech before each show, explaining to the audience where we were in the process. We got the opportunity to see our work before a non-industry audience—at least for a while.

SONDHEIM: Also, it was "Mister Broadway goes off-Broadway."

LAPINE: How did that feel? You were the oldest guy in the room when we went into rehearsals.

SONDHEIM: Loved it. And what I also loved was that it wasn't a commercial vibe I was getting from you or that theater. You just put on the play. If it doesn't work, it doesn't work. You're not letting sixty-four backers down. It's an off-Broadway, nonprofit, subsidized theater. I thought, This is the way I want to work the rest of my life. I loved it.

LAPINE: That's amazing. And I felt like I was going in the other direction. Leaving Gertrude Stein behind.

SONDHEIM: You were entering the tunnel, and I was coming out of it.

ANDRÉ BISHOP

BISHOP: The first time we had performed the show was very exciting, and like all first previews, certain things went incredibly well and others did not. The end of Act One, even at that early stage, had the impact that you and Sondheim had intended it to have, and we could tell the audience was very taken with the show. It was a unique experience for them as well as us. At the end of the evening after the audience and actors had left, you, Sondheim, and a group of us stood in the lobby chatting about how the show went and what would be the plan of attack for the next day. I didn't really say anything. I was very shy then. So the next day I was upstairs in my office, and the receptionist buzzed back and said, "Stephen Sondheim is on his way in to see you." I thought, Oh, my God, what's this about, because he never dropped in to see me in my office. So he walks in and without even saying hello he says to me, "André, you did something unforgivable last night." And I stammered, "Oh, what did I do?" And he said, "You're the producer of this show, and we just had our first performance, and we were all standing and talking about what had just transpired and you didn't say one word about the show or what you had seen or how you felt, and you didn't even congratulate the authors. And that is terrible manners and you must never, ever behave that way again." And I said, "Oh, I'm so, so sorry," and he left. Of course, I was very taken aback. It wasn't like I didn't say anything because I didn't appreciate the show or didn't have one or two things to say. I was young and had never worked with someone of his stature. It was stupid of me to presume he didn't care what I thought. I had thoughts and opinions, and I should have shared them. But of course that came across completely differently to him. And I came to realize that even legendary artists as experienced and successful and knowledgeable as Sondheim needed to be bolstered and supported.

LAPINE: Steve was vulnerable and maybe a little insecure, like the rest of us. As we now know, those feelings don't go away, no matter how old you are or who you are or what your accomplishments have been—you're putting a piece of yourself out into the world and you wouldn't be human if you didn't manifest some vulnerability. Oddly enough, that was also what the show we were writing was about.

BISHOP: I was shattered, not because I thought what he was saying was wrong; what he was saying was right, but my essential shyness had gotten in the way of whatever effectiveness I could have had. And I always point this out as the greatest piece of advice that anyone has ever given me about producing—plays, musicals, readings, whatever; you must always say something supportive.

One thing we discovered in our first few previews was that the character of Dot seemed to disappear after the first studio scene and the song "Color and Light." Steve had almost finished the song "Everybody Loves Louis" for the second park scene, but in the meantime, she had nothing to do but appear on Louis's arm. The playwright John Guare, an old friend of Steve's, came to a performance the first week. We were chatting with him afterward and discussing the character of Dot, and John just casually suggested it would be wonderful if we could see Dot learning to read rather than her just alluding to it. It was one of those great ideas that can make a huge difference. Often it's the person who comes in cold who can see your show more clearly and toss out a valuable idea you hadn't thought of. I went home that night and wrote a scene for Dot with her lesson book; this moment then reverberated through the piece to the end of the second act.

When it comes to sharing ideas with colleagues, I am reminded of a story Sondheim told me. During the run of A Little Night Music, *based on the Bergman film* Smiles of a Summer Night, *when the great director came to New York to see the musical, everyone involved was a bit nervous that he wouldn't like the adaptation and the changes that were made from his film. After the show, someone finally asked him how he felt about the changes in the musical adaptation. He shrugged and responded: "We all eat from the same cake."*

Frayed Nerves

Once we started dealing with audiences, the vibe really changed and the stress ratcheted up to another level. We were working all day making changes to the show and then putting them in at night. I would go home after a performance and make notes for the actors, as well as continuing to write the second act. Next morning, I'd come in early to address tech issues before rehearsal began in the afternoon. It was both grueling and exhilarating. However, as we went into the second week, we had a situation.

MANDY PATINKIN

PATINKIN: An audience was coming and watching a completely unfinished piece. All kinds of things weren't written, particularly for my character. And still, the majority of what I had to do was say nothing: just draw, sit on the stage, walk to the X, say "I've got to finish the hat," walk to another part of the stage, and say something else. I was in quite a state. I thought I was a very old, experienced actor at thirty. I didn't realize how inexperienced I was. But the idea of being in front of people without a role—well, I thought you were all crazy. Well, good for all of you, but I'm the one out here on the stage and I don't know how to do this! I had never done anything like it before. I didn't know what a workshop meant.

LAPINE: Well, it was a bit of a new phenomenon. I don't think anyone had done this kind of full workshop production with an audience.

PATINKIN: I wasn't calm, cool, and collected; I was terrified. As positive as I am and as clear as I am now, I was the polar opposite at that moment. I knew people in the business were coming—it wasn't just these subscribers—and this was embarrassing to me. So I said, "I'm out of here. Just replace me."

LAPINE: Of course, you didn't express what you were feeling, because you were right in the middle of a crisis moment. You just stormed out of the theater one day.

PATINKIN: When I was younger, I had a bad habit of trying to fix my problems by running away. One thing I've tried to learn through the years is to sit with the discomfort. But I had no idea how to do that then. I like the theater because you rehearse it. You don't get to rehearse life. So, I thought this was insane, and you were to blame. You know, who else was there for me to blame?

LAPINE: Yeah, I think I went running out of the building and chased you down Forty-second Street.

PATINKIN: You did, and you stopped me and said, "Your wife and your agent are coming tonight. I'm asking you to please put aside your rage and your feelings and your terror, and just give everything you have to this performance. That's all I'm asking." With total "James directing" adultness, you said to me, "If they agree with you that you should walk away, fine."

LAPINE: I don't remember freaking out about your walking out, actually.

PATINKIN: You didn't. Not one iota.

LAPINE: I learned that lesson when I did *Table Settings*. Our lead actor was a bit of a star and he wasn't having a good time. I spent a lot of valuable hours working and talking with him to keep him on board. It was a commercial production and somehow I felt his notoriety was important to the success of the show. Eventually, he quit, and I was very upset until my producers said to me, "Why do you want to have an actor in your show that doesn't want to be there?" It was great advice. And I recast the role and the show was a success. So, at that moment with you, as much as I wanted and needed you to stay with the project, I knew you had to make that decision for yourself.

I called Kathryn Grody, Mandy's wife, a talented actress and writer, and told her about the situation.

KATHRYN GRODY

LAPINE: You know what you said to me when I called you?

GRODY: Remind me.

LAPINE: You said, "Just tell him you love him." Boy, was that *not* in my wheelhouse. Besides, I was feeling very little love coming my way from Mandy.

GRODY: James, you didn't realize how insecure everybody is.

LAPINE: You're absolutely right about that. I often felt inexperienced, but I never really felt insecure about the work, if you know what I mean. There were questions about the piece that were not filled out and to which I didn't have the answers. But I knew the answers were there and that we would discover them. But I did feel kind of helpless at times because I couldn't find the way to connect to certain people, Mandy prominently among them.

GRODY: You make an assumption that somebody like Bernadette or Mandy, who had this huge ascendance, is confident, but nothing fills those empty centers.

LAPINE: Bernadette didn't feel that way to me.

GRODY: I think Bernadette has probably had other ways of expressing insecurity.

LAPINE: Actually, Bernadette tells you immediately when she's feeling insecure about the material or something she's doing. She tells you right there. She doesn't let it fester, which I think is what happened with Mandy. So, you guys came to the show and we had a meeting at that little restaurant next door, Chez Josephine, with you and Mandy's agent, Jeff Hunter. Mandy eventually joined us there.

Kathryn Grody, Mandy
Patinkin, their son Isaac,
and Paul Ford

MANDY PATINKIN

PATINKIN: That moment was powerful for me, because my wife and agent
both looked at me when the show was over, and they went, "You're not
leaving this show. This is unbelievable."

LAPINE: I'm not sure I trusted you after that moment. You know, it's hard to
trust somebody who's going to go running out the door.

PATINKIN: Absolutely. It's also hard to trust yourself when you know you're
that person that might run out the door.

*It was not exactly smooth sailing after Mandy recommitted to the show. Ralph
Byers, who played the role of Jules, was expecting his first child. Of course there were
no cell phones then. He kept telling the young person at the Playwrights switch-
board, "If my wife calls, I've got to know immediately." Well, I guess his wife called
and nobody gave him the message. When he found out, he got so angry he slammed
his hand down on the dressing room table and ended up breaking it rather badly. He*

had to leave the show and we lost valuable rehearsal time putting his understudy, Kevin Marcum, into the role.

KELSEY GRAMMER

GRAMMER: At one point early on in rehearsals you asked me to move downstage but you were pointing upstage, and I thought to myself, You know what? Honestly, you need to know what downstage and upstage are.

LAPINE: Oh, God! It was a strange dyslexia I had for years. Same with remembering stage left and right.

GRAMMER: So that was my initial impression of you: that you didn't quite know what you were doing. And then once when we were performing, I was having trouble with one entrance—I just hadn't rehearsed enough. I couldn't quite figure it out. We were having a note session with the company and you said to me something like: "You fucked up that entrance again," and I thought, How dare you! And I barked at you something like, "Don't ever talk to an actor like that again."

LAPINE: You actually stood up and let me have it in front of the company. I was completely stunned and speechless. You know, the interesting thing about doing this book is when you go back and replay these moments—particularly in light of everyone else's memories of the experience—you begin to understand things you never understood at the time. That was one of those moments, and I was terrified of you after that.

GRAMMER: Well, I'm sorry.

LAPINE: No, you don't have to say you're sorry. I get it. I wish you had just pulled me aside to have that conversation. I would have been grateful for it at the time.

BRENT SPINER

SPINER: When Kelsey called you out at that note session, we could tell that was the stake that went into the heart. That was a big moment.

LAPINE: Yeah. I never mentioned it to Steve. I just kept that to myself.

SPINER: Well, let me just say this: You didn't know that wasn't okay to say at a note session. I think there is a protocol that you hadn't learned. I mean, I don't think it occurred to you.

PAUL GEMIGNANI

GEMIGNANI: You'd get angry sometimes during rehearsals.

LAPINE: When did I get angry?

GEMIGNANI: When shit wasn't working for you and you were struggling to find a solution. You were mostly angry with yourself, but sometimes it came out at us. But as far as I was concerned, that's okay, because you were also cutting to the chase. You'd say something like, "This is fucking bad," and then you'd try to figure out where you were going next. The fact is, it's not a popularity contest. Get the job done.

LAPINE: When I finally just accepted the fact that everyone didn't like me and moved on, the better I got at my job.

GEMIGNANI: It's hard when people don't like you. I've experienced that.

LAPINE: It took me a long time to learn that getting people to like you is not part of the job description.

DANIELLE FERLAND

LAPINE: Were you aware that there were certain dramas going on around you?

FERLAND: Nah. The biggest thing that happened to me when we were at Playwrights Horizons was that I had my first crush—it was on the son of Kurt Knudson, the actor who played the role of Mr. Randolph.

LAPINE: How did you meet his son?

FERLAND: He was just hanging around. I think he was my official first kiss. I was like eleven.

"Finishing the Hat"

At the beginning of the third week of performances, Steve came in with a new song for George called "Finishing the Hat," and it was a turning point in our production. The character of George is not an easy person to know or care about. He's a cool character: driven and passionate and supremely self-absorbed. This song gave us that moment to let the audience hear directly from this artist. It also helped Mandy, who was just desperate for that musical moment to express what his character was feeling underneath that seemingly detached façade. The song also cleverly brought coherence to the beginning of the second park scene as George reviews his sketches, singing the first line again from each of the short songs that make up "The Day Off." Just as each of the park characters expressed themselves as George sketched them, now it is the artist's time to turn that laser gaze inward.

LORETTA ROBERTSON

ROBERTSON: We were going over our stage management notes after rehearsal and Steve came in. He had just written a song and he wanted to play it for you. I remember thinking to myself, How cool is this?

LAPINE: Let me guess: That was "Finishing the Hat."

ROBERTSON: Yes, it was. I told myself to imprint this moment on my brain. It was just one of those *wow* moments. You were thrilled when you heard it, and the next day Steve came back to teach it to Mandy.

STEPHEN SONDHEIM

SONDHEIM: I met Mandy across the street at that restaurant—

LAPINE: The West Bank Cafe, our auxiliary rehearsal space.

SONDHEIM: It was a very hot July day. I was sweating on sixty-four levels before playing the song for Mandy. He just took to it and insisted on putting it in that night. We'd had one rehearsal with it before we brought it across the street to sing it for you.

NANCY OPEL

OPEL: We were in rehearsal, doing our thing, when Mandy and Steve walked in. You stopped whatever we were doing and told us that Mandy was going to sing a new song that he had just learned. So we all parked ourselves somewhere and Mandy sang the song. There was a sort of gobsmacked silence at the end, followed by everyone clapping very enthusiastically. Finally, you said, "Okay, let's get back to work." Everybody just sort of wandered back to whatever they were doing before. Steve was standing down front and I was on my way to the stage and I said, "Steve, I have to go home." He said, "Why, are you sick?" And I replied, "No, it's the most beautiful thing I've ever heard in my life." And he looked at me and said, "Did you really like it?" You know, that's when I finally realized, This is really special—to be involved with something like this show.

MICHAEL STAROBIN

STAROBIN: Late in rehearsals one day, I heard some of the actors muttering something to the effect of, Why are we doing a show about this obnoxious artist? There was a lot of skepticism until the day "Finishing the Hat" came in. I remember watching Mandy rehearsing it and lighting up like a flare. It was just this exciting moment that this character sud-

denly had. This moment of explaining himself: why he's so hard on his partner and also why he's so hard on himself. The piece didn't make sense until that song came in. The finale was already there, which was wonderful. Bernadette's opening was already there. But it was missing that moment—and when it came in, it pulled the show together.

IRA WEITZMAN AND ANDRÉ BISHOP

WEITZMAN: I happened to be the person making the speech the night that "Finishing the Hat" went in; and I remember saying in my intro, Steve Sondheim finished a new song today and Mandy is going to be singing it tonight. The audience, in one fell swoop, gasped at the idea that they were going to hear this hot-off-the-presses new song. The hushed attentiveness that came with the first hearing of that song was really like nothing I had ever experienced. Of course, it was such a beautiful, heartfelt, meaningful song that really seemed to sum up the idea of George's struggle to create, and the joy of finishing his creation. It just left us all in awe.

BISHOP: In some ways, it was the best Mandy ever did it. It was utterly pure. Any actor would respond to a song about creation and creating, but he had no time to work on it. That night he put the lyrics in his sketch pad, but he barely looked at them. He sang it beautifully over many, many months, but there was something so complete and pure that first time he sang it that I'll never forget.

In the final week of our presentations, Steve and I went off during the dinner break to Curtain Up, a nearby restaurant. It was a beautiful summer night and we sat outdoors. I ate while Steve, who doesn't do early dinners, probably just had a drink. His presence was clocked by many of the diners and as we were chatting, I noticed a history professor of mine from my college years sitting at a nearby table. I'd gone to school in a small Pennsylvania town, and it was unusual for me to see someone from that chapter of my life in New York City. I wondered if he even remembered me. He didn't look our way. I figured I would say hello after our dinner and maybe gloat a little when I introduced him to Stephen Sondheim.

After some small talk, Steve said to me out of the blue, "I want to write my next show with you." I was completely caught off guard. "What?" I said. He responded, "I want to write my next show with you." My immediate response was, "We haven't even finished writing this one." I don't much remember where the conversation went from there. Internally, the one-foot-out-the-door part of me was a bit panicked about anything that smelled of a commitment, whereas the healthier part of me was thrilled beyond belief. I had never felt that kind of trust coming at me. It's difficult to put into words the feelings that were bouncing around inside me at that moment. I glanced over at the table where my old history professor was sitting, but he was gone. And, I realized, so was an old part of me.

The Music

STEPHEN SONDHEIM

LAPINE: After "Finishing the Hat" came into the show, the score for the first act was essentially finished. I'm curious about how you connected your score musically. From the first song, "Sunday in the Park with George," onward, how conscious were you about how your score would connect?

SONDHEIM: The arpeggios at the top of the show set up everything. Everything.

LAPINE: So, in a sense, they created the building blocks of the score?

SONDHEIM: Often, yes. It depends. In the case of this show, and *Sweeney Todd*. For lack of a better term, you create leitmotifs: where you take something and it keeps developing. I thought, What's going to hold this whole show together? It is one long arc of a story as opposed to incidents. You do it in the script, too. There are leitmotifs in your work as well.

LAPINE: I suppose that's true.

SONDHEIM: In your script there are phrases that come back. I don't know whether, when you write a phrase, you think that's going to be useful in the second act when she comes back, then it can be repeated. That's what I do.

LAPINE: I wouldn't say I do that consciously. But characters do speak and express themselves in a certain way—and yes, expressions and the use of language can come to define them. I'm not consciously aware that I do that until I read it over. Then yes, I use it.

SONDHEIM: It's a matter of degree, James. Obviously, a lot of my work comes out unconsciously. But I do make a plan, too. Even within a song, I will sketch out what I think the harmonic scheme is going to be. This is something I learned from my composing professor, Milton Babbitt: Have a motif. Okay, what does this phrase imply harmonically? So, we'll put that harmony, say, in the beginning. Then in another section of the song I decide we'll put the second harmony. So when it's all over, it's like one long version of this little melody.

LAPINE: I'm pretty sure you went directly from the song "Sunday in the Park with George" to "Color and Light," if I'm not mistaken.

SONDHEIM: Generally, I like to write it in order.

LAPINE: In this case you jumped ahead and then went back to the next song: "No Life." I think you went ahead to "Color and Light" because it was a continuation of the George-Dot storyline. Also, it had an unusual structure, weaving in and out of the dialogue.

SONDHEIM: I always think in terms of, how do you hold a score together when there's dialogue in between? No doubt that's why I wrote "Color and Light" next. Generally, though, I find if I don't write in order, I will find that I'm repeating myself. Whereas, if I write in order, I say, "No, I've said that already. No, I've said that already."

LAPINE: And by that you mean lyrically, or musically?

SONDHEIM: In every way.

LAPINE: Do you think of the whole score before you write the first song?

SONDHEIM: Yeah.

LAPINE: And that's why you're you. Many theater composers just jump in and write a song, and then another song, without giving enough thought to the entirety of a score.

SONDHEIM: My methodology comes from studying with Milton Babbitt. If you're going to ask someone to listen to something for three minutes, just like asking them to listen to a forty-five-minute symphony, how do you hold their attention? If you're telling a story, it's what happens next?

LAPINE: You keep bringing the audience back to something you have implanted in their ear, even if they don't realize it.

SONDHEIM: Exactly. You're telling a story with motifs, with phrases and things like that. And in a musical, because each song exists by itself—and then sometimes there's dialogue in the song—that makes it even harder to have some kind of coherence, because you don't want reprises all the time. You want something that says, that character sings this kind of music.

LAPINE: Well, it's such an appropriate approach for writing about this painting, too. I thought a lot about how the characters were portrayed visually—where they were in the painting, their scale in relationship to everyone else, etc.

SONDHEIM: Remember the way I started? I had this brilliant, pretentious, terrible idea that since Seurat had twelve colors on his palette and there are twelve notes in an octave, I suddenly thought, Everything's going to be seconds, two notes together—a possible analogue to Seurat's close juxtaposition of different-colored dots, the closeness of the notes on the piano.

LAPINE: Didn't you once consider doing it all on the white keys?

SONDHEIM: Yes, I did indeed. And then I thought, this is exactly the kind of intellectual idea that is completely useless. How did Seurat hold his painting together? Oh, I'll do the same thing.

LAPINE: We didn't know how lucky we were by picking this painting. The painting is brilliant, because it's endlessly inspirational.

SONDHEIM: And no one knew who Seurat was, so we could make it up. If you do a musical about Van Gogh, you've got to cut off the ear.

LAPINE: Seurat did us a favor: he died young.

SONDHEIM: And he never opened his mouth.

LAPINE: And he left very little of himself behind. His only writings were theoretical, not personal.

SONDHEIM: I don't think he would have been any fun to have dinner with.

The Book

The first credit of "book by" in a musical was in 1895. Credits until then were usually "libretto by," "written by," or just plain "by." It has always struck me as a strange credit. Now that I have written a number of books for musicals, I am often asked by playwrights for advice on the craft. (I don't know any individuals who solely write musical books these days.)

Having never written a traditional book for a musical before Sunday—and having seen few musicals—working with Sondheim became my education. I learned as I went along, pretty much writing in order without an outline, and figuring out the show in tandem with my composer-lyricist. It's a real mind shift for a playwright to suddenly be in collaboration with another writer. Finding that common voice is a challenge. Steve had to know who these characters were and where their story was going before he began writing. (If we had been writing an adaptation of existing material, it would have been completely different. We would have had a common frame of reference.) I wish I had the gift to be a lyricist, but I don't. Likewise a poet. But I do enjoy writing monologues for my characters. Getting inside their heads helped Steve know who they were, how they spoke, and what they were thinking about at a certain moment in time. Also, it helped him get to know me. These characters will undoubtedly reflect what's on my mind and why I'm telling their story.

Our other two collaborations, Into the Woods and Passion, were developed completely differently. My initial intention on Woods was to write an original fairy tale. After several attempts I discovered that fairy tales by their very nature are short and often their plots can turn on a dime without any logical explanation. That's when I hit on the idea of inventing original fairy-tale characters and intermingling their story with characters from the well-known tales. I wrote a rather lengthy first scene that set up each of the three main plots and handed it to Steve, declaring, "This does not lend itself to being a musical." I thought it too lumbering and I couldn't see how music could tie it together. Suddenly, our roles had switched. As Steve questioned whether songs could be integrated into the initial Sunday in the Park scenes that I had written, I was the one now saying what I had written did not lend itself to musical treatment. In retrospect, that was probably a great psychological move on my part—tell Steve that there is something that can't be done, and he will show you that you're wrong. To this day, the intricacy of the opening number of Into the Woods still amazes me.

Our third collaboration was Steve's idea. He saw the Italian movie Passione d'Amore, by Ettore Scola, and thought it would make a great musical. I was less convinced when I saw the movie, but once I discovered that it was actually based on a novel by Iginio Tarchetti and read the source material, I found my way into the story. I advocated to Steve that it be "sung through" because it felt so operatic in tone. As we began writing, Steve wrote a great deal of music. We had an informal reading of the first few scenes—maybe a half hour in length. As we walked out of the rehearsal room, Steve was a bit agitated. He stopped me when we cleared the building and said, "This can't be sung through. The ear needs a rest so the music can be 'heard.' We have to restore more of the book." And of course we did, and he was right. Speaking with the producer Emanuel "Manny" Azenberg, he put it rather succinctly: "The book of a musical is a very underrated thing. It's a vital organ that gets dismissed and nobody knows who wrote it. But if you have a book that doesn't engage, you don't really hear the music."

I point out these three examples in order to say that there is actually no one method of writing the book of a musical. And what works for one may be in no way appropriate for another set of collaborators. There are any number of musicals that have been sung through and done so successfully—from my own collaborations with William Finn, the Falsettos shows, to the Andrew Lloyd Webber musicals, notably Evita. That doesn't mean they didn't have a "book." The book writer's most important contribution may be that of creating the structure of the show and the development of the characters; how the story is to be told and how music figures into the equation; and what dramatic and thematic purpose a song serves. This is something that Sondheim understands and helped me to understand: where and how a song functions most effectively. At the time, when it was taking him so long to write the first song, I didn't understand what he meant when he would say he wasn't sure that what I was writing needed songs. But looking back, I think it was a more simple and fundamental question: Why is this a musical and not a play?

One thing to come to terms with immediately if you are writing a book for a musical: the audience has come to your show to hear the actors sing, not talk. So, if you happen to have a big ego, this may not be the line of work for you. Also, if you choose to write a book for a musical, be prepared to do a lot of rewriting. Some of your best material is likely to be absorbed into song. That's the way it works, and should work.

If Sondheim and I have a fault in our writing—and I am not saying we have only one fault—it's that we have too many ideas. Too many things we want to say. We often have had to remind ourselves why we're writing our show. What is the one central idea that drives the project? I usually write a sentence or two to remind myself what I want a play or musical to speak to thematically and tape it to my desk. It brings focus to the writing. When you collaborate, there are even more opportunities to lose your focus, to let important details slip through the cracks. This was the big lesson of Sunday in the Park in previews. When the show was not landing with an audience, it was important for us to stay true to our vision and make sure that we were always writing the show we wanted to write. That doesn't mean we didn't pay attention to the audience and listen when we were offered feedback from friends and colleagues. But at the end of the day, we had to stay true to our initial impulses and write the show we had intended, not the show these people had wanted to see.

A side note: In our current era, the major movie companies have come to realize that the old films in their libraries could be further monetized if they were adapted into musicals. Of course, musicals have been based on movies, plays, and stories since their inception. But more times than not, those projects were driven by their authors because they had a passion to say something that was echoed in the source material, and to say it with music. You can feel the lack of passion when a musical doesn't have an inherent impulse "to be." All the craft in the world can't make up for a song that doesn't have a truly personal cri de coeur at its center.

Then there is the Disney phenomenon. Take your successful animated musical movie. Produce a stage production of it next. Then make the live-action film. I too have written a book adaptation for Disney, for a stage version of The Hunchback of Notre Dame. *It was an interesting challenge. I loved the gorgeous Alan Menken–Stephen Schwartz score and I am grateful that I got the opportunity to work on the project. I learned that transferring the magic of animation to the stage is no small challenge. I made the mistake, however, of reading the Victor Hugo novel, a brilliant but very dark affair, and realized that these were two very different animals. My most memorable moment of the experience came during an early note session after a rehearsal presentation when the then corporate chairman of Disney said to me, "You know, James, if the hunchback can get the girl at the end of the show, we'll make a lot more money." (At the end of the Victor Hugo novel, Esmeralda and Quasimodo are both quite dead.)*

The Final Week

Steve and I had agreed to do two presentations of the first act as a benefit for the theater. Tickets were set at $250. Up until that time, only Playwrights Horizons subscribers had been able to attend, so here was an opportunity for the general public (who had money) to see what we were cooking up.

STEPHEN SONDHEIM

SONDHEIM: Those benefit performances were nerve-racking.

LAPINE: Of course. Many of the people attending were your friends. André and I sat in his office on the second floor and looked out the window as the audience arrived. He pointed out all the notables, many of whom I was not familiar with.

SONDHEIM: Oh, yes. Those were my favorite moments. Again, nonprofit—it's all a family. We'd smoke up there.

LAPINE: Yes, we'd do that often before the performances. Getting stoned and watching our audience arrive.

SONDHEIM: Then you would say, "Magic time," and we'd go down to our little theater. I just loved that. God, that's so much more fun than the Imperial or the Shubert.

LAPINE: And that benefit night was amazing, seeing this well-heeled group of people together in this small, funky theater. You were downstairs in the lobby greeting people. André pointed out Lee Remick, who I of course recognized. Richard Avedon. Mrs. Hammerstein. Mrs. Rodgers. Leonard Bernstein.

SONDHEIM: And then there was Arthur Laurents. I think he came with Terrence McNally. We all met afterward. I'm not going to go into that story.

LAPINE: Oh, must be a good story!

SONDHEIM: He was, to put it mildly, ungenerous about the show. Terrence liked it a lot, but Arthur . . . he was in rehearsal for *La Cage aux Folles*.

LAPINE: I can only imagine. Leonard Bernstein came right up to me in the lobby after the show—I'd never met him—and he planted a big kiss on my mouth.

SONDHEIM: And the tongue inside, because he always did that.

LAPINE: The tongue may have tried to get in, but I think I held him off.

SONDHEIM: Yes. He did that with everybody. Aaron Copland called him "the kissing bandit."

LAPINE: It was hilarious, and then he said to me, "If I give you another $250, can I see the second act?"

SONDHEIM: That's kind of nice.

Act Two

At the end of our last week, for three performances, we made the bold move of mounting what we had of our second act as well. Steve brought in two more songs, both of which were complicated to teach. The curtain rises on the same tableau we had left at the first-act finale, and the characters sing an amusing song called "It's Hot Up Here"—about what it's like to be stuck in a painting. At the end of the number, Seurat walks out and delivers a monologue about the days before his death at the age of thirty-one. This is followed by a series of eulogies from the people in the painting, each of whom leaves the stage after he or she speaks, leaving us in the empty park, which then also disappears.

The second scene suddenly transitions to the present day, and we meet the modern-day George, played by Mandy. He is Seurat's great-grandson, a performance artist, and we are at the Art Institute of Chicago, where he has been commissioned to do a performance-art piece honoring the painting of La Grande Jatte on the occasion of its one hundredth anniversary. His grandmother Marie, played by Bernadette, joins him. The performance piece I created was pretty bizarre in tone.

After George's presentation, the assembled join a reception that is held in front of the painting. A musical number called "Gotta Keep 'Em Humming" provides a commentary on the twentieth-century art world.

(right) Mandy and Bernadette doing God knows what . . .

(below left) Judith Moore and Carmen Mathews

(below right) Kevin Marcum and Mary Elizabeth Mastrantonio

STEPHEN SONDHEIM

SONDHEIM: When we put up what we had of the second act, I got up and did the introductory mea culpa, at your suggestion. "Ladies and gentlemen, there's only one act of our show, but tonight, we are going to

BOATMAN
They all wanted him and hated him at the same time.
They wanted to be painted -- splashed on some fancy
salon wall. But they hated him, too. Hated him because
he was so much taller. Hated him because he only spoke
when he absolutely had to. Most of all, they hated him
because he had the final word!

When the BOATMAN exits, the stage is empty. LIGHTS change.
MUSIC. Enter and old woman in a wheelchair. She is ANNETTE(played by
DOT), George's grandmother, and she is dressed in the same outfit
as the OLD LADY. She begins chanting the following as she
slowly moves, eventually assuming the OLD LADY's pose.

ANNETTE
There are boats on the Seine. There are boats,
boats, boats.
There are sails on the boats. There are sails,
sails, sails.

She is followed bye DEE, George's girl-friend, who is dressed
in a similar fashion to CLARISSA. She assumes her pose as
she chants:

DEE
There is dew on the grass. There is dew,
dew, dew.
There is sun on the dew. There is sun, sun, sun.

Enter JED, who moves to the BOATMAN's position.

JED
There is glare on the water. There are sparkles
ripplig past.
There are sparkles in the ripples. There are
ripples trippling fast.

Then comes NAOMI, who, with parasol in hand, portrays a CELESTE.

NAOMI
There's aroma everywhere. There are scent
smelling treats.
There is music in the air. There are songs
playing sweet.

And, finally, GEORGE, who moves grandly about the space.

GEORGE
There are boats on the Seine with snapping
sails in the wind while the dew on the grass
meets the ripples of the sun as the music in
the air smells the scents of this scene splashing
sparkles of the light on the --

In the middle of his chant, there is a sudden dimming of the
LIGHTS and fading of the ELECTRONIC MUSIC. Everything goes
black for a second and the actions stop. George lets out
a tempermental shout.

First page of the transition into the performance-art piece

share with you what we have of the second act," etc. You made me get up, because it was my fault.

LAPINE: Oh, I didn't make you get up.

SONDHEIM: Yes, you did. You said, "Steve, André can't do it tonight and I think it would be better if you did it. I think people want to see you."

"Gotta Keep 'Em Humming"—Bernadette Peters, Melanie Vaughan, Mandy Patinkin, Kelsey Grammer, and Christine Baranski

Well, I didn't mind. In a theater that size, you feel like you're talking to a small group of friends.

LAPINE: I don't quite remember the performance-art piece. Maybe I've blocked it.

SONDHEIM: There were umbrellas and George carried around a big paintbrush and all that. It was really terrible—not a good idea.

LAPINE: It was bad. That came from my downtown days; the last vestiges of Gertrude Stein. The audience did not know what to make of it. What we learned from that experience, though, was that we had to make the second-act George a very credible artist.

SONDHEIM: Right. We had our first pass at the cocktail party song, "Gotta Keep 'Em Humming." I don't think the song was finished. I don't have a memory of an ending.

LAPINE: Sounds right. And then there was no other music until the end of the show. I kind of whipped together that finale, the reprise of "Sunday." Funny, that never changed.

MARY ELIZABETH MASTRANTONIO AND NANCY OPEL

MASTRANTONIO: It was like cramming for exams to do that second act. That song, "It's hot and it's monotonous . . ." was terrifying. We were in our places for the painting tableau so you couldn't look to your fellow actor for your cue or to the conductor.

OPEL: I played George's girlfriend, and we were on the island of La Grande Jatte, and I came in with a picnic basket, a bottle of wine, and smoking a joint. Not kidding. Do you remember that?

LAPINE: No, but it sounds like something I would have done.

OPEL: Mandy was sitting there reading Dot's red lesson book. I just wanted to kill him, because I was like, Look up at me once, just once, just look at me once, please, when I'm saying my lines. I ended up sort of leaving him alone to his thoughts. We had no real rehearsal time for the second act. We were holding scripts. So, everyone had to really take a stab at who their character was and just go with it.

As painful as it was at times, we learned a great deal about our second act from those three performances. After a totally exhausting two months, when we'd rehearsed for five weeks, introduced eight new songs—including two in the second act—and done twenty-five performances in front of an audience, our little adventure was over. We closed on a Saturday and the next day Sondheim generously threw

a party for the cast and crew at his home. During the evening Steve made a toast and pointed out that one hundred years earlier to the day, Seurat had stepped onto the Île de la Grand Jatte to begin his first sketch for the painting.

Until then, I'd had no time to consider what the next step would be for our show. Of course, the fact that Bernard Jacobs of the Shubert Organization—along with his friend the influential producer Emanuel Azenberg—had attended the workshop didn't escape anyone's notice. But interestingly enough, I was not in the circle of discussion about a Broadway transfer, if in fact there was such a circle. Steve and I didn't speak of it. Exhausted, we went our separate ways for the summer. A few weeks later, we learned that the Shubert Organization, with Azenberg, wanted to transfer our show to Broadway. For the upcoming season no less.

Lapine
Goes
Broadway

Broadway: Preproduction

Steve and I did not work together over July and August of 1983. I think we both needed time off to recover from the nonstop intensity of the workshop. We also needed a little distance from the project so we could come to the next round of rewrites with a fresh perspective.

Right after Labor Day, I was to have a meeting with Manny Azenberg, who would be not only producing the show with the Shubert Organization but acting as its general manager as well. (The general manager oversees all aspects of mounting a production and handles all financial concerns.) At the time, Azenberg was considered one of Broadway's top producers, having presented a host of highly acclaimed plays and musicals, including some eleven by Neil Simon.

I had rented a funky barn upstate, where I'd go to write and get out of the city. On the day I was to meet with Azenberg, I got caught in traffic coming back and didn't have time to shower, shave, or change. I was a bit mortified as I walked into his midtown office in dirty jeans and a holey old sweater. The first thing Manny said after "Hello" was "I love the way you're dressed." Well, that's a good sign, I thought.

MANNY AZENBERG

AZENBERG: My oldest daughter and I debate how many shows I really produced in an era when there weren't thirty people above the title. It's either sixty-six or seventy, depending upon how you define Broadway. But it was a different time. In the period of *Sunday in the Park*, I was also producing Stoppard's *The Real Thing* and Neil Simon's *Brighton Beach Memoirs*. I don't think that that era could be replicated, because it's just much more difficult now and the equilibrium between money and art has changed—it's much more about money than art.

LAPINE: So, you had been involved with the Shubert Organization on many projects. I'm assuming you had a close relationship with Bernie Jacobs, who ran the organization along with Gerald Schoenfeld, and that he asked you to get involved with *Sunday*?

AZENBERG: Yes. He called me up and said let's go see the new Sondheim musical at Playwrights Horizons. If you recall, the Shubert Organization in the early seventies was in desperate straits, and that's when the lawyers Bernie Jacobs and Gerry Schoenfeld took over the company, which up until then had been run by members of the Shubert family. Shortly thereafter, *A Chorus Line* came into the Shubert Theatre and took them off the ventilator, as it were. I always said that Bernie didn't bet on the horses, he bet on the jockeys. Michael Bennett comes up with a musical. Mike Nichols comes up with a play, Neil Simon with a play. You try to get their shows in your theaters. So Sondheim comes up with a musical— you say yes. William Goldman used to say, "Nobody knows anything. Every time out, it's a guess." So Bernie put his money on those jockeys.

LAPINE: In Sondheim's regard, though, he was not commercially as viable as, say, Neil Simon and Mike Nichols. They had real blockbusters.

AZENBERG: Producers and theater owners—well, there's always the fantasy of being involved with the "art" part of the theater. That was the impetus.

LAPINE: So Sondheim really represented "high art"?

AZENBERG: Absolutely. I think of it as "Sondheim intimidation." The Sondheim name intimidated Bernie, and that made him want to do *Sunday in the Park*. He didn't care that *Merrily* failed. When we left the workshop and walked down Forty-second Street, Bernie said, "We're going to do it." I said, "Wait a second. There's no second act!" And he just repeated, "We're going to do it." No matter what objections I brought up, he stood firm. Why? Because it was Sondheim. End of conversation.

LAPINE: When I think that someone would move forward to produce a musical on Broadway without having a finished second act—it's kind of mind-blowing that Jacobs was so determined to produce the show. You know, we did do the second act for three performances at Playwrights. Why didn't you two come back and see it?

AZENBERG: I was afraid.

LAPINE: But you were committed to producing the show!

AZENBERG: Think about the era. There were empty theaters then, unlike today. Bernie was in the business of filling his theaters.

LAPINE: So what did you think of the show?

AZENBERG: It was intimidating and baffling.

LAPINE: Then why did you get involved?

AZENBERG: Because I thought "Finishing the Hat" was really good. I didn't get the show until I heard that song. You don't really know if you can maintain some sort of a balance between your taste and your ignorance and know that there's something past your ignorance that might be good. You go with that.

LAPINE: Why did you have any confidence in me—a neophyte who'd never worked on Broadway?

AZENBERG: We didn't. We didn't know who you were. You were a graphic artist or something like that. From Cleveland.

LAPINE: I wish. Mansfield.

AZENBERG: Whatever. The man is from Ohio. But you were Sondheim's choice.

LAPINE: Okay. So who put up the money for the show?

AZENBERG: It was a $2.1 million budget, as I recall. Bernie said, I'll get the money, don't worry. You do the show.

LAPINE: Wasn't ABC one of their partners?

AZENBERG: I think so. There were other investors, too, but the Shuberts put up a third of it.

LAPINE: Imagine that today. And, in 1984, being an investor didn't necessarily mean your name went above the title as a producer.

AZENBERG: Bernie was very smart. If you take a show and you put it into a theater that you run, you have two streams of income. The rent income might far exceed the production income. But we were going into the Booth Theatre, which has only eight hundred seats. It made no sense to put a musical in there. That was a courageous decision. Not only were we doing it, we were putting it into this little theater.

LAPINE: Well, Bernie did show me a few other theaters. He tried to get me to do the show in the Lyceum—maybe the Belasco and the Cort as well, but it was the Lyceum he kept pushing. I was so naïve. Nobody sat me down and explained the economics involved, or I might have been persuaded to go with a larger house. But I was making an artistic choice. I knew it would never look as good anywhere else.

AZENBERG: The economics would have been worse in the Lyceum. That second balcony is in Montreal!

LAPINE: Where was Gerry Schoenfeld in all of this?

AZENBERG: It was Bernie. He was the one who pulled the trigger.

LAPINE: Gerry was around the theater a lot. Frankly, I didn't have much interaction with either of them until we got into the theater.

Schoenfeld, Azenberg, and Jacobs

PUTTING IT TOGETHER

Steve and I were thrilled that the response to the workshop was generally positive, and that the show was moving forward. Of course, at Playwrights Horizons, it was judged as a work in progress; allowances were made for whatever seemed unfinished or rough. I think the audiences were genuinely excited to be part of the process of a Sondheim show. Because I was a newcomer, I didn't really register how unusual it was for a show like ours—a musical—to jump so fast from an off-Broadway workshop to Broadway.

STEPHEN SONDHEIM

LAPINE: *Sunday* began previews on Broadway just a year and half after we came up with the idea. Had any of your other shows come together that quickly?

SONDHEIM: Oh, sure, yes. *Gypsy* was six months from starting to write it to opening night.

LAPINE: Wow.

SONDHEIM: Yes, and on *West Side Story*, we had a deadline because Lenny was taking over the Philharmonic in the fall of '57. We had to finish that quickly as well. It came together in less than two years.

LAPINE: What about *Sweeney Todd*, my favorite show of yours?

SONDHEIM: Six to eight months. That was the fastest of any with my own music.

LAPINE: That show feels like the writing burst out in a rush of inspiration. So . . . maybe there's a theory here, that the best shows are written quickly.

SONDHEIM: I think much of the best art is made quickly, and some of it not. As far as I'm concerned, there's no real relationship between the length of time you spend and how good it is. You can work for three years and it's terrible. You can work for six months and it's terrific.

LAPINE: I'm an impatient person. Maybe sometimes I work too fast.

SONDHEIM: Like Arthur Laurents, you work all the time. It's not like working toward a deadline. You have a way of—

LAPINE: Banging it out?

SONDHEIM: Utilizing your energy. And if you don't feel inspired, you still write.

LAPINE: For better or worse.

SONDHEIM: I've always been a lazy writer. My habits are strictly from college. I was very good at my classes, so I never bothered to study until the night before the exam. Then I would cram and had no trouble. In the same way, I wait, I wait, I wait; and then, Oh, my God, you need this song on Tuesday, and it's Monday night—

LAPINE: Well, I'm not sure that's accurate. That's what I thought, too, until I started going through your papers recently. You may not have been writing, but you always seemed to be thinking about what you were going to write. I was so surprised to look at the volume of notes you made on each song before you even got around to working on the lyrics and music.

SONDHEIM: Oh, I didn't mean that I write songs overnight—though I have, once or twice.

LAPINE: Well, on *Sunday*, I gave you a deadline. I went ahead and scheduled the Playwrights workshop even though very little of the score had been written. I think it was pure naïveté on my part to do that. In retrospect, it's interesting that you didn't object.

SONDHEIM: As the date approached, I got more creative.

LAPINE: Right. Well, what was interesting was that we were writing in front of an audience.

SONDHEIM: That's the difference between writing for the theater and writing in any other medium. You can work with the audience. It's helpful, even though it can present obstacles—as when flaws reveal themselves that you didn't know existed.

LAPINE: I am not as fearless now, in the age of the Internet, when shows are literally being reviewed on social media the very first time an audience shows up. We didn't have that worry then.

On September 27, a surprise came in the mail: another letter from Ed Kleban. I knew he had come to see the workshop, but, as I had not heard back from him, I'd assumed that he understood our project had nothing to do with his show, Gallery. This letter said otherwise and was again copied to his lawyers. Kleban wrote that "as a moral man . . . I had no choice but to hold off on Sunday until Gallery was produced."

LAPINE: I've been going through a lot of the papers, and discovered a letter from Ed Kleban saying that Burt Shevelove had played you the songs from *Gallery*. So, suddenly, he was implicating you as well as me in ripping him off.

SONDHEIM: Really? Totally wrong. I didn't hear *Gallery* before I wrote the score of *Sunday*. I did hear it, but years later.

LAPINE: As you know, I met your agent, Flora Roberts, through Ed. Did she ever discuss this issue with you?

SONDHEIM: No.

I wouldn't say I panicked when I got Kleban's letter, but I definitely became very concerned about what it might lead to. I decided to get a lawyer to assist me in my response—which was cordial in tone. I told him we simply could not hold off on our production. I was concerned that news of Kleban's threat might lead the producers to pull the plug on our project; nevertheless, I informed them of the situation. In fact, they remained wholeheartedly supportive, and took out indemnity insurance to protect Steve and me in the event of a lawsuit.

At the first few Broadway previews, Ed was apparently in the balcony taking notes throughout the show, but I never heard from him again. Sadly, he passed away three years after Sunday *opened, at the young age of forty-eight. In 2001, many of the songs from* Gallery *were incorporated into a Broadway revue of Ed's work called* A Class Act. *His score earned him a posthumous Tony nomination. In his will, Ed established the Kleban Prize in Musical Theatre, a generous financial award given annually to a lyricist and librettist. Through the years, this recognition has gone to more than two dozen talented artists in our field.*

Moving On

When we began meeting in anticipation of Broadway, Steve and I took a hard look at our second act. Based on the workshop, several people had suggested we jettison it altogether and just expand the first act.

BRENT SPINER

SPINER: I couldn't have been more shocked when I got the phone call saying the show was going to Broadway. I thought, Really? So soon? Everybody in the cast was sure that the first act was going to be expanded into a full-length play and what we'd done as the second act would be thrown out.

ANDRÉ BISHOP

BISHOP: Toward the end of the Playwrights run, many people felt that the first act was a perfect evening, particularly those who saw the sketchy second act. What you and Steve tried to do was very hard—to begin all over again with a new hero. The second act has always been a bone of contention for some, even after the show opened on Broadway.

Steve and I never considered dumping the second act. There was always going to be a second act. We were working toward a bigger idea and a more emotional show. As we continued hashing out our plan, we revisited the first act for cuts and trims. When we'd been doing the workshop with just the first act, we had the luxury of not being concerned about its length. But with two acts, it was something we had to consider.

STEPHEN SONDHEIM

SONDHEIM: In the number "The Day Off" we had all these individual sketches of the people in the painting, and you said, "That's filler. It's interesting . . . but we need to get back to Dot and George. These other characters have to remain peripheral in George's life." This was very smart.
LAPINE: Maybe so, but I was the one who had to tell those actors that their songs were being trimmed or cut altogether. I did it before we got to the first Broadway rehearsal, so at least it wouldn't be a shock.
SONDHEIM: Oh, God.

LAPINE: They were a talented cast, but that's the way it goes. And that's the way it continued to go as we went into previews and we cut even more of their material.

The first matter of business was figuring out the character of our second-act George. It became obvious when we saw it performed that making him a downtown performance artist was not going to work. First and foremost, we had to make it clear to an audience that he was a talented and credible artist. The avant-garde world was too foreign for most people and made George a laughable figure. Seurat was a respected artist who happened to be a commercial failure in his lifetime. We decided that contemporary George should be just the opposite: commercially successful but at a crossroads where he's lost touch with his artistic vision.

As we continued work on writing the show, we also had to begin making casting decisions. First and foremost, we needed to get commitments from our two leads.

KATHRYN GRODY

GRODY: Mandy had been offered *Death of a Salesman* with Dustin Hoffman, but it would have been in direct conflict with *Sunday in the Park*. He was tortured about it, because he had idolized Dustin Hoffman as a kid, and playing his son in this great play would have been a joy for him. While he was mulling over the offers, we went to see the musical *La Cage aux Folles*. At the end of that show, he turned to me and said, "There's no way I'm not doing *Sunday*." He loved *Sunday*. He couldn't believe he was offered *Salesman*, but he made up his mind rather quickly.

STEPHEN SONDHEIM

SONDHEIM: We didn't get an immediate answer from Bernadette about her commitment to the Broadway transfer, so you and I went to Atlantic City to see her club act and speak with her afterward. She voiced her concern that her character didn't have a moment in the first act to express herself—the way George did with "Finishing the Hat."

LAPINE: Bernadette was very up-front. What Bernadette said was: "I feel I drop out after the first couple of scenes, after 'Color and Light.'" Adding the primer scene helped keep her character alive in the park and present in the first act. But Dot still didn't have a musical moment to express her frustration with George. Bernadette's instincts are excellent.

SONDHEIM: It was never selfishness. Remember, the producers wanted to give Bernadette first billing and she said no, it's called *Sunday in the Park with George*, not Dot. The character got lost. It wouldn't have mattered who played the role.

LAPINE: You first wrote a song called "Nowhere to Go," which eventually became "We Do Not Belong Together." I believe that was the first thing you tackled after the workshop. It dramatized George and Dot's conflict and drove the plot forward. It helped the show enormously to hear from Dot at that moment, and made the song "Beautiful" that follows—and the whole scene between George and his mother—even more moving.

With the addition of a new song for Bernadette, we assessed the rest of the score and went about the task of cutting down the first act. Steve trimmed "No Life" and rewrote the "Soldier Song." We also tightened all of the secondary characters' music in the "Day Off" sequences.

Show Business

In Sondheim and Furth's Merrily We Roll Along, *two of the protagonists are writers of a musical. In one scene, they appear on a television talk show and the interviewer asks them, "What comes first, the music or the lyrics?" The more cynical of the two collaborators quickly answers, "The contract."*

In 1919, the Dramatists Guild was formed as an advocacy organization for playwrights, lyricists, and composers. Because writers for the theater own their own work and license it for production, they are not considered "employees" and therefore are unable to form a union. The Guild's council has been made up of leading writers in the theater, and its past presidents have included Sidney Kingsley, Richard Rodgers, Oscar Hammerstein, Moss Hart, Robert Sherwood, Frank Gilroy, and yes, Stephen Sondheim.

Of course, the big question, as in any business, is: Who gets the profits? In 1926, the Guild negotiated the Minimum Basic Production Contract with Broadway producers, which included a minimum royalty of 6 percent of a musical's weekly box office gross for the authors. That was usually split evenly among the book writer, composer, and lyricist. (Musicals traditionally make much more money than plays, as they are usually in larger theaters and have a higher ticket price.) Producers were not happy with this arrangement but eventually capitulated. Later they filed two antitrust suits against the Guild—one in the 1940s and another in the 1980s. Both attempts failed. The last suit resulted in a new agreement called the Approved Production Contract, which is still in effect to this day.

In 1982, the producers of the play Children of a Lesser God were the first to reach an alternate agreement with an author (which the Guild subsequently agreed to approve). That production created a "royalty pool" where writers no longer got their royalties off the gross receipts but rather shared a percentage of the net operating profits, along with other royalty participants and producers. (It is interesting to note that Azenberg and the Shubert Organization also produced that production.) That year, Nine became the first musical the Guild gave its approval to for a royalty pool. When I asked the lawyer John Breglio, who was involved in this negotiation, why the Guild agreed to a pool, he simply replied, "Because the producers were not going to do the show without one." The situation was a bit more complex than that, but suffice it to say, the financial landscape for authors and producers was beginning to change. And Sondheim, as a former president of the Dramatists Guild, was not going to sign a contract that was not approved by the Guild.

As previously mentioned, I had met Steve's agent briefly when I had my dealings with Ed Kleban. Flora Roberts was someone I would come to love and respect. She represented an era of our business when civility and class reigned. Also, she was one of a very few women agents in the theater, and a powerful one at that. At the time of Sunday, she had just taken on an associate, Sarah Douglas. Flora passed away in 1998.

SARAH DOUGLAS

DOUGLAS: When Steve came off Merrily, he was very depressed.
LAPINE: I met him a few months later.

Flora Roberts

DOUGLAS: Flora called him up and she went out for a drink with him. She said, "So, do you want to give up writing?" He said, "Yeah, I'm going to give up writing." She said, "Do you know who's going to care? Nobody but you and me."

LAPINE: They clearly were very fond of one another.

DOUGLAS: I learned a lot from Flora. She had a strong moral center. She was very discreet. She would never, in my entire time working with her, say anything bad about a client's work. She also could be tough. Frank Weissberg, the lawyer for the Shuberts, called her up about a deal they were making for one of her clients. He began by saying: "This is what we're going to do." Flora stopped him dead in his tracks: "I'm an agent. I don't take dictation."

LAPINE: What was her role in the Kleban project I was briefly involved with?

DOUGLAS: That was before my time. Flora was so supportive of Ed in the face of many, many challenges with that relationship. I saw her influence better behavior in people. Ed was kooky and wasn't helped by his very divisive, cantankerous lawyer. He was not the first client that Flora represented who had wild success in an initial outing, which then became crippling.

LAPINE: How involved was Flora in making the deal?

DOUGLAS: Oh, she was involved. Of course she worked along with Steve's lawyer, John Breglio. Flora was very good friends with Manny Azenberg. He was always more sympathetic and approachable than Bernie Jacobs. She took the position that *Sunday* was an opportunity for the Shuberts to actually show their mettle as producers as opposed to just theater owners. Many young writers today say to me, "I want a career like Steve Sondheim's." I've heard that my entire time in the business, and it sort of makes me chuckle because I go, "You don't even know really what's behind that career. It hasn't always been a slam dunk." *Sunday* was a perfect example where the red carpet wasn't rolled out for him. What I saw in Flora was that she was passionately in love with *Sunday*—she had a kind of determination about that project you didn't see every day. One of the things that Flora was very good at was her psychology dealing with the various parties involved. When things got really tough and ugly, she had a way of just stepping back and having perspective. She used to call on other people to bring their "higher self" to the conversation. This, sadly, does not happen anymore.

As for the business side, royalty pools were a new phenomenon, and Flora didn't understand them. She said, "We'll have Manny Azenberg come to the office. We'll have sandwiches over the desk, and he'll teach us about pools." He came in, and that's what happened before the meeting with the Dramatists Guild.

Steve's lawyer, John Breglio, worked out of the prestigious office of Paul, Weiss, Rifkind, et al. Besides Sondheim, he represented Michael Bennett and a host of other superstars in the theater. My agent was George Lane, a man younger than I was. I believe I was his second client.

GEORGE LANE

LANE: I first met Flora and Breglio at her office on Fifty-seventh Street. We all sat at that kidney-shaped desk and discussed the project. I made a proposal—I was trying to tie your directing deal to the writer's deal and get you a fifty-fifty split with Sondheim, with your directing fees joined with the writer's fees. Flora didn't care for that idea. Her way of expressing that was actually not to express it, but to leave the room. And then I had to go back and forth with Breglio at some length. We worked out a deal—and it wasn't my proposal. That said, Sondheim being Sondheim could have asked for more than he was getting—which is what I expected when I went into that meeting. He only wanted the Guild minimum. Sondheim was always very, very generous.

LAPINE: Yes. And after *Sunday* we actually did do a fifty-fifty split on our future two projects. And that was something Steve suggested.

JOHN BREGLIO

BREGLIO: We had a meeting at the Dramatists Guild offices, and we all sat around. Peter Stone was president of the Guild at the time. We had a real problem because you were putting the show into a tiny theater. *Sunday* was a trailblazer going into a "play" house. Now, of course, there are a number of musicals playing in what were then theaters considered too small for anything but a play.

LAPINE: Economically, that forced the Dramatists Guild to make some concessions?

BREGLIO: Yeah, it was very tense. Bernie would talk to me privately. He really wanted me to do whatever I could to help negotiate an arrangement that made economic sense. Steve's instructions always to me were, "I will not do anything without the certification of the Guild." Keep in mind, there had only been one royalty pool approved for a musical by the Guild at this point. That was *Nine*, which had opened two years earlier at the 46th Street Theatre, which had thirteen hundred seats. Now we're talking about the Booth, which had eight hundred seats—almost 40 percent less. So the challenge was to figure out how we could put a square peg into a round hole. Peter Stone, the president of the Dramatists Guild, was being very aggressive. He was still very angry about the notion of a royalty pool. He said that gross deals were a birthright for writers in the theater. Bernie knew he was in a very delicate situation. I had told him, "Look, this has got to be drawn as a Guild deal, whether you like it or not. If the Guild doesn't go along, Steve will not agree." And I assume you would have been in the same position.

LAPINE: Yes, though I don't even think that I was a member of the Guild at that point, to be perfectly honest. But of course I was going to do whatever Steve wanted to do.

BREGLIO: Well, it became clear that *Sunday* would have to have a royalty pool if it was going to be in any way economically feasible. At this point there were very few people who knew how pools worked. Peter Stone tried to manipulate the numbers as best he could. I believe the pool for *Sunday* was unprecedented. I don't think anyone has ever done one like that again. I told Steve, "This is totally justified. I don't see how they can make much money." Everybody would complain about Bernie, but he was very passionate about certain things. He wanted to do the show, but he was also a tough businessman. I'm pretty sure that Gerry Schoenfeld told me at one point: "I don't know why Bernie wants to do this. This is sort of insane, putting the show in the tiny Booth Theatre."

LAPINE: Yeah, I was being intractable. Funny to look back on that now: I had no sense of the repercussions at my insistence that this show go into the Booth Theatre. I just picked what I thought was the best space for the show.

BREGLIO: Peter Stone wanted to make sure that everyone knew that this deal was unprecedented and that the Guild would not agree to something like this again. Of course, as the years went by, the Guild had to accept many, many formulas.

Steve and I were asked by Bernie Jacobs to attend a meeting about the show up at the Shubert Organization offices. We arrived to find Flora Roberts, John Breglio, George Lane, and Biff Liff, who was a senior agent at William Morris, also there.

LAPINE: I'm not quite sure why Bernie invited Steve and me up to the offices, but it became clear that there was to be a discussion of our deals. After a few niceties were exchanged, Steve just looked at me and said, "We're getting out of here," and we left.

LANE: Bernie told everyone where to sit. He then went and literally turned up the heat on the thermometer and said to the assembled, "We're not leaving this room until we have all our deals in place."

LAPINE: One deal that was not set was for me as director. From what I gather, I was expected to take the minimum payment and you wanted to get me more. I have to add here I have no recollection of even discussing deals on this project. I just presumed agents would do their job, and I stayed out of it.

LANE: At one point Gerald Schoenfeld walked into the room. He looked around and said, "Which one of you is George Lane?" I raised my hand; he nodded, stared at me for a moment, then turned around and left the room.

LAPINE: Why do you suppose he did that?

LANE: I don't know. Intimidation? Or to embarrass me? At that time, I had nothing to lose, so I thought I was in a pretty good negotiating position.

LAPINE: So, did I end up being paid more than minimum?

LANE: No. *(laughter)*

Casting

I gave serious consideration to which actors from the workshop production I wanted to use. During the lowest moments of rehearsals, I'd felt I was not being supported by some of the actors, one of those being Melanie Vaughan. She'd been valuable to the show, but frankly, I didn't know if I could deal with her negative energy. She seemed unhappy all the time.

MELANIE VAUGHAN

VAUGHAN: You invited me out to lunch one day between the workshop and the Broadway production. I knew it was because we had not gotten along. I had lentil soup and we talked about whether it would be a problem for me to work with you on Broadway.

LAPINE: Were you surprised that I invited you to lunch?

VAUGHAN: No. Well, yes, maybe the lunch part was a surprise.

LAPINE: Some of the actors hadn't seemed too happy with me during the workshop. Frankly, I wasn't sure what they thought of the show, either.

VAUGHAN: It wasn't that we didn't like the show. Some of us just didn't like you. I mean, you were very nice—you were never anything but nice. I never knew you to be rude to anyone. You never snapped at anyone. You never did any of those temperamental things. Maybe you were too nice.

LAPINE: Maybe.

VAUGHAN: You said you wanted to make sure that things were clear between us. And I said, "You know, I think I have come to terms with my anger issues. It's anger at myself."

LAPINE: Well, I was relieved to get my discomfort working with you off my chest. And once you admitted you had issues to deal with, I decided to offer you the Broadway role. I think we got along a little better on the second round.

VAUGHAN: I had gotten used to you by then. I had gotten used to your directing style, which I hadn't liked, and I was not alone in that regard. I liked working with Mary Elizabeth [Mastrantonio], but I always looked at her and said, My God, you are so beautiful. Why am I in the room with you? Let me get out of the room. She was very nice, I must say. But then you cast Mary D'Arcy—there was something about working with her that just clicked.

Mary Elizabeth Mastrantonio took a starring role in The Human Comedy, *which was being presented by the Public Theater on Broadway. We replaced her with another Mary, Mary D'Arcy, also an accomplished soprano. Mary was a former Miss New Jersey who came in fourth at the Miss America Pageant in 1978. She would be making her Broadway debut.*

MARY D'ARCY

D'ARCY: My first audition was just with you, Paul Gemignani, and Steve. I sang an abbreviated version of "Glitter and Be Gay."

LAPINE: That's not an easy song to sing.

D'ARCY: Yeah. I couldn't do it now. I had promised to sing at a wedding that day, and it was right after the audition. I was wearing a sexy red dress and all this makeup. I gather Steve's reaction was, "I don't think that's a Celeste." I was told to come back dressed in a very innocent fashion, which I did, and I guess it worked.

LAPINE: What was the experience like for you, walking into a show where many of the cast had already done a workshop?

D'ARCY: It was interesting because I had never originated a role, so I was

Mary D'Arcy, Robert Westenberg, and Melanie Vaughan

PUTTING IT TOGETHER

playing a little catch-up—but I kind of *was* Celeste. I don't think I got half the jokes that I was telling. Melanie's Celeste was bossy. Well, Melanie *is* kind of bossy. So I just played off that.

We also needed a Soldier who could cover the role of George. Kelsey Grammer was a baritone, and we needed someone who could sing in the tenor range. Also, given the contretemps Kelsey and I had had during the workshop, I was nervous about getting in a rehearsal room with him again. For the role of the Soldier and George's understudy, we hired Robert Westenberg. Bob had been studying in a seminary for a year and a half before he acted in a play directed by a fellow student. That led him to discover his true calling; he left the seminary and went to San Francisco, where he studied acting at the American Conservatory Theater. When we auditioned him, he had already appeared in a few off-Broadway shows and had recently made his Broadway debut, opposite Anthony Quinn in the musical revival of Zorba. *As for Kelsey, things turned out just fine.*

MANDY PATINKIN

PATINKIN: At the end of the Playwrights workshop, Steve threw a party for the cast. A friend of mine who was running Paramount at the time was looking for interesting new comics. I thought Kelsey was pretty hilarious, so I told him at the party, "They are looking for somebody for this show called *Cheers*. Why don't you check it out?" And he said, "I don't know anything about that show." I said, "Well, call this friend of mine."

When Mike Nichols came and saw the show at Playwrights Horizons, he was taken with Christine Baranski's performance and subsequently cast her in his production of Tom Stoppard's The Real Thing. *We replaced her with Charlotte Moore, a friend of Steve's. An accomplished actress, Charlotte was a two-time Tony Award nominee and Drama Desk Award winner. She came in and gave a terrific reading of the scene and, though singing was not her strength, she passed muster with the music department. We immediately hired her.*

For our fourth Jules, we were fortunate to get Charles Kimbrough, who had worked with Steve when he was in the original cast of Company. *(After Charlie left*

Sunday, *he was cast in the sitcom* Murphy Brown, *which became a smash hit and ran for ten years.*)

CHARLES KIMBROUGH

LAPINE: We had already done the workshop when we met.

KIMBROUGH: I know that very well because I had auditioned for Mike Nichols in August of that year and he'd said, "If you see anything while you're here in New York, see the workshop of *Sunday*. It's just great."

LAPINE: Did I have you come in and audition?

KIMBROUGH: Oh, yes. It was a very happy audition because you were delighted right away with what I was doing. I sang the same song that I'd sung for my *Company* audition, thirteen years earlier.

LAPINE: You were perfect for the role. Did you get to know Steve very well when you were doing *Company*, or was he off writing most of the time?

KIMBROUGH: As we started rehearsing the numbers, he was right there.

LAPINE: What was he like back then?

KIMBROUGH: He was always gentle. And a little dangerous. And he was more of a mess. The cigarette never left the corner of his mouth; his hair was all over the place. And he was the young firebrand genius. He was very polite to everyone, but I always understood that there was this sort of furnace working in there.

LAPINE: How so?

KIMBROUGH: The first interval in the song "Sorry-Grateful" is a seventh. It's not a full octave, and I got lazy and I was singing it incorrectly. He came backstage and said, "If it was a mistake, I understand. But if you're doing that every night, watch it!" I just said, "Yes, yes . . . absolutely . . ." Of course, I was a bit intimidated. On *Sunday*, it was very different. I was grateful that he was there for staging "No Life" because he's so specific. Everything is clarified. There's not a smudgy corner when he's done.

LAPINE: And when you did *Company*, what was your sense of Hal and Steve's relationship?

KIMBROUGH: I always thought they might be lovers.

LAPINE: Oh?

KIMBROUGH: But they weren't. I was green as grass. And I was from Highland Park, Illinois, so what the fuck did I know about anything like that?

LAPINE: Collaborations are a sort of marriage. It's very personal and intimate when you are putting something out there in the world for all to see.

KIMBROUGH: Yeah.

LAPINE: The reason I ask about their relationship is because *Sunday* was Steve's first show without Hal after years of working together. I was wondering if that was reflected in any way that you noticed.

KIMBROUGH: Well, Hal was very rough on Steve. He just blew up at him one day. Just blew up and said, "There's no endings to these songs! There are no buttons! I want buttons. It just blends all together. It's weak!"

LAPINE: Did he say all that in front of the company?

KIMBROUGH: In front of everybody. It was in the theater. He just yelled, "I can't do this. I can't work this way. Songs have to have buttons!" Steve just sat there, you know, and took it. I think Steve took a lot. I mean, Hal loved him, but the atmosphere was a bit stormier on *Company* than on *Sunday*. Hal can only do work by stamping his foot—it's part of his energy. He can't *not* do it.

LAPINE: Steve and I were just getting to know each other during *Sunday*. By the time you came in, I think we had really bonded.

KIMBROUGH: It was wonderful that you came into the theater the way you did—from outside and away from the Broadway thing. I think it all eventually worked to your advantage completely.

LAPINE: Steve loved having the experience of being surrounded by younger people. I think it took a lot of guts to go from Hal to me—but of course he won't agree with me on that.

KIMBROUGH: Well, he wouldn't. From what I saw, he was completely comfortable with you, which was a huge thing. You and Hal have very different temperaments. Hal would just scream sometimes, but we always knew that he kind of loved us. He wanted us to love him so badly that we did. But *Company* was much more turbulent than *Sunday*. Much more.

In the workshop, the Old Lady (ultimately revealed to be George's mother, whom I chose to not identify in the program so the reveal would pay off) was played by the late Carmen Mathews. Carmen was a lovely actress with a warm presence, but not quite right for the role. I had imagined George's mother to be colder, with a more eccentric edge. For Broadway, we cast Barbara Bryne, a British actress who had come to Canada in the 1960s. Barbara had been a member of the Stratford Shakespeare Festival and later a company member at the Guthrie Theater in Minneapolis. She'd made quite an impression on Steve and me when we'd seen her off-Broadway in Joe Orton's Entertaining Mr. Sloane. *I spoke with Barbara via Skype at an assisted living home in Minneapolis. She had recently turned eighty-nine.*

BARBARA BRYNE

LAPINE: Do you remember the rehearsal process at all?

BRYNE: Yes. I remember asking you about the meaning of some of the things you wrote, and you were noncommittal. You wanted us to find our way ourselves and be organic about it.

LAPINE: How did you feel about that?

BRYNE: Well, I thought it was good. It made us think. For instance, I didn't know quite what to make of the tree business . . . why the tree disappeared on my character in the first scene.

LAPINE: It was to let the audience know that you were in George's world as he drew you. But you wouldn't have understood that as the character.

BRYNE: The only thing I do remember was the audience always laughed when George called me "Mother" at the end of the scene.

LAPINE: One thing you did that always amazed me: you would be in your costume and ready to go at half-hour, and you would sit very quietly offstage in the wings waiting for the show to begin.

BRYNE: I always did that. I wanted to feel a part of the world before I entered it and also take the temperature of the audience. I would sit there during the show as well. I liked to listen to it as it went along.

LAPINE: Interesting. I've never known an actor to do that. I asked you once how you kept your performance fresh. Do you remember your answer?

BRYNE: Well, I tried to change something in every performance, to trick myself—change a line reading or piece of business. Somehow it affected what preceded that moment and what followed it.

LAPINE: Did someone teach you that, or is that something you just came to understand?

BRYNE: It was a Russian director who I worked with at the Guthrie.

LAPINE: Most of your scenes were with Mandy.

BRYNE: Yes. He was very good and very sweet. He was always telling me that he liked my singing and said, "My mother sings like a bird." Once, in rehearsals, we three were talking about a scene and Mandy was saying to you that I needed to do the scene a certain way and I just said, "Excuse me. I'm sitting right here, and I'm going to do it *my* way." When you acted with Mandy, you were never sure what you were going to get. I liked that.

Design Team

I'd never had the luxury of a large budget for a production. Not that I hadn't had the opportunity to design some very beautiful shows on a limited budget. The ones at the Public Theater were built in-house. The ones at Playwrights Horizons were bid out to non-union shops. Generally, you would design your show and present the designs to whoever headed the scene shop at the theater or the scene shop that was being hired to build the show outside. They would say, "Yeah, we can do that." Or, "No. Go back to the drawing board."

Preparing for the Broadway production, I worked with Tony Straiges on our design, which we expanded considerably from the workshop, now making the most of the fly space and trap room below the stage. We worked in tandem with our technical director, Peter Feller, whom Tony had done his previous Broadway shows with. We then sent the drawing and model out for bid to several union scene shops. The bids came back and the producers awarded the job to—surprise, surprise—Feller Precision. Yes, Peter Feller also had his own scene shop!

TONY STRAIGES

STRAIGES: The set came in at $350,000 [approximately $860,000 today], a reasonable sum at the time. You were pretty specific about what you wanted. I remember showing you the two *Sunday* paintings in progress, leading up to George's finished canvas. After the first park scene, when we go to his studio, we only see the figures in the painting that appeared in the previous scene. You said you wanted the unfinished figures to be white—ghostly. Then, the next time we come back to George's studio, we see all the subsequent characters George had been sketching, so the audience can track the progress of the canvas as it becomes populated with the characters they have met. You wanted the painting to be the exact size of the real one, which it was. You went to the island of La Grande Jatte in Paris and you gave me pictures of the construction sites that were there and the skyscrapers. And I did research on that.

LAPINE: I tried to make the script very specific, because I was writing for Steve, trying to give him a sense of what things were going to look like.

STRAIGES: That was a result of your graphic design background. A lot of directors don't have a visual sense and rely completely on the designer, but other directors, not very many of them, have a good visual sense of what they want and how the show will move. You're one of them.

LAPINE: Well, I see it before I write it, generally. It's just kind of my orienta-

"Color and Light"

tion. We were going into a pretty small Broadway theater and we had to fit a lot of scenery in there.

STRAIGES: We had to figure out the rake of the stage to give the painting a certain perspective in the final tableau. We never did get the rake that would have looked the best because the actors would have gone crazy— it would have been too steep. So, our rake was a half inch to a foot, an incline that actors could work with.

LAPINE: The Shuberts had to take out a row of seats to accommodate an orchestra pit, and tear down a wall in the basement to get a grand piano into it.

STRAIGES: They also had to make accommodations in the basement to allow for the pop-ups from beneath the stage. There was a lot of scenery squeezed in everywhere!

Renderings for Dot and
the Soldiers

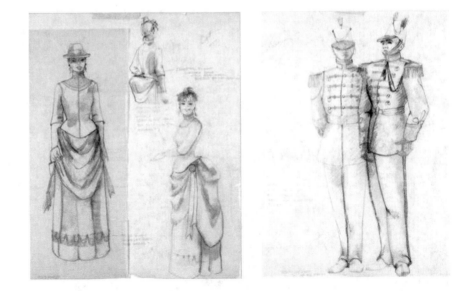

ANN HOULD-WARD

HOULD-WARD: We had been given a costume budget of fifty thousand
dollars [approximately $120,000 today]. I think after we sent our draw-
ings to the shops, our budget number came in at sixty or sixty-five
thousand, which sounds ridiculous now. A little off-Broadway show
has a fifty-thousand-dollar budget today. When the shop bids came in,
there was a call from Bernie Jacobs's office that he wanted to see Patricia
[Zipprodt] and me to discuss the budget. Patricia was smart enough to
send me in alone. So I bring the sketches up to Bernie's office and I'm
in that Chinese lacquered red room alone with him and his huge desk.
And I'm a virgin. I don't know what to do. I'm laying out the sketches
and trying to tell him why we need this costume and that and doing my
best to convince him that we needed every piece of clothing, and he just
looks at me. He's so kind. He's so patient through my whole song and
dance. Then he says, "You know that Theoni Aldredge is going to win
the Tony Award for her costumes for *La Cage aux Folles*, don't you? We're
not spending any more than fifty thousand."

LAPINE: I didn't know any of that before the meeting we had a few days later. Gerry Schoenfeld was there, as was Patricia, dressed beautifully and as classy as ever. She made a very impassioned speech about how this was a show about a painting, and the clothes had to reflect the patterns in the painting and the fabric had to be hand-painted, and Bernadette had to have this many costume changes, and there was a certain level of craftsmanship that was necessary and expected for a show like this . . . and on and on. I was impressed.

HOULD-WARD: Patricia had been through this before.

LAPINE: She turned the charm on, and when she was finished, Bernie just looked at her and said, "The budget is fifty thousand dollars." Patricia got kind of teary-eyed, as I recall, and said she would see what she could do to bring the budget down, and then you guys left the room. Bernie looked at me and kind of laughed and said, "She's not gonna cut one damn penny." It was like this game that Bernie and Patricia knew they had to play. I'm sure she did spend every penny she needed, and you guys made a gorgeous show.

HOULD-WARD: It was beautiful.

LAPINE: She was amazing. It was your very first Broadway show and mine, and Patricia and Steve were the veterans who opened the door for us.

Steve and I continued to discuss exactly what kind of artist our second-act George was going to be. We talked about him being a creator of holograms, but that seemed too difficult to pull off visually and, again, perhaps too abstract for an audience to grasp.

STEPHEN SONDHEIM

SONDHEIM: I was concerned right from the beginning about our concept for the second-act George's "art." That was the big thing that worried me about the transfer to Broadway. If we can't make that work, then the entire second act may not work. If George's piece of art is not inventive and impressive, then our contemporary George is no good. And if he's not a good artist, then what are we writing about?

After much discussion, we knew we had to create something concrete for the audience to see—which led us to the decision to make George a sculptor and multimedia artist. His work had to be impressive and cutting-edge, but also have an interactive element for the purposes of the narrative I had written. Like his great-grandfather, he would have to have an interest in science. And that inspired us to use the notion of "chromoluminarism"—the fancy name that art historians coined after the fact for Seurat's theory of separating primary colors into "dots" or "commas," allowing the eye to mix the colors into a third color. (This was also sometimes called "divisionism.") Thus, we came to call contemporary George's sculpture the Chromolume.

When I discussed this idea with Mandy, he introduced me to Bran Ferren, a multidisciplinary engineer and designer whom he knew from his work on Evita. Bran immediately struck me as the perfect person to tackle this challenge.

BRAN FERREN

FERREN: I read the script from the workshop and was curious about how it was going to come together. It seemed like a set of interesting vignettes and ideas. I believe we had a pleasant discussion about surrealist painters and I was intrigued at thinking about the contemporary George as an artist rooted in a sensibility of light and pointillism, and how to interpret that.

LAPINE: Steve and I came out to East Hampton and met with you in your studio, and you demonstrated some things. Did you work at all with Tony Straiges, the set designer, or did you design the machine yourself?

FERREN: I designed the machine. Tony and I had talked extensively. I worked as well as I knew how to integrate my design into his. Technically, what we did was the first use of projection mapping ever, and it was done before video projection was possible. We actually ended up writing computer programs to geometrically warp the images on film and project them onto the sphere atop the sculpture. We were thirty years ahead of normal.

LAPINE: You had to fulfill a number of my needs. We had to see that George was an accomplished sculptor, so the machine had to look very

Bran Ferren

impressive. It had to serve my purpose of having visuals to accompany the character's presentation at the museum show. And you did that wonderful thing of having the images be an organic piece of the sculpture.

FERREN: Yes, and it was something that no one had seen before. That, for me, was important.

LAPINE: But then, most importantly, the object had to do something really crucial for the storytelling: it had to "paint with colored light," as Seurat had hoped to do with his paintings.

FERREN: The Chromolume was conceived in three acts, if you will. The first act was light rays going through the air behind it. For that, we had to build a twenty-thousand-watt, water-cooled xenon source into the base of it. So, it was a little like a Josef Svoboda design giving off the sense of light curtains behind it. We moved from there into images of stars coming at you on the sphere, wrapping around the sphere before the entire lid of the sphere rotated and this brilliant light source shot out, accompanied by smoke and colorful theatrical lighting. Finally, the laser beams started shooting across the proscenium, creating this sort of amazing, chaotic web over the audience's head.

LAPINE: The first time you showed me the Chromolume was, appropriately enough, a Sunday afternoon. You and your team had the theater to yourself. I was totally thrilled that everything you designed worked exactly as you had described it. I called Sondheim to give him the good news, because we were both worried this gamble might not pay off.

FERREN: It thrilled me getting your reaction, because there was no way for you to really visualize what I'd been talking about until we were in the theater.

LAPINE: Right. It was totally a leap of faith. We had no video or computer renderings to see in those days. What really put it over in the production was Sondheim and Starobin's scoring, which used synthesizer music that continued to build. It was definitely a departure from the feeling of the music in the first act.

FERREN: I could believe that, like Seurat, this artist had created something unique, that he was in his own category.

LAPINE: It wasn't just a piece of scenery, for sure. It represented the character and informed the story. Of course, when I initially broached the idea of it with the producers, they were a little like, "What the fuck?"

FERREN: Terror.

LAPINE: It wasn't cheap.

FERREN: It wasn't . . . and I appreciated your confidence that I could pull it off. Creating big effects is never cheap, and we were buying two sixty-thousand-dollar lasers and stuff like that. The producers were whining, which is typical, so I made adjustments to try to come up with the best balance. But they were supportive. I mean, it's always an issue when a new thing appears in the budget. It can put everyone in a state of panic.

LAPINE: Yeah, I hadn't quite warned them about this because the idea evolved sometime after the workshop. The Chromolume ended up costing the same amount as the entire set: $350,000. They never challenged me on it. Fortunately, it was the days when we had only three producers to deal with and they didn't have to answer to a million investors. This was more a prestige project than something like *Cats*, where an audience is paying for spectacle, but they went for it.

FERREN: I did have to spend a fair amount of time saying, "Trust me." I remember you being nervous about things, feeling all the pressures on you.

LAPINE: Frankly, I didn't know anything about you or your work. But you were a good salesman.

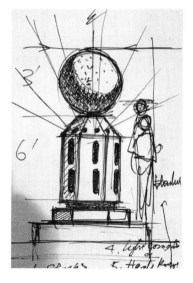

FERREN: It's a living.

LAPINE: There was such confidence in the way you talked about what you could do. You also helped me understand the character I was writing. He ended up having something of you in him.

TONY STRAIGES

STRAIGES: The first time we saw the Chromolume perform, I was standing in the back of the theater with Richard Nelson, our lighting designer. This big object came out to center stage and did all these things that were really pretty amazing. I turned to Richard and said, "Does this make you nervous? Is this where the theater is heading, all this technology and stuff?" We had a good chuckle. It was impressive, but also not our world.

Sound

In 1984, the sound department was not considered to be in the same realm as the other design elements. Our sound person on Sunday was Tom Morse, a veteran de-

signer who had worked frequently with Manny Azenberg. Tom had begun as a stage carpenter. Around 1974, sound in the theater began to take hold and, as there were very few people familiar with the technology, Tom moved into the field.

TOM MORSE

MORSE: When I began, it was primarily foot mics, placed at the edge of the stage, that were used to augment the actors. Wireless microphones were very rarely used. My first Broadway tour was Pearl Bailey's *Hello, Dolly!* at the Kennedy Center. We had one wireless microphone, and that was on Pearl. The device came into common use rather quickly after that. When I did *The Wiz* in 1974, we had twelve wireless mics. That was considered a huge show at the time.

LAPINE: And you operated the sound as well, yes? Or did you just design it?

MORSE: I operated the sound. In those days the sound designer was also the operator. It always sounded good from where the operator sat, but often that was not the case in other parts of the theater. That's when the division between designer and operator came to be, so the designer could sit in various sections of the theater and take notes so that no matter where an audience member sat, they were hearing the same show.

LAPINE: For the workshop we used Scott Lehrer for sound, but his job was mainly to wrangle the synthesizer we were using. We had no need to mic the cast there. This was my first Broadway show with an orchestra in a pit, so I was learning the complexities of balancing the band with the singers.

MORSE: When I spoke with you and Gemignani, I understood that the plan was to have a very "acoustic" sound.

LAPINE: Yes. We didn't want head mics for the actors. Steve endorsed this idea. After all, there was no amplification when Ethel Merman and the cast of *Gypsy* used to belt out to the back row of the 1,760-seat Broadway Theatre—why should we amplify in an intimate theater like the Booth that had a thousand seats less?

MORSE: We kept it very minimal. A show today will have 165 inputs on the consoles, all digitally controlled. We had a twenty-four-input analog console for *Sunday*.

LAPINE: I'm assuming we had foot mics and that the orchestra was mic'd.

MORSE: Yes. A lot of the mic'ing in the orchestra is just for onstage monitors, though, so the performers can hear their cues and pitches. The monitor speakers we used on *Sunday* were really small. This was a very low-key show in terms of audio. Back in that era, you'd actually get a bad review in *The New York Times* if they could hear a sound system, so you would totally try to avoid that if you could. I go to straight plays now and look at the sound systems, and they're larger than what I used in musicals—much larger.

LAPINE: Audiences have become very lazy listeners.

MORSE: I used to stand on the side of the orchestra on a first or second preview and just watch the audience. Their body language would tell me whether or not they could hear—whether they were getting it or not. I could actually see that some sections were hearing differently from others. Our job, primarily, is to create a conduit from the performers to the audience—to make sure the audience gets the information. Of course, this isn't always achievable if the actors have poor diction. I used to make a deal with the performers: "If your voice reaches the balcony rail, we'll take care of everything else." Now it's the second row, and even then it's hard.

LAPINE: Sondheim's lyrics can be very dense. In this show, it was particularly true of the number "Putting It Together." We were lucky that we had Mandy singing it, because his diction and breath control were exemplary.

MORSE: Yeah, you had a great cast.

The Poster

Given my background in graphic design, I was very interested in seeing what the artwork for our show would be. Steve and I met with the ad agency's designer, Frank Verlizzo.

FRANK VERLIZZO

LAPINE: Out of curiosity, how did you get involved in doing graphic design for the theater?

VERLIZZO: I went to Pratt Institute in Brooklyn and David Byrd was my teacher. David used to hold the class in his studio. At that time he was working on the poster for the musical *Follies*, and I would actually see it taped to his drawing table when he was in the process of doing the airbrushing. It was such a fabulous poster. That immediately hooked me on theater and theater posters.

LAPINE: You know, Hal Prince once joked, "We sold more posters than tickets to that show."

VERLIZZO: That poster is longevity personified.

LAPINE: So how did you come to do the *Sunday* poster?

Georges Seurat, *A Sunday Afternoon on the Island of La Grande Jatte*, or *A Sunday on La Grande Jatte—1884*, 1884–1886

Georges Seurat, oil sketch for *A Sunday on La Grande Jatte*, 1884

(The Art Institute of Chicago / Art Resource, NY)

Georges Seurat, *Landscape, Island of La Grande Jatte* (study for *La Grande Jatte*),
1884, 1885, painted border 1889/90 (Private Collection)

Georges Seurat, *Young Woman
Powdering Herself*, 1888–1890
(The Courtauld Gallery)

Georges Seurat, *The Models (Les Poseuses)*, 1886–1888 (Barnes Foundation)

Set model for Playwrights Horizons workshop (Courtesy of André Bishop)

The finale of Act One on the tiny stage at Playwrights Horizons (© Gerry Goodstein)

Model rendering for *Bathers at Asnières* (Courtesy of Tony Straiges)

Georges Seurat, *Bathers at Asnières*, 1884

(© The National Gallery, London)

"No Life"
Foreground: Dana Ivey and
Charles Kimbrough

(Martha Swope / © Billy Rose Theatre Division,
The New York Public Library for the Performing Arts)

Costume designs by Ann Hould-Ward, 1984.
Photocopy, with hand-coloring and graphite on paper,
with fabric swatches (Collection of the McNay Art Museum, Gift of
Robert L. B. Tobin)

TOP LEFT: Mother; **TOP RIGHT:** Soldiers;
BOTTOM RIGHT: Jules.

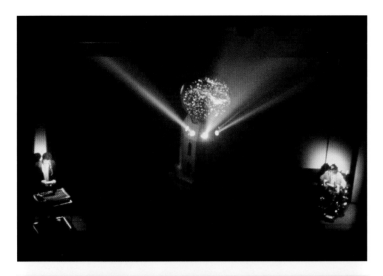

The Chromolume

(Courtesy of Bran Ferren)

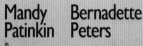

Poster design by Frank Verlizzo

LEFT: Patricia Zipprodt, *Sunday in the Park with George* costume sketch, 1984

(Billy Rose Theatre Division, The New York Public Library for the Performing Arts)

RIGHT: Costume for "Everybody Loves Louis"

(Martha Swope / © Billy Rose Theatre Division, The New York Public Library for the Performing Arts)

One of Stephen Sondheim's work pages for "Children and Art"

(Courtesy of Stephen Sondheim)

One of Stephen Sondheim's work pages for "Lesson #8"

(Courtesy of Stephen Sondheim)

"We Do Not Belong Together"

(Martha Swope / © Billy Rose Theatre Division,
The New York Public Library for the Performing Arts)

"The Day Off"
Foreground: Nancy Opel
and Brent Spiner

(Martha Swope / © Billy Rose Theatre Division,
The New York Public Library for the Performing Arts)

"Children and Art"

(Martha Swope / © Billy Rose Theatre Division,
The New York Public Library for the Performing Arts)

Barbara Bryne as The Old Lady in Act One and as Blair Daniels in Act Two

(Martha Swope / © Billy Rose Theatre Division, The New York Public Library for the Performing Arts)

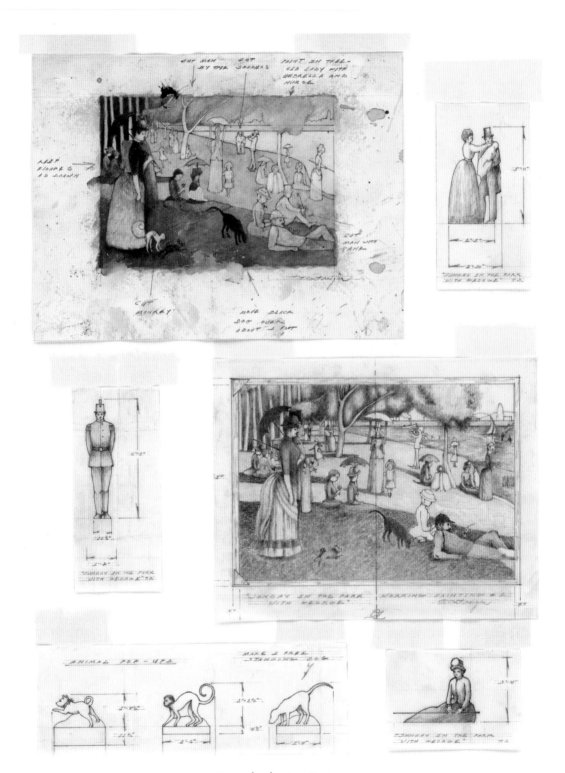

Set studies by Tony Straiges

(Courtesy of Douglas Colby)

The endlessly rehearsed Second Act number "Putting It Together"

(Martha Swope / © Billy Rose Theatre Division, The New York Public Library for the Performing Arts)

The finale of Act One on Broadway

(Martha Swope / © Billy Rose Theatre Division, The New York Public Library for the Performing Arts)

RCA recording session, May 1984

(Photograph by Peter Cunningham, courtesy of Sony Music Masterworks)

VERLIZZO: David Byrd suggested I go work at the theater ad agency Blaine Thompson after I graduated. From there I went to Serino Coyne, which was representing your show. Manny Azenberg knew my work and asked for me.

LAPINE: So what was your process? You had the script, I assume.

VERLIZZO: Yes. I was also lucky enough to have seen it at Playwrights Horizons. I had designed three different concepts, three different posters. The Shubert Organization at that point then got very involved, and I went to their office to show them the comps. They really zeroed in on the one that we used. And, in fact, when I showed you and Steve, you also chose that one. The original background color was turquoise, and Bernie Jacobs asked me to try other colors. That's where the orange came from.

LAPINE: There's so much orange in the painting.

VERLIZZO: I know, absolutely.

LAPINE: And then did you present it to Steve and me?

VERLIZZO: Yes, and when I showed it, you made a suggestion about the woman's legs—and this is something else that helped me a lot. I had just legs in a straight position at that point. I cut them out of a magazine. You suggested that they be in motion—like a gavotte. Then I went ahead and had a photo session and showed you a couple of variations, and that was the one you chose.

LAPINE: Was Steve around for that?

VERLIZZO: Yes, you both were. And when we were all looking at the final rendering at the Shubert offices and Bernie asked, "Is there any way you can put music notes on this?" I tried not to make a face, but I was like, Oh, my God. Before anybody said anything, Sondheim said, "Bernie, it says it's a musical; you don't need music notes." That was the end of that conversation, which was lovely.

LAPINE: When it came to the discussion of credits, I wanted my name at the bottom and listed as: "Book and Direction by" but Steve insisted that my name appear near his as a writer. He said, I don't want to be up there alone under the title.

The Music Team

STEPHEN SONDHEIM

SONDHEIM: I spoke with my usual orchestrator, Jonathan Tunick, about joining us when we knew we were going to Broadway. At that time, he was focusing on his own work as a composer. He may also have had a conflict. He commended Michael Starobin for just the little stuff he had done at Playwrights, and told me, "Take Michael. He's terrific. I just have one piece of advice. Have an orchestra reading, because it's a whole other business, orchestrating on a Broadway scale." He said, "Listen to what Michael does, because he hasn't dealt with a large band before." And sure enough, this was very valuable advice.

MICHAEL STAROBIN

LAPINE: How would you define what an orchestrator does?

STAROBIN: If I had to define my job as an orchestrator, it's to continue the composer's work of coloring the character's emotions with harmony and rhythm by adding color and counterpoint. This first requires that I understand what the composer is doing, both dramatically and compositionally. And, while the lyric is structured in lines and stanzas, the music has to connect the thought patterns of those lines. So even if the sung language stops for punctuation and the actor's breathing, the music should make his emotion as continuous as his thoughts are.

LAPINE: And how did you approach orchestrating this show?

STAROBIN: It really helped that I had been the assistant rehearsal pianist for the workshop. This allowed me to get to know the score intimately and to hear the actors' voices and vocal colors. It's rare nowadays that I get this access to the score before working on it—that I actually get the score "into my fingers." *Sunday in the Park* is the only job I "auditioned" for. The shows I had done prior were much smaller. When I was hired for *Sunday*, I had never worked with a band bigger than six or seven players. For my audition, I was told to use ten or eleven. It felt like such a luxury to have so many players. A number of classical pieces kept floating around in my head as I prepared the audition. The most obvious were two French Impressionist chamber pieces: Debussy's Sonata for Flute, Viola, and Harp and Ravel's Introduction and Allegro. But for some reason, I also kept thinking of Elliott Carter's Double Concerto—because of its use of the harpsichord. I thought this might be a useful sound for Stephen's musical evocation of pointillism.

LAPINE: What did you do for the audition?

STAROBIN: I orchestrated "Color and Light" and "Beautiful" and then took a bunch of friends into a studio to play them for Paul and Steve.

STEPHEN SONDHEIM

SONDHEIM: They played Michael's orchestration and it was too busy. I knew exactly what had happened. Michael was used to orchestrating for shows in which he had to supply some of the music himself—because there wasn't enough counterpoint.

LAPINE: He overdecorated?

SONDHEIM: Exactly. But in my case, I overdecorate myself! So it compounded the felony. I was glad to be able to say to Michael, "Please, underdo that, because if anything, my music is already too busy." That was useful. Michael went back into the studio and reorchestrated those songs and maybe one more. He took my notes and got the job.

MICHAEL STAROBIN

STAROBIN: I learned from Steve that I didn't need to sell his songs. They work. I was adding too much material of my own.

LAPINE: Well, when we worked together with Bill Finn on *March of the Falsettos*, you were really serving a different purpose.

STAROBIN: With Billy I was notating and really acting as an arranger. Stephen doesn't need an arranger.

LAPINE: What is the difference between arranging and orchestrating?

STAROBIN: Orchestrating is simply putting music onto the instruments. If I just took the piano part and reworked it for other instruments to play, that would be orchestrating without arranging. But no one does that, because what you write for piano is pianistic. For a show, you don't touch the melody line; the voice supplies the melody line. You only double it occasionally, for effect.

LAPINE: So when you got the job, did you talk to Steve in more depth about what he wanted?

STAROBIN: The one question I asked him was, "You have this artful show, yet you have this kind of funny musical-comedy number up top. Why?" He said, "Because it is an arty show and we need to tell people they can relax and laugh during it."

LAPINE: So, he had you point that up in the orchestration?

STAROBIN: Yes.

LAPINE: Well, you got to get arty later.

STAROBIN: Absolutely. And this was a great show for me for that reason.

STEPHEN SONDHEIM

LAPINE: Was the process of working with Starobin different from working with Jonathan Tunick?

SONDHEIM: I've done so many shows with Jonathan. I play every song for him and then I make a tape. He likes to have a tape because he says that the way I play influences the way he orchestrates. It helps him get my intentions. And I guess he does this with everybody he orchestrates for.

LAPINE: Do you sing it?

SONDHEIM: Yeah, I sing and play. Then, when he's familiar enough with whatever I've written, which may not be the whole score—in fact, it usually isn't—he'll get a feeling of what the sound of the orchestra should be. Then he'll sketch out for me what his plan is for the instruments.

LAPINE: With Michael, you had the advantage of the workshop. Hearing the songs the way the actors performed them. You got to see some version of the show up on its feet before you discussed the orchestration.

SONDHEIM: Right. My piano copy was very complete. I don't hear instruments, although Milton Babbitt, my teacher, said that I do. I just don't recognize that I do. But I write a lot of counterpoint and things. Jonathan takes all my piano lines and just says, "Oboe, clarinet, et cetera, et cetera." Because I worked out the counterpoint, which is what the orchestrator has to do. I write horizontally, as opposed to vertically—meaning chords. And that's because of my classical training. I'm sure that's one of the reasons Michael got to know the score so well during the workshop—because he saw all the lines that were going on.

PAUL GEMIGNANI

GEMIGNANI: When Michael auditioned for the job, he did a mock-up or two of the arrangements. I helped him as much as I could. I thought he was great. I couldn't read what he wrote at first, but I got used to it. He's just a genius.

LAPINE: What was the difference between working with Jonathan and Michael?

GEMIGNANI: Jonathan is more methodical. More exacting. Michael will just jump into the water. He will just go for it, and if it's wrong, fuck it, he'll fix it. You can talk colors with Michael: how you feel about something. Maybe some can do it with Jonathan, but I can't. He did help me early in my career. He did say, "Why don't you give him a break? See if he can conduct," that kind of thing. I believe if he had done *Sunday*, it wouldn't have been the same show. You would not have been happy. Jonathan has very negative energy.

LAPINE: We all worked happily together on *Into the Woods*. You were both total pros. I never noticed any tension between the two of you. And Steve loves you both.

GEMIGNANI: Well, yeah, because Steve doesn't have to deal with the bullshit. I respect an orchestrator's work, but if I see that something has to be changed, I change it. All I have to do is say, "Michael, I changed this today because . . ." and I give him the reasons. If I say that to Jonathan, I get back, "What did you do that for? Why didn't you call me? What's wrong with it? Probably those guys weren't playing it right." It's not a collaboration.

MICHAEL STAROBIN

LAPINE: So did you dive right into writing once you got the job?

STAROBIN: Actually, one of the first things I did was call Jonathan Tunick. I knew he was busy with other projects, but I asked if I could take him to lunch and sound him out about the process. So, we became friendly at that point. It just felt like these were his shoes I was stepping into, even if just for one show. It ended up being for two shows.

LAPINE: Did he give you advice?

STAROBIN: Yeah. Watch out for Paul Gemignani!

LAPINE: What did he mean?

STAROBIN: He said that Paul was a very political animal and to just be careful.

LAPINE: Oh, so it wasn't so much about the music . . .

STAROBIN: No, not about the music. Just that politically, I should be careful.

LAPINE: They do have very different personalities. Paul is a powerhouse, there's no question about it. I was very intimidated by Paul at first. Were you?

STAROBIN: Very much so, and I don't think he trusted me at first. But we became *very* good friends. He brought me in on many, many shows. Jonathan and Paul are the best music department Broadway has ever seen, at least in my time.

LAPINE: Well, sometimes that tension can help create great works. They are both smart and talented.

STAROBIN: Their work together on shows like *Pacific Overtures* and *Sweeney Todd* is just remarkable.

LAPINE: So, once you got the gig, you probably began writing the orchestrations?

STAROBIN: Yes, I had a head start because of the workshop.

LAPINE: How did you go about choosing your instruments?

STAROBIN: I knew I would start with the two keyboards and percussion we had used at the workshop. MIDI—the language synthesizers use to speak to each other—had just been developed, and it allowed me to store many sounds on a synthesizer and recall them at the touch of a button. I knew I would want strings. I had worked with strings in *March of the Falsettos* and found I had an affinity for scoring them. I had never worked with a full quartet [cello, viola, and two violins], but some of Stephen's piano writing was asking for a quartet. Woodwinds have always been present in theater orchestras and Broadway players have developed the art of doubling, sounding good on several wind instruments—flute, piccolo, clarinet, bass clarinet. A number of them can also play saxophone. And double reed specialists are expected to play all of those as well as oboe and English horn. This is an invaluable asset for an orchestrator. Having players with the ability to change instruments within a few bars allows variations of color. Because Stephen stylized the song "Beautiful" with a Ravel-like accompaniment, the use of a harp seemed like it might be called for. This was my first time using one, and I learned the often-ignored fact that a harp is not a piano and cannot be scored like one. Beth Robinson, our harpist, taught me a lot. Finally, we chose to do what we had done in the workshop, and use a French horn for brass. Actually, two French horns: a regular F-one and a high D-flat horn, which, when you press a certain button, gives you high notes. We needed that for the final calls at the end of each act. I earned a reputation for not knowing how to write for French horn, because what I wrote was way out of the range of a regular horn and very hard to play. Often, players crack on those notes. It was Paul's player, Ron Sell, who suggested the special horn, and he always pulled it off.

LAPINE: I held my breath at the end of every show when there was a sub on.

STAROBIN: When it worked, it was great. But we chose to use a trumpet on the original cast recording. Another concern is that you have to make sure the actor can hear the beat and harmony clearly enough to comfortably perform. And you have to also write comfortably for the players. This is something I didn't quite accomplish in *Sunday*, due to my inexperience. I didn't know any better. I learned to take chances.

LAPINE: Did Steve have input into the instrumentation?

STAROBIN: We discussed it, but he deferred to me.

LAPINE: And Gemignani?

STAROBIN: Paul pushed me in certain directions. I used a synthesizer in addition to the piano on the first keyboard chair. The second keyboard was an all-synthesizer chair. I also abandoned using a bass in the orchestra because of budget. I was only given eleven pieces for the band, so I put the bass on the left hand of the synthesizer.

    The pit was so small we had to slice the bass drum in half and use, like, a half bass drum.

LAPINE: You mean you literally sliced it in half?

STAROBIN: Yes, so we had a circle with one skin instead of the full bass drum that has a skin on either side. We didn't get the same resonance, but we got the low frequency somewhat.

LAPINE: Your off-Broadway ingenuity served you well.

STAROBIN: I used pots and pans for the "Boatman" song.

LAPINE: Well, you're brilliant at maximizing the use of your instruments. How many instruments were the reed players playing?

STAROBIN: Each reed player had about seven or eight instruments, including flutes, clarinets, and saxophones. One of the players was a reed doubler, so he also played oboe and English horn.

LAPINE: It must have been a slower process to orchestrate in 1984.

STAROBIN: Yes, it was all by hand on onionskin paper with pencil. Pages were about thirteen inches high, so you couldn't Xerox anything.

LAPINE: Would you say you were ever intimidated or nervous?

STAROBIN: I would say I was too ignorant to be intimidated. I really didn't realize where I was. When we got to Broadway, the whole experience felt bigger than we expected it would be. By then I truly understood Stephen's position in the theater.

LAPINE: Yeah. I had my support team around me at Playwrights. That was my turf. Once we went to Broadway, we were definitely at the grownups' table. Did I confide in you once we moved uptown?

STAROBIN: We talked some. The thing is, once we were doing the Broadway production I disappeared because I had to go off and write. I was not there in rehearsal as I had been when I was the pianist. That's one of the things I regret about being an orchestrator: I'm pulled out of the process of watching the show come together, which is the really fun and interesting part.

For the Playwrights workshop our first rehearsal pianist was Tom Fay, who often worked with Paul Gemignani. He and Paul were scheduled to work on the new Kander and Ebb musical, The Rink, *the following season, starring Chita Rivera and Liza Minnelli. Once* Sunday *was scheduled for Broadway, Paul decided he would leave* The Rink *after it opened and work with us and would leave Tom Fay behind to become their conductor.*

Gemignani brought his second pianist, Paul Ford, over to Sunday. *Though Ford had toured with first-class productions and subbed on Broadway, this was his first time working on a new Broadway show. Paul grew up in Atlanta and moved to New York straight out of high school, and he had an encyclopedic knowledge of musical theater.*

PAUL FORD

FORD: Being a huge fan of Sondheim's work, I was very excited to be a part of his latest show. I had the music for only a few weeks, and of course I was freaked out for a lot of reasons. Oddly enough, I don't think we had a sit-down read-through the first day of rehearsal. I came in and almost immediately went upstairs with Steve and Barbara Bryne and started going through the song "Beautiful." As he went along, he made me transpose it into three different keys.

LAPINE: Were you nervous?

FORD: Oddly, no. He paid absolutely no attention to me. It was about teaching the song to Barbara and seeing where it sat best in her voice. He was totally focused on that.

Ted Sperling was a twenty-two-year-old recent graduate of Yale who came on board as our second rehearsal pianist. Gemignani hired him after Sperling asked him for a recommendation for an internship grant. When the grant fell through, Paul gave him a job. Now a noted musical director in his own right, having conducted shows such as The Light in the Piazza, The King and I, *and* My Fair Lady, *Sperling first met Sondheim at Yale, when he and a group of friends mounted a production of* Merrily We Roll Along.

TED SPERLING

SPERLING: When *Merrily* closed abruptly, some of my fellow theater geeks and I vowed to do a production of it. We had to get permission from Sondheim, and we had a nice correspondence. I was getting daily packages from Pat Sinnott, his wonderful assistant, who sent us the materials since the show hadn't yet been licensed. I ran to the post office every morning to see what was waiting for me. We did it in a classroom on graduation day, so the framework of a graduation ceremony had a lot of resonance. And doing it with all college-age kids seemed natural; no one questioned people playing different ages. We had a great success with the show, and I sent a cassette to Sondheim. He wrote me a lovely note back. When I got the job on *Sunday*, a friend of mine, Jesse Green, who's now a critic for *The New York Times*, told me that he had some of the music from the show at his apartment, and if I wanted he would play it for me.

LAPINE: How did he get that?

Paul Gemignani, Al Hunt (reeds), Les Scott (reeds), Karl Bargen (viola), Ted Sperling (synth), Paul Ford (piano), unidentified woman, Adrienne Wilcox Ostrander (percussion), Marilyn Reynolds (violin, concertmistress), Beth Robinson (harp), Stephen Sondheim, Ron Sell (horn), Michael Starobin. Missing from photo: Cecelia Hobbs (violin), Eileen Folson (cello), and Bob Ayres (percussion)

SPERLING: Jesse had been Paul's intern on *A Doll's Life* and had befriended Mathilde Pincus, Sondheim's music copyist. So I went to his little Greenwich Village apartment and he played me the title song and "Beautiful." And I remember thinking that this was wild—unlike anything I had ever heard on a Broadway stage before. I sort of couldn't believe I was going to be playing these things myself.

LAPINE: What was working with Gemignani like?

SPERLING: Paul was really great at keeping the atmosphere light. I remember the rehearsal period being very fertile. I learned a lot from him. I admired how he worked with people who weren't singers foremost. Barbara Bryne, for example, was very nervous about her song. It had no clear beat. It was very hard to tell when she was supposed to come in. And instead of saying something like, "It's a half-note rest," he would say, "Just watch me, and I'll point to you." He never talked to people about eighth notes or used the words "phrasing" or "legato." He never used any Italian. He would just talk to them about what the point was and what the character might be feeling, or what we needed to understand about a song. I remember Steve saying, later in the process, that my experience on *Sunday* reminded him of his own experience on the Rodgers and Hammerstein musical *Allegro*: the first time he was working in a room of professionals.

Choreography

After the Playwrights workshop, it was suggested—by whom I don't remember—that I hire a movement person to help with the Broadway staging. This may have had something to do with the amount of time it had taken me to stage the musical numbers during the workshop, especially the first-act finale. I didn't much like the idea of "choreography," and, since I had done the musical staging for March of the Falsettos, *I found that I rather enjoyed doing it myself. But a choreographer I was not. Understanding the pressure I was going to be under—and knowing that writing and directing were quite enough to tackle for my first Broadway show—I began to look for the right movement collaborator.*

Randolyn Zinn, and in
the background, Charlie
Blackwell and Loretta
Robertson

Randolyn Zinn, and in
the background, Charlie
Blackwell and Loretta
Robertson

*Ira Weitzman and John Lyons recommended the choreographer Randolyn Zinn.
Zinn had been a dancer and actress before moving into choreography, and had
worked with Garland Wright and Liviu Ciulei at the Guthrie and with Michael
Kahn at Juilliard—all directors I admired. We discovered that we were both from
small towns in Ohio and our fathers were both traveling salesmen.*

RANDOLYN ZINN

ZINN: Once we met, you asked me to go and meet Steve. It was a very cold
winter day, and I think I owned one warm sweater. When I arrived at
Steve's house, he asked me very graciously if I'd like something to drink
and served me a silver thimble of red pepper vodka, which warmed me
right up. I think it was at that meeting that I suggested there be a place in
the show for a ballet. But the script was very set, so there was going to be
no way that anything new could be imagined. I was the choreographer

of a musical with no dancing. And I'm proud of that, actually, because it was a bold experiment that worked.

LAPINE: So, what are your memories of the rehearsal process? I know you worked with Bernadette on her "Color and Light" section.

ZINN: She was so open to ideas. My job was to get into the interior of that character, her fantasies, and find the perfect movement and language, and to do it with humor. You know, Dot is somebody who had lots of dreams and wanted to be in the Follies. So, at one point, we had her pick her foot up and try to get it to stretch all the way out and it doesn't work. Bernadette got that immediately.

LAPINE: That was a nice touch. And Mandy?

ZINN: I didn't do so much specifically with him, but I did work on the number "Putting It Together." I designed the movement vocabulary of the people in the party scene so that it would feel like it was from his point of view. I asked the actors to come up with a few gestural sentences to use while they were singing. Now, this is standard practice in modern dance, to ask performers to come up with interstitial movements. It's not done so much on Broadway.

LAPINE: We had different approaches to things.

ZINN: You would sketch things out on paper, while I tend to see staging spatially. That's just the choreography gene kicking in. But our two approaches were not mutually exclusive.

LAPINE: Yeah. I had to walk into the rehearsal room with a plan on paper.

ZINN: I totally get it. I mean the pressure, my God.

LAPINE: Did I seem like I had a lot of pressure on me?

ZINN: I remember once sitting backstage during previews and you came in late. We were all waiting for a production meeting when you rushed in and said, "Sorry. I just had to have a meeting with the book writer."

LAPINE: As you were new to the production, what was the vibe like?

ZINN: Tense.

LAPINE: And where did you feel the tension was coming from?

ZINN: It was a Broadway show. Time and money. I was friendly with Pat Zipprodt. She was constantly concerned about budget.

LAPINE: Did we have any kind of conversation when we began rehearsals?

ZINN: You asked me to do some warm-ups, and also for my input in staging. To be honest, I was a bit sensitive because I wasn't being given a choreographer credit, because the producers didn't want to hire a dance captain.

LAPINE: Is that right? You know, I thought they didn't want a choreographer credit because they were concerned that an audience might expect dancing when there wasn't any.

ZINN: That's what my agent told me. So I went into the project already feeling a little—

LAPINE: Knocked down?

ZINN: A little bit.

LAPINE: Well, you made an indelible contribution to the show. At the end of the show, when Dot brings the modern George around to face the characters in the painting—something we did in the Playwrights staging—you added the company bowing to him at that moment. That was such a marvelous and moving gesture.

ZINN: I know it was a small thing, but I was very proud of that moment.

Stage Management

Manny Azenberg brought in the very experienced production stage manager Charles Blackwell to work on our show. Charlie had stage-managed The Wiz, Promises, Promises, Nine, *and a host of other productions, so he knew his way around a Broadway stage and the birthing of a new musical. He had also been an actor and a dancer, and had received a Tony nomination for writing the book of the musical* The Tap Dance Kid *the previous year. We were very lucky to have him guiding our show. I also thought it important to bring along our stage managers from Play-*

(opposite) 1. William Parry, 2. Judith Moore, 3. Mary D'Arcy, 4. Melanie Vaughan, 5. Fred Orner, 6. Danielle Ferland, 7. Loretta Robertson, 8. Charles Blackwell, 9. Paul Gemignani, 10. Johnna Murray, 11. Fred Nathan, 12. Charlotte Moore, 13. Charles Kimbrough, 14. Robert Westenberg, 15. Stephen Sondheim, 16. Ted Sperling, 17. Mandy Patinkin, 18. Bernadette Peters, 19. James Lapine, 20. Paul Ford, 21. Cris Groenendaal, 22. Barbara Bryne, 23. Michael Starobin, 24. Randolyn Zinn, 25. Nancy Opel, 26. Brent Spiner

wrights Horizons, Fred Orner and Loretta Robertson, because of their knowledge of the show and our company. I had not worked with them before the workshop, so I left the final decision about using them to Charlie, whom they would be working directly under.

LORETTA ROBERTSON

ROBERTSON: Fred and I first met Charlie when he was deciding whether to hire us as his assistants. This would be our first Broadway show. I said to Charlie, "I think there are just such amazing, wonderful things going on in this show; I love it, and I know it forward and backward." Fred said, "Well, there is so much more work to be done. I'm just not so sure this show is actually going to work." Charlie responded, "Fred, if you're going to come on board, you need to find a way to love this show. If you don't love this show, then you don't need to come along." Fred came along.

MANNY AZENBERG

LAPINE: You insisted we hire Charlie Blackwell, your go-to stage manager. In retrospect, that was a very wise move. At the time, I didn't realize he was also your eyes and ears in the room.

AZENBERG: Yes.

LAPINE: I came to learn later that that's why producers are so involved in deciding who will stage-manage their shows.

AZENBERG: Charlie was experienced. He also was black, six foot five, and 225 pounds. Nobody argued with Charlie.

LAPINE: He had a sweet manner and was very good at his job. I always felt supported by him, but when he needed to assert himself, he did. But Charlie had no agenda other than to serve the production. He turned out to be a godsend for someone who had never worked on Broadway.

Rehearsal for Broadway: February 9, 1984

In the five or so months we had off before the first rehearsal, Steve and I met several times to hammer out our game plan before writing even began. Between our workshop and first rehearsal for Broadway, Steve drafted a song for Dot called "We Do Not Belong Together," which was to end the second studio scene. We also significantly trimmed the entire "Day Off" section and cut the short song "Yoo Hoo."

In the second act, Steve transformed "Gotta Keep 'Em Humming" into "Putting It Together," a long and complicated number that encompassed the third scene of the act. He was also working on the penultimate song for George and Dot, "Move On." I rewrote the scenes for the second-act George—particularly the cocktail party—to conform to his new persona.

And, of course, I spent considerable time auditioning new members of the company as well as understudies. And then there were the weekly design meetings. The time went by quickly. Too quickly. Before we knew it, we began our five-week rehearsal period. I felt like I was in a perpetual state of trying to catch up to a train that had already left the station.

On our first day of rehearsal, we did the usual meet-and-greet and the designers presented their models and sketches. Then we dove right in and began teaching the music to the new people. A few days later, we sat down and read through the script with music. The company sang the songs that they knew, and when we got to one that hadn't been taught, Steve played and sang.

ROBERT WESTENBERG

WESTENBERG: Seeing Sondheim play his music for the first time was amazing. He sang with such childlike joy; he was absolutely into it.

LAPINE: I always found his commitment to singing his material full-out so inspiring. There was nothing tentative about it. I bet that came from the early part of his career, when he had to audition his songs for prospective producers.

WESTENBERG: It was also so informative to those of us who'd have to sing his songs. He really acted them.

LAPINE: What was the rehearsal process like for you?

WESTENBERG: I loved watching you be puzzled by something—some transition that wasn't working—and then figure out how to get us from here to there. Gemignani would jump in and make suggestions. It was a real eye-opener for me because I'd never been involved in the development of a new show.

We began our first rehearsals with Randolyn Zinn leading the company in some movement exercises, similar to what I had done in the workshop: promenades and such. Some of the cast made it clear yet again that they didn't much like these exercises, but I thought it was important for Randolyn to see how people moved and took direction. She needed to know how comfortable they were in coming up with their own postures and gestures—who was game and inventive and who wasn't.

We had hardly gotten into the second week when it became clear we had a problem: Charlotte Moore just wasn't the ideal choice for the role of Yvonne. When we'd auditioned her, her singing seemed fine for what would be expected of her character. Though "No Life" might appear to be a rather short and simple number, it proved to be more musically complicated than you would think. As rehearsals progressed, we discovered that we needed a stronger singer in the role.

I had the unenviable task of letting her go. This was made harder by the fact that she was a friend of Steve's, but he'd agreed that we had no choice in the matter.

I had learned my lesson about this the hard way; if you know in your gut an actor is not going to work out, it's best to cut ties as soon as possible. The longer you wait, the more difficult it becomes for everyone involved. This is not the most enjoyable part of a director's job.

Charlotte couldn't have been more understanding. It should be noted that she went on to cofound the Irish Repertory Theatre in 1988, where she directed many of its acclaimed productions.

We quickly contacted Dana Ivey for the role, and she stepped into the rehearsal process rather seamlessly. Dana was relatively new to New York City, though she had worked consistently on American and Canadian stages, often doing classical work. Just prior to auditioning for Sunday, *she appeared on Broadway in George Bernard Shaw's* Heartbreak House *with Rex Harrison, Rosemary Harris, and Amy Irving. Though Dana's singing voice was on a par with Charlotte's, she had the kind of natural musicality that gave her the requisite confidence to put the song across effortlessly.*

DANA IVEY

IVEY: I was called to come in at lunchtime, when the cast had left the rehearsal hall. I'd learned the scene, learned the song, did it for you, and then went home.

LAPINE: I had admired you as an actor. I don't think I had ever seen you in a musical, though.

IVEY: No, I hadn't been in a musical in New York until *Sunday.* My agent called at the end of the day to say that I had been hired, and I started rehearsals the next day.

LAPINE: Tell me a little bit about what the rehearsal experience was like for you.

IVEY: It was a wonderful room, a wonderful cast. There was a sort of joy and energy that was palpable. When we were working on the finale of Act One, you were trying various stagings and one of them gave me such chill-bumps. You didn't do it again, and I thought to myself: That was the right staging! When we moved into the theater, you went back to it, and I was so excited: Yes! That's it!

CHARLES KIMBROUGH

KIMBROUGH: James, you had a tuning fork thing going when you were staging. You would go, "Take a step to your left; no, take a *half* step to your left. Yes. Okay. Okay. That's your mark. And then when you come in, no, too far in. Hold it there." It was like that.

LAPINE: That must have been maddening.

KIMBROUGH: But I could work with it.

LAPINE: Well, *you* could. Others had a harder time.

KIMBROUGH: Yes, they did. But it was composed. You were painting. And Dana and myself, we felt solid and were happy to go with it. It was a unique job for me, because I had to depend entirely on you to figure out how I fit into the picture, if you will. When you were staging the song "Sunday," we were moving toward that place where you would call, "Stop!" When everybody stopped, the picture was complete. That's it. I'd never had an experience like that. The power of the music with that staging, it just killed me when I finally saw the show myself.

Dana Ivey and Charles
Kimbrough

PUTTING IT TOGETHER

The rehearsals for Broadway moved apace, with little drama. The new actors got up to speed quickly, and by the third week we had staged the entire show and did a run-through for Steve and the designers. It went very well and everyone was in high spirits.

As rehearsals continued, periodically the actors were sent to Barbara Matera's costume shop for fittings. It happened to be right at 890 Broadway, where we were once again rehearsing. All of Michael Bennett's designers had their studios in that building—even the cobbler who made the shoes for his shows. It saved an enormous amount of time not to have to send actors across town for fittings—time much better spent in rehearsal.

ANN HOULD-WARD

LAPINE: I'd never been to a high-end costume shop and was enthralled when I joined you and Patricia at Matera's for Bernadette's first fitting. I sat there as you draped colored fabric on Bernadette, discussing what colors suited her skin tone and showing me how texture could be used to give the clothes a pointillist feel. It was so interesting to me. And the grapes! You put out a little spread for the actor in case they got hungry during the fitting. It was all so elegant and classy. You made the actors part of the process right from the start. I'd never had that kind of experience before, probably because I had never done a show with that kind of budget.

HOULD-WARD: To me, you seemed like you were totally in control of what was going on. You knew exactly what you wanted and you were very able to communicate it. It's funny, isn't it, our point of view as young people? What we felt inside and what we projected?

LAPINE: I've never felt that confident about costumes. They are not the strongest aspect of my game. I've worked with designers whose drawings, beautiful as they may have been, didn't represent the garment we ended up with. It might have been the color or fabric or fit. But your drawings were very accurate. And the way you worked with the actors was so informative. What was it like for you, working with "stars"?

HOULD-WARD: Well, you know, I had assisted on a lot of things involving stars. I think I was reasonably fearless. My whole background made me look at people as just *people*, and say, "Hey, we're in this together." One of the wonderful things about working with Bernadette is that she lets you do the fitting; she allows you to do all the fiddling with the costume right on her. Then, when you're finished, she walks to the mirror, gives herself the once-over, and shares her thoughts. She's a consummate professional and she lets you be one, too.

LAPINE: Yes, she immediately gives you her trust. Sometimes actors make you earn it.

HOULD-WARD: I think Bernadette enjoyed bringing her character to life with the creation of the clothes. Mandy, on the other hand, had really studied the character, so his questions would arise out of that research. Were his clothes aged and worn? What would have been comfortable for him to paint in? He was quite exacting.

LAPINE: It was an education, watching you and Patricia work.

HOULD-WARD: James, you had this kind of quiet, gentle way, but there was the strength of steel underneath it. It's an enjoyable thing for a group of designers to funnel our collective creativity into that final product. But we have to be in sync with one another to succeed.

LAPINE: The visual element was the part of the process where I felt most confident. I knew that language. Also, it was easy for us to discuss our common design goals because we had an iconic image to reference. Seurat brought our vision together.

HOULD-WARD: Your writing is so visual, too. That also makes our work somewhat easier.

LAPINE: One thing we talked a lot about was how we were going to translate pointillism. We never really got those dots literally, did we?

HOULD-WARD: We got textures; we painted into these garments after they were built.

LAPINE: That's right, yes. And the thing is, literal dots would never have really registered at that distance from the audience.

HOULD-WARD: We did a lot with overlays, using a net or another fabric to give a shimmer under the lights. That along with the painting of the fabric, that's really how we got the sense of shimmer into the costume—that thing Seurat was after.

LAPINE: Apparently, David Hockney stormed out at intermission. Someone heard him complain, "Where are the bloody dots?!"

During the final week of rehearsal, Sondheim delivered the penultimate song in the second act, "Move On." It was an exciting boost for Mandy and Bernadette to have this glorious and passionate number toward the end of the show. And dramatically, it was a big step in bringing our second act into focus. Yet, as the clock ticked down, there were still two songs to be completed for Act Two: "Children and Art" and "Lesson #8." Comforted by the fact that songs had come in quickly during our workshop, no one was particularly concerned.

Just prior to moving into the theater for tech rehearsals, we had our sitzprobe—*German for "seated rehearsal." This is one of the most exciting moments in a musical's creation. It's when the singers and musicians come together and the cast hears the orchestrations for the first time.*

MICHAEL STAROBIN

STAROBIN: The sitzprobe was probably the most stressful moment of *Sunday* for me.

LAPINE: It's always thrilling for the actors and the writers.

STAROBIN: It's thrilling—but this was my first Broadway show, and it was the moment my work would be judged. That can be really difficult. If the players are still grappling with what they're doing, your ideas may not be coming through. The work is being judged too early.

LAPINE: So that's where you, Steve, and Paul really have to come together.

STAROBIN: Yes. And it took Paul and me a couple shows to develop a relationship where he would eventually say, "Are you sure you want this here?" He appreciated the fact that I would go out on a limb to try something. I tell this story: In the middle of writing a chart, I came down the stairs and said to my wife, "They're going to fire me." "Why are they going to fire you?" she asked. "Because I'm doing something so crazy that when they hear it they'll fire me." She got very upset. Well, this habit continued after *Sunday*, and she learned to just ignore me. I realized recently what I was doing was cutting myself loose, going directly to the worst-case scenario.

LAPINE: I think that's pretty endemic to our trade. I think it's a safety measure we all rely on.

STAROBIN: It's useful. It says, Okay, it doesn't matter what I do. I'm getting fired anyway, so I might as well have fun and do what I think is right for this song or this show and take a chance.

LAPINE: Have you ever been fired or had to fire someone?

STAROBIN: Yes to both. I was fired from Frank Wildhorn's *Dracula*. And when I was a music director once, I had to fire my girlfriend, who wasn't playing well enough.

LAPINE: And you remained a couple?

STAROBIN: Yes. I think I followed firing her with a proposal of marriage. That was the worst relationship in the world.

LAPINE: Sounds it. So, moving on from your personal travails. How would you characterize Gemignani's conducting?

STAROBIN: I've always said that Paul is the best conductor on Broadway because he doesn't conduct songs, he conducts acts. He shapes the entire act, while most conductors conduct a song and don't worry about the flow of the show as a whole. People think his tempos are fast because he's bored. No, they're fast because he's trying to put the actors at speaking rhythm—to get them to sing in the rhythm in which they speak. He's one of the few music directors who have a great relationship with both the stage *and* the pit. You know, it's usually one or the other.

Shortly after the sitzprobe, we moved into the Booth Theatre to begin two weeks of technical rehearsals. The mood of the company was very bullish. We were ready to get out of the rehearsal room. And personally, I was surprised to find how exhilarating it felt to be working on Broadway.

The
Booth
Theatre

Technical Rehearsals: March 19, 1984

CHARLES KIMBROUGH

KIMBROUGH: James, you were tough.

LAPINE: Tough?

KIMBROUGH: You know how I discovered that? You were standing at the back of the orchestra, in the standing-room section, just before the actors were about to assemble for our first tech rehearsal. You were leaning on the rail and staring at the set. And I came up next to you and you said very quietly, "It's just what I wanted."

LAPINE: Really?

KIMBROUGH: That can only be said by somebody who has a little toughness in him. You didn't say, "Oh gosh, I'm just so happy." You'd known exactly what you wanted and you got it. No big-hit director could have taken your book and your idea for this show and done that production. It was absolutely your eye that made *Sunday*.

LAPINE: Nice of you to say.

Rendering of Dot's
mechanical dress

BERNADETTE PETERS

LAPINE: When we got to Broadway, you seemed very confident. You were
the "pro" in the cast, after all, with more Broadway shows under your
belt than anyone.

PETERS: I had my concerns. First of all, there was that dress I had to wear
at the top of the show: the "mechanical" dress that I had to step out of
for my first number. I was a bit nervous about how that was going to
turn out.

LAPINE: You had approval of that dress in your contract and we were all
aware how important it was that we come through for you.

ANN HOULD-WARD

HOULD-WARD: The idea for that first dress Bernadette wore was sketch-
ily realized in the workshop production, but for Broadway we had
some money to spend. We put moon-walker legs inside of it, like those
modules have that land on the uneven surface of the moon, so it could
stand on its own. We were working on a raked stage, so the legs had
to telescope down and find their footing. There was a gas container
in the back of her bustle that, when signaled, sent the legs down. The
front opened up and closed on a signal from the stage manager. Basically, he operated it with a garage-door opener from offstage. Bernadette
didn't have to do anything. It was going to be a magical moment—if it
worked.

TED SPERLING

SPERLING: When we moved to the theater, the actors had a costume pa-
rade, which I don't think people do anymore. It was done in the order
of the show, so one of the first things that happened was the "Yoo Hoo"
people came out as figures in Seurat's *Bathers* painting, and Nancy Opel
was dressed as a boy. She thought it was the funniest outfit she'd ever
worn and we all had a good laugh. And then the next person out was
Bernadette, because it took her a while to get into her first very elaborate
costume. It was still in process, but I didn't understand that. So, after all
the jocularity with Nancy, the mood was very light, and when Bernadette came out onstage, I said from the house that she looked like Joan
Sutherland. It was one of those outfits that really gave her a lot of bosom.
I think everybody thought I meant she looked fat, because Sutherland
was a large woman. Immediately, Pat Zipprodt ran down the aisle and
chewed out Paul Ford, who was sitting next to me, thinking he had
said it. I was cowering there, and Sondheim grabbed me and yanked me
into the lobby. He gave me a lecture about how you always tell the star
she's beautiful, no matter what. And frankly, don't offer an opinion if

not asked. I slunk back into the room and sat down very quietly next to Paul, who had been so generous to me in taking me under his wing. We sat in silence for a little bit, and then he whispered, "Somebody had to say it," just to make me feel better.

LAPINE: I absolutely wanted to kill you. You had no idea how much effort went into that crazy dress and trying to make this impossible idea I dreamed up work.

SPERLING: Yeah, it was a horrible moment.

LAPINE: I mean, in retrospect it was no big deal, but at that particular moment you pressed a lot of people's buttons!

BERNADETTE PETERS

PETERS: I was so focused on that dress. The first one they gave me made me look like I weighed three hundred pounds. Eventually, they were able to make it smaller and still hide the mechanics beneath it. Then, there was always the question of whether the legs that kept the dress standing when I came out of it would come down. And on top of that, the dress didn't always open; sometimes I had to manually open it.

LAPINE: What a great way for an actor to start a show and sing the title song. You never were quite sure what you would be dealing with. I do have to say that it was magical when it worked.

PETERS: It was a little touch-and-go there at first. Would I get stuck in the dress? Once they showed me how to operate the "emergency exit," at least I knew I had some control over the situation.

ANN HOULD-WARD

HOULD-WARD: During previews, I remember sitting in the back praying the dress would open properly. One night she got out fine, but toward the end of the number, when she headed back to get into it, the dress suddenly shut.

LAPINE: She couldn't get back in?

HOULD-WARD: No! So, when the scene was over, she just grabbed the dress under her arm and walked off with it.

LAPINE: That must have gotten a big hand.

HOULD-WARD: Yes, and a big laugh. Bernadette was a good sport about it.

BERNADETTE PETERS

LAPINE: As far as I could tell, you only felt really insecure about one thing: playing Marie, George's ninety-something-year-old grandmother, in the second act. That was a tall order.

PETERS: That's where I had to really trust you. I said, "I don't think this is any good." You said, "No. No, don't lose your confidence. Don't crash out on me now." I remember thinking, Oh. He knows what I'm feeling. That was so important to me—that you knew that I was feeling insecure. I didn't know what I was doing, and you told me, "You really are doing a wonderful job."

LAPINE: That's because we found Marie by going outside in. In the rehearsal room it was abstract because we didn't have the wig and costume. We worked on how you could communicate the age without being a cartoon. I remember this very specifically. I think that's what helped you, because we talked about her lack of energy and her speaking voice, all the physical things that go completely against what acting is—to *not* have energy, to *not* emote.

PETERS: You have to trust that.

LAPINE: You were stuck in that wheelchair, without the use of your body. You really had to trust that the spirit of Marie was there in the writing. Once you kind of got that—once *you* accepted that people would accept you in that part—you had a ball with it. It was great when the audience arrived.

PETERS: Right.

LAPINE: As a writer, I didn't know if that conceit—of you going from playing young Dot to old Marie—was going to work, either. I was so amazed and relieved when it did, especially given all the other aspects of the second act that weren't fully realized yet. You had to walk a very fine line in that role. Was your mother around at that time? I know I met your father.

PETERS: My mother had died the year before.

LAPINE: Didn't she pass away on the dance floor?

PETERS: Yes. She was dancing and she said, "I feel dizzy." And then she just passed. One of her sisters went the same way. I'm looking forward to that.

LAPINE: Maybe you channeled a little of her as Marie.

PETERS: Every night was a party for my mother.

The tech period moved very slowly. I was used to working without union rules, but in a union house, we were required to take a certain number of breaks. It took me a while to learn that I wasn't permitted to move furniture or props, that I had to ask a stagehand to do that for me. Overtime was enormously expensive. There were so many more elements to pull together than in anything I had done previously. It seemed to take forever for the lighting and set cues to get written by the stage manager and then rehearsed with the crew and cast. And, as a director, you must always do a certain amount of restaging once you get on a set. You can only envision so much in a rehearsal room. Before I knew it, the band arrived, and that introduced an entirely new element to iron out.

Our first audience was coming and I hadn't finished teching the second act, let alone running it. We had scheduled two invited dress rehearsals, primarily for Playwrights Horizons subscribers. That had seemed like a good way to do a test run before the paying customers arrived.

First Preview: April 2, 1984

It was early April, and we were hit by an unexpected heat wave. When the first audience arrived, the air-conditioning had not yet been hooked up, the lighting designer had not finished lighting the show, I hadn't done any full run-throughs, the crew hadn't had a chance to practice the set transitions, and we had no amplification because I wanted a natural sound in this small theater. On top of all that, we were still missing two important songs in the second act. In their place the actors were performing monologues.

It was quite a first performance. The theater was sweltering. The audience couldn't hear the show and sometimes couldn't see it. The first act ran an hour and forty minutes. Many people walked out at intermission and more during the second act. By the end of the show, people were so desperate to get out of the theater that if I'd stood in their way, I'd have been trampled.

STEPHEN SONDHEIM

LAPINE: It was not a good start.

SONDHEIM: It was terrible. I remember the look on your face. You had never been walked out on before. You had never experienced that because you had been writing for off-Broadway, where nobody ever walks out because the weirder or more boring the show is, the happier they are to be there. I wanted to say, or maybe I did, "It happens to me all the time, James. Get used to it."

LAPINE: The actors could feel the resistance of the audience. They were also pouring sweat onstage. I really thought I was going to have a heart attack that night, and I was kind of hoping I would so I wouldn't have to come in the next day.

SONDHEIM: Welcome to commercial theater . . .

PAUL FORD

FORD: The first performance of the first act was an hour and forty minutes, but that length was normal for the classic musicals in their day. *Gypsy* had a first act that was an hour forty. And, as for the second act, there was a time when it was not unusual to have mostly reprises and a dream ballet. Look at all the Rodgers and Hammerstein shows. Their second acts have maybe three new numbers and several reprises. So, I didn't notice any big problems with that first performance. I left the theater thrilled that I had played the first public performance of the new Sondheim musical. As I walked into Shubert Alley, I saw this actress I knew from Atlanta who had recently been in *Nine* for two years. I went up to her excitedly and said, "Oh, my God, I can't believe you were here tonight!" Her response was, "How can you play that horrible music?" That was shocking. I never saw her again. My expectations of people are often too high, but that was out of bounds.

I went home that night half dead and did triage on the script, cutting out anything that didn't land or seem necessary. I staggered in early the next morning to work on tech. I told Richard Nelson, our lighting designer, that in places where we hadn't properly lit a scene, he should just turn up the lights; I didn't care what it looked like.

This was the only time I got bossy with the Shuberts, insisting that the air-conditioning be working by that night's performance. When the actors came in, I incorporated all the cuts. Then I drilled the crew on the transitions in an attempt to cut down the running time. Meanwhile, Tom Morse dealt with our sound issues.

TOM MORSE

MORSE: We immediately put mics on Mandy and Bernadette, as well as one on Barbara Bryne—George's mother. I had one additional mic we passed around as needed, mainly to the little girl or if a character was far upstage. There were no backstage sound people on the show, so wardrobe had to change a microphone out when necessary.

LAPINE: I did some restaging to bring people closer down to the foot mics.

MORSE: I also added a mic upstage for the final song of the first act, because we had a lot of chorus that we couldn't mix into the blend. When we first hung it, that mic fell like a half an inch below the scenery. Tony Straiges burst into tears. He thought it was the worst thing that ever happened to man, so we moved it out of sight.

LAPINE: Yeah, Tony would have noticed that immediately.

The second night, the reception was more encouraging, if not enthusiastic. After that, the paying customers arrived—and it became immediately clear that we were in real trouble. There was so much that needed attention! I had to reshape and rewrite the book, trim some of the songs, and refine the staging—and then there was the second act. Because we had only three songs, I had to try and fill in those moments that were missing by adding temporary dialogue and underscoring. Fortunately, this was before the Internet. Today, theater aficionados would be running home after the first preview to review the show on social media.

STEPHEN SONDHEIM

SONDHEIM: There may have been no Internet, but the naysayers were doing damage by phone.

LAPINE: That's probably true. And then there was the fact that the Shuberts had sold so many discounted seats to benefit parties.

SONDHEIM: Oh, yes, there were a lot of theater parties.

LAPINE: When people attend a theater party to benefit Mount Sinai Hospital, they want dance numbers, not *Sunday in the Park with George*.

SONDHEIM: Theater parties are always deadly.

LAPINE: As previews progressed, people were still walking out at intermission or in the middle of the second act. And even those who stayed were walking up the aisles during the curtain call. Understandably, the actors were discouraged.

MICHAEL STAROBIN

STAROBIN: I actually remember not being able to hear the bow music. So I went to the sound operator and asked if he could make it a little louder. He said, "No, I can't. I'm turning up the stage mics to make the applause sound louder because it's so weak."

LAPINE: Who told him to do that?

STAROBIN: He told me it was an old Broadway trick.

ANN HOULD-WARD

HOULD-WARD: I was leaving the theater after the show during an early preview and people were literally ripping up their programs and throwing them into the waste receptacle. I never had any experience like that—working on something that gave people such an extreme emotional response. Now, I'm old enough to look back and say, "Wow, the show really touched people, both those who liked it and those who didn't." At another performance, I was standing in the back of the theater watching the show. There were so many people leaving during the second act that Bernie Jacobs got out of his seat, came up the aisle, and held the door open for them because it was squeaking every time someone left.

MANNY AZENBERG

AZENBERG: There was an audience that thought this was the second coming and there was an audience that would have thrown grenades on the stage if they had them. There were people who walked out in tears and people who walked out wanting their money back. Word of mouth was: 25 percent of the audience thought it was the best thing that had ever happened; 50 percent thought it was the worst thing they'd ever seen; and 25 percent were just . . . baffled.

JOHN LYONS

LYONS: The birthing of the second act was scary and difficult.
LAPINE: What were you hearing on the street?
LYONS: It was sort of like this: "Love the first act. I don't know what the hell they're doing in the second. What happened to all those beautiful pictures and costumes?" People found it jarring to be brought into the present day. They wanted to stay in the nineteenth century. And they clearly experienced the second act as unfinished. This didn't faze me,

because I wasn't under the same pressure you were. And also, I was accustomed to Playwrights Horizons, which was always so process-oriented. The writers would work on the material until a show opened, so it didn't seem odd to me that *Sunday* wasn't finished yet.

LAPINE: Of course, Broadway audiences pay top dollar and they expect to see a finished product, even in previews.

LYONS: It's funny to see the show now. It would never even occur to me that those two acts weren't born at the same moment and all of one piece.

LAPINE: I know it was tough for the actors to come out in the second act and see so many empty seats. Even so . . . many have told me now what a great time they had working on the show.

LYONS: Oh, I remember several actors who were *not* having a good time. I think they initially thought, Oh, I'm going to be doing this new musical with Steve Sondheim! It'll be like *A Little Night Music* or *Sweeney Todd*. I don't think they realized it was going to be nonstop work and figuring the show out in front of an audience.

LAPINE: I find that, in retrospect, people tend to forget the difficult parts and remember the good. Naturally, I tend to remember only what was difficult.

LYONS: Well, it was a good cast. And to think that when I moved to New York, I wouldn't have even known what a casting director did.

TED SPERLING

SPERLING: My parents came to early previews, when people were leaving at intermission or during the second act. They were very concerned that their son's job might be in jeopardy, and—unbeknownst to me—they wrote a note to the Shuberts.

LAPINE: Saying?

SPERLING: Saying, "This show's in trouble. You've got to do something," or words to that effect.

LAPINE: You must have been horrified!

SPERLING: I was.

LAPINE: Did they identify you as their son?

SPERLING: I think they must have.

LAPINE: I'm glad I didn't know about this at the time.

As we headed into the second week of previews, it became clear that we were going to have to postpone our opening. Looking back at the calendar for the show, I don't know why we scheduled so few previews. I can only assume that, having never done a Broadway show, I didn't understand how it would go. I was used to working in non-union houses, where we'd pull all-nighters if necessary to get a show ready.

We certainly couldn't open with two songs missing, so we postponed from April 23 to May 2, the Tony Award eligibility deadline. There was general relief that we would have a bit more time to finish things, but the prospect of an additional week of rehearsals was daunting for the already exhausted company. And for some, there was disappointment that relatives and loved ones who had planned their trips from afar to be at our opening might now miss out on it.

Previews

CHRISTINE BARANSKI

BARANSKI: When musicals go right and everything works, it's the greatest collaboration. It is the biggest high. When things aren't working, it can be the depths of hell. I had a very unhappy experience on the musical *Nick and Nora*, which previewed for eight weeks. This led Richard Maltby to declare, "Previewing a musical in New York is like having a gynecological exam in Times Square."

DANA IVEY

IVEY: About the second week, I had people I thought were friends come to see the show. They were incredibly rude and made stupid, awful remarks. I mean, they just were *down on it*. I loved the show. I was a happy camper. I was physically exhausted, but I thought the show was saying something wonderful and I was terribly proud to be a part of it. I was appalled when these people said really dismissive things. I thought, Well, they don't know what they're watching. I didn't take it to heart. I just thought it showed what rubes they were, and that they didn't know how to behave.

MARY D'ARCY

D'ARCY: We had hecklers. That was a first for me. One night when we started Act Two with "It's Hot Up Here," and Yvonne sang the second line, "It's hot and it's monotonous," someone yelled from the audience, "It sure is!" People laughed. It was horrible to hear that.

LAPINE: At least you were on the stage. I had to sit with them every night. I just wanted to strangle people. Unfortunately, it wasn't the last time I had that experience. When Steve and I did *Passion*, it was even worse in previews.

BARBARA BRYNE

LAPINE: Barbara, you were always in such good spirits when we were in previews. The audiences were not too friendly. Did you notice that?

BRYNE: I heard that there were men pacing in the foyer during intermission, muttering, "Where are the dancing girls?"

LAPINE: People didn't know what to make of the show.

BRYNE: I found that actors loved it, and artists of all kinds—painters and writers. They knew what it was about and could follow it and had no problems. I think it was ahead of its time.

NANCY OPEL

OPEL: When we started performances at the Booth, I began to realize that the audience didn't like our show. We would get into that second act and rows of people would get up and stomp out. At least that's how it felt. And then, as we worked on it during the day, it felt like we were cutting the show in half.

LAPINE: Well, yes, your parts were getting smaller. We had discovered that we really needed to concentrate on the main story of George and Dot in the first act. And we had to find and shape that second act.

OPEL: Yeah. That was hard, but you know, I think we just kind of said, "Okay, if it's between having a show that's successful and having a big part . . . you know what? We'll take the successful show."

DANA IVEY

IVEY: During previews, we were working so much during the day and then performing at night . . . I think I fainted one day. We were working in our corsets on that raked stage. My shoes were like buskins. I've since developed a terrible hatred for rakes. It was just physically exhausting, those few weeks. We would go over and over things. There would be small changes, not major ones that affected me particularly, but it was essential work because the show was incomplete.

LAPINE: I was in my work bubble. I know a lot of the cast were sitting around and waiting a lot.

IVEY: Yes. We were all called in every day, but we weren't all used a lot every day. It was a strange time, because we also had to have the energy for the performance that evening.

LAPINE: Yes, I have since learned you don't want actors sitting around doing nothing unless you have no choice—particularly when they are performing that night. You must have been aware that not everyone in the company was happy. The crew thought we would be closing on opening night.

IVEY: I must've been living in cloud-cuckoo-land. I was having a ball. I mean, I knew it wasn't finished during previews, and that new things were coming in. I don't remember being unsure of the piece, though. I know I felt very sure of what I was doing, what my character was doing, where I fit in—and I was just so happy to be there.

WILLIAM PARRY

PARRY: When you're working on a new piece, no one is quite sure whether it will come together. For me, it was exciting. That whole thing of not having the second act was like, this is when the great discovery happens. It's when the cast either bonds or they don't, and our cast really bonded.

LAPINE: When did you all bond?

PARRY: Probably when we discovered that the audiences weren't with us. Nobody was sure what was going to happen with the show. On a dinner break one day, someone asked, "How long do you think this show will run?" We were kind of laughing and no one bet longer than six months. This was early in previews.

LAPINE: I'm shocked that anyone thought it would last six months!

PARRY: Most didn't. I didn't know whether it would have a broad appeal.

STEPHEN SONDHEIM

LAPINE: I asked you to come in and speak with the actors.

SONDHEIM: Yes. I'd been through my fair share of rocky previews.

LAPINE: You told your *West Side Story* anecdote.

SONDHEIM: Yes. At the first preview of *West Side Story*, after the opening number, I saw a couple rise from their seats and begin to leave the theater. I caught the man's eye and I could just see in his expression, I've had a hard day at the office. Dancing gang members? Not my thing. And I totally understood it.

LAPINE: I think hearing from you about your experiences on other shows helped a lot.

SONDHEIM: It helped . . . and they knew I would eventually come through with the last songs. That was the other thing.

MANDY PATINKIN

LAPINE: During those bumpy previews, whom in the cast did you talk to about the show?

PATINKIN: I was close to Bernadette, but we didn't talk about it. I don't think I ever talk with another actor about the work while we are doing it. We do the talk while we're working. We put the talk into the work.

LAPINE: But you must have sensed that people in the company were unhappy and felt insecure about the show.

PATINKIN: I don't remember that, honestly. I remembered that we had this jewel of a first act from Playwrights, with a little piece of "Putting It Together" as a possibility for a second act. But I could just feel that the second act wasn't working. This idea of the second act—it was a big idea, but I didn't know what it needed. I didn't know how to fix it. I didn't know what Stephen or you were working on. I was just up there with what I had, and I couldn't make it work—although my hubris was so enormous at that moment that I thought, Of course I'll fix it. I'll find a way to fix it. There must be something I'm not doing.

BERNADETTE PETERS

PETERS: I had done a few successful shows prior to having the lead in a big Broadway musical, *La Strada*. It ran one night.

LAPINE: How did you navigate the uncertain preview period we had?

PETERS: It was nothing like *La Strada*—nothing like when there's no writer showing up. And the composer! Lionel Bart, who had a serious drug problem, initially wrote the music for *La Strada*. We were out of town in Detroit, and on the stage, when the director, Alan Schneider, said, "There's one thing that bothers me," Larry Kert, who was my costar, responded: "It's called *La Strada*." We were in big trouble, big trouble.

LAPINE: That may have a lot to do with why you were so calm during

Sunday when other people were seriously worried. I mean, you never seemed to have a moment of jitters or uncertainty.

PETERS: No. I had been through so much of this before, when the product was not up to snuff. I knew we had something very special. Every day was so exciting. You and Steve never lost your focus. That's when shows go wrong, when the creators lose their point of view. The show just takes a left turn—loses its center. You and Steve knew where the show should go, even if you hadn't finished getting it there.

Philip Smith, the former chairman of the Shubert Organization, was its general manager when they produced Sunday.

PHILIP SMITH

SMITH: There was a real concern in the Shubert Organization about the way the preview period was going. You know, bottom line, the show had to work.

LAPINE: I would imagine it didn't have a big advance in those days.

SMITH: It didn't.

LAPINE: If Bernie was worried about the second act, he never spoke to me about it. My guess is he didn't speak with Steve, either.

SMITH: He trusted you two. He'd say to me, "Phil, if they don't see it, we certainly can't see it." When Gerry Schoenfeld would jump in and try to make suggestions, Bernie would say, "Gerry, don't you think they've thought about that a hundred times?" Gerry would have sat down and written the second act for you if he could have.

STEPHEN SONDHEIM

SONDHEIM: Considering that it was so uncommercial by nature, I was quite surprised that Bernie and Gerry liked it—but they did. They were behind us all the way, through thick and thin. When everybody was walking out of previews, they were on our side. Twice in my professional life have they done something as startling as that. The other one was *Pacific Overtures*. You would have expected them to say, "Get out of here," when we needed a theater. Not at all. They supported it.

Once we got through our first two weeks of previews and the pressure of an imminent opening was off our backs, the real, intense work began: shaping every scene and every moment; finding the rhythm of the show. There were not many huge changes in the first act. Mostly, we continued to trim the park scenes and refine the staging.

As previews went on, of course there were still people who didn't like the show, but there wasn't the degree of hostility and bafflement we'd experienced in the beginning. We still didn't have the last two songs, but we went about trying to make the second act work as best we could. I think we only got about four hours of rehearsal time a day—then you take away the mandatory union breaks, the time to get in and out of costume, a good half hour of notes about the previous evening's performance—there really wasn't all that much time. We only had four days we could rehearse each week, given matinee performances, so we were really under the gun.

We were having problems with the blocking for "Move On," the number at the end of the second act. After one performance, Mandy said, "I'm not leaving this theater until we set the blocking." Bernadette wholly agreed. It was a big union no-no to use the stage after hours, but we kind of hung around until everyone was gone and then the three of us worked for about an hour with just the ghost light. We had no accompaniment, no stage manager—we just put our heads together and blocked that sucker, after which we drilled it a number of times so we could all go home and sleep knowing that we had nailed it. Those two actors never stopped dedicating themselves to making the show work.

PAUL GEMIGNANI

LAPINE: When we were having big problems in previews, you were really a stalwart for everyone. Recently, Barbara Bryne said, "Well, I had Paul there in front of me, and he was always listening and involved with what we were doing. He was our audience. When he laughed at something I did, it meant the world to me." Nobody conducts like you do because you have a real relationship with actors.

GEMIGNANI: That's great to hear, because most of the time I never hear that, but I think that's the job. I mean, any moron can wave a baton, but where's the connection? Where's the presence that makes the actor comfortable enough to do his or her best work? I don't mean that to sound lofty. I mean, that's what I think the job is. When I see conductors sitting at the piano just focusing on the music, it makes me nuts, because they don't really see what's going on onstage.

LAPINE: I remember getting very annoyed with you because once, in the middle of a show, you started slapping your hand on the stage to get an actor's attention. They were off tempo or whatever.

GEMIGNANI: Yeah, he was just doing his own thing. I've thrown things before, too. Sometimes you're so in the moment that you do strange things. You were right to be annoyed when I did that. But what is lonelier than standing on a stage with a light in your face and you can't see? Where's the connection? Particularly if you are not getting the response you would like from an audience. Also, when you look at an actor's face and they're singing, you can push them to go somewhere further. An actor, especially somebody like Mandy, can go anywhere he wants because he knows the conductor is there. When the actors feel secure, they have more freedom to grow and expand the song. Also, I think of it as a big part of my job to keep the orchestra engaged, too. They're in a hole. They can't see anything. Nobody makes a big deal about them most of the time. With the level of concentration that's required to play your and Steve's material, there's no room for wandering.

LORETTA ROBERTSON

ROBERTSON: Once we got to Broadway, the vibe really changed. Every minute costs money, and we put in a lot of overtime. I appreciated that Charlie Blackwell understood the crew and the rules and regulations. I think Manny Azenberg knew that Charlie could get the crew on board. After the first few previews, they all thought the show would close on opening night. They called it *Sunday in the Dark and Bored*. Their other little joke was *Sunday in the Park with George; Monday on the Truck with Waltons.* Waltons was the trucking company that would come haul the set to the dump when a show closed. A few of the crew got the show, but a lot of them . . . well, their favorite musical was *42nd Street.* Add to that the fact that it was the eighties and a lot of the crew was doing drugs.

LAPINE: Really?

ROBERTSON: Charlie Kimbrough came off the stage once and said, "Is the follow-spot operator on drugs or what?" "Yes, he is," I said. "If I go confront him, you are never going to have light on you again." That's just the way it was. I knew not to fight the crew. I had to choose my moments carefully, so when it was important, I could go to them and say, "Look, please pull your act together here. I need this done."

LAPINE: What did they make of me?

ROBERTSON: You know, the fact is that they didn't pay that much attention to directors, or even to Sondheim. They tended to focus on which actor was a pain in the butt. I literally had to say to crew members, "You are *not* dropping a sandbag on Mandy's head. We need this man for the show." "Okay," they'd say, "we're just going to kidnap him and dump him in the middle of the Bronx."

LAPINE: I guess they thought he was difficult?

ROBERTSON: If Mandy heard two people whispering offstage, he would get upset. He was just such a pain in the ass. When we got to rehearsals, Charlie Blackwell designated me as "Mandy handler" because he thought he'd listen to me. "Mandy loves you," he said.

LAPINE: It's true. He did love you.

ROBERTSON: We had one episode during a show when Mandy came offstage and screamed at me. I wanted to punch him out, but I knew I couldn't do anything. I couldn't even shout back, so I just turned around and started to cry a little bit, and Charlie Blackwell saw me and asked what was going on. I said, "It's nothing, it's nothing; Mandy just yelled at me, and I'll deal with it." Well, next thing I knew, Charlie took Mandy aside and said, "Don't ever yell at Loretta. If you've got a problem, you come to me." So Mandy came over, *very* apologetic. He told me he loved me, then said, "You're like Kathryn; I talk to you like I talk to my wife." It was really interesting. Mandy left the show temporarily at one point during the run for another job. When he came back, he was a changed person. He was so much fun to work with and have around! I asked him about it and he said, "You know, I really thought that my talent was tied up in my being difficult; that if I reined in my personality, then I would lose my talent." Through it all, I absolutely loved Mandy. It was love/hate sometimes, but we were very close. When I left the show, Mandy gave me a going-away party at his apartment and even invited the crew.

MARY D'ARCY

D'ARCY: I played George's ex-wife in the second act. That character was developed during previews and there were days when you were handing us new pages and we would go on that night and do them with barely a rehearsal. And I was scared out of my mind to do a scene with Mandy Patinkin with no rehearsal. I was so nervous every night I couldn't relax. Mandy's work is so extraordinary, that he could be so present that it was different every night, and you really needed to know who you were playing. Mandy never did the same thing twice, and I was used to working with actors—even someone like Richard Harris, for example—who had a particular performance and stuck to it. But with Mandy, I never knew what he was going to throw at me, or what his mood was going to be, and I was terrified of disappointing him and not being able to rise to the occasion. One night, he really snapped at my character and I started crying in the scene. Afterward, I thought I might have done something wrong. When the show was over, I went and knocked on his dressing room door and said, "Um, Mandy?" and he said, "No! No, no, no, no. No, go away. Go away! Everything's fine. Really. Go. Go." He didn't want to spoil the spontaneity by discussing it. And I thought to myself, Okay. I'm doing all right.

LAPINE: Mandy and I are alike in a certain way. If we're not happy with something, we let you know it. If things feel right, we're less likely to talk about it. Now, I tell my actors the first day of rehearsal, if I don't say anything to you about your work, it means I'm very pleased.

By the third week of previews, there was a general sense of despair over the fact that we were still losing audience members at intermission, despite all the good work we had done. We'd gotten the first act down to a reasonable seventy-five or eighty minutes, and audiences seemed to like it, but clearly, word was out about our second act. They sold hearing devices in the lobby of the theater. There was a sign that read, "Rent a Headset. Don't Miss a Word!" Underneath it, someone had scrawled, "Miss an Act!"

MANDY PATINKIN

PATINKIN: Manny Azenberg was not helpful. He kept saying things that would upset me.

LAPINE: What kind of things?

PATINKIN: He let me know he didn't think the show was very good. I couldn't believe it. This is a producer of ours! I've known Manny over the years, and I've never really brought it up to him. I hope he reads this.

LAPINE: I'm going to ask him about it.

PATINKIN: Good, good, good, because it was very difficult, as a young actor, to hear an experienced producer—the guy who did all of Neil Simon's plays—be critical of the show you're in. I thought, Oh, he must be right. So it was just hell, and really irresponsible in the long run.

MANNY AZENBERG

LAPINE: You said to me once, when we were well into previews, "I don't care about these people onstage"—or words to that effect.

AZENBERG: That's absolutely true.

LAPINE: Did you like the show?

AZENBERG: No, not really. Which is neither good nor bad. Producing it was an act of a strange kind of loyalty: we were doing the show because Sondheim wrote it and because the head of the Shuberts said, "We're doing it." I got "Finishing the Hat." Emotionally, I mean. It took me a while. I got the show when you finally did the full second act and I heard "Children and Art." I told Stephen a month later, "I get it." It took a while.

LAPINE: What was your relationship with Mandy?

AZENBERG: Strange. We're friendly when I see him now, and in certain things he's sensational. In other things he's not.

LAPINE: Did you interact with him during the show?

AZENBERG: Very little. I thought he was weird. But in the final scene in the first act, Mandy was wonderful. That strange quality that he has, that high voice, it just worked.

LAPINE: The reason I ask is because I talked to him about it. He felt, I think, that you weren't behind the show—and from what you're saying, maybe that was true.

During the day, I would be in the middle of rehearsal and see Bernie Jacobs and Gerry Schoenfeld watching in the dark, from the rear of the orchestra. These two older men in trench coats were like spectral figures, just staring, expressionless. I'd go about my business, and when I'd turn to see if they were still there, they would be gone—just like that.

At one point, Bernie asked Michael Bennett to come see the show. I don't recall whether he asked my permission. I had never met the man, but I was happy at the prospect of having his input. When he came to the performance, he didn't want to sit; he wanted to stand with me at the back of the theater.

STEPHEN SONDHEIM

SONDHEIM: We had dinner with Michael afterward, and when it was over, you said that it was kind of perfect watching the show with him because he was not saying, "It seems to me the theme needs to be this . . ." He said, "Turn the lights on earlier when she comes onstage and later when she goes off."

LAPINE: It was primarily technical feedback that he offered. "What's wrong with you?" he said to me right after the "Dog Song" was finished and there was a seamless segue into a chorus of "The Day Off." "Your lead actor just delivered a great number. Let Mandy get a hand. You've got to let the audience clap." I made the adjustment the next night, and of course Mandy got a big ovation. It made a huge difference and taught me something important. An audience needs to be able to show its appreciation. It helps validate their enjoyment and encourages anyone on the fence to get on board.

SONDHEIM: Exactly.

LAPINE: On top of that, everything that followed the number played better. Bennett's notes were few, and most were about small things, but they were all interesting. I tried most of what he suggested. Some things worked, some didn't work at all. He was Mr. Showbiz, and that wasn't my skill set. I'm not sure Michael Bennett liked the show, but he respected it and he certainly worshipped you. I think his report back to Bernie Jacobs must have been positive.

SONDHEIM: The Shuberts did support us throughout that awful period.

LAPINE: Yes, you're right. Any other producers would have been freaking out.

SONDHEIM: Absolutely.

LAPINE: Actually, anybody else would probably have fired me and brought in someone more experienced.

SONDHEIM: Yes, probably. Or had Neil Simon come in and write some jokes. Michael Bennett had his other side. He wanted Neil Simon to come in and fix *Follies*.

LORETTA ROBERTSON

ROBERTSON: One of the things that helped turn the company's spirits around was when Johnny Cash came to the show in previews. One night, Nancy Opel—our expert "celebrity spotter"—came backstage and told everyone Johnny Cash was in the front row. At intermission we were like, "Okay, is he going to stay or leave?" We were so used to people leaving at intermission that we were excited that he stayed for the second act! All I heard was people singing Johnny Cash songs for days after that.

MANDY PATINKIN

LAPINE: The preview period dragged on, and I remember one rehearsal day when you were very withdrawn and unhappy. I just felt you hated me, or were taking out whatever frustration you were feeling on me, and consequently, I can't say that I was wildly fond of you. I was already feeling so much stress and tension. You were the star of our show and I think it was obvious to everyone that you did not have confidence in me. I felt I was being tested every minute.

PATINKIN: Maybe. Or maybe you were taking things too personally.

LAPINE: Could be. We were all exhausted. I know I was not feeling supported, but I might have been mixing that up with not feeling "liked." And I might not have been likable. I was concentrating on the things that were not working, which is what a writer does. As the director, I probably neglected to let the company know what I *liked* about what they were doing. I was not big on praise. I have learned through the years to try and be more supportive of my actors. I'm not sure I have always succeeded. I can't fake it and sometimes I can get very lost in the details of the work.

BERNADETTE PETERS

LAPINE: The chemistry between you and Mandy was electric. You were so amazing together. George was a tortured and difficult and complicated character, and sometimes during rehearsals Mandy became tortured and difficult and complicated. Others were not as patient with that as you were, myself included.

PETERS: I think Mandy was really always thinking, How do I make this moment work? No. That didn't work. Let me try it again. Let me do it like this. He was looking for his character. He was *in* the creative process.

LAPINE: I don't think he trusted me as a director to help him find that.

PETERS: I don't know if he would have trusted anyone. I think he had to find it for himself. He probably would have gone through it the same way with any director.

MANNY AZENBERG

AZENBERG: As the preview period progressed, there were complaints.

LAPINE: Complaints?

AZENBERG: I had this conversation with Mike Nichols once. Mike said our major job as a director is to seduce, and you don't do that.

LAPINE: I certainly didn't do that then.

AZENBERG: Well, you learned that part of the job is to seduce an actor into being better. And I'm not talking about doing that physically, but to get an actor to trust you. Anonymous notes came to the producers during previews. One or two of them said, "I think Sondheim should come down and watch rehearsals." But that happens on 50 percent of the shows I've ever done. There's always an actor or actress who's unhappy.

LAPINE: That's not quite how I heard it. Who was it that asked Steve to come watch because he thought Mandy was hijacking rehearsals?

AZENBERG: That was Bernie.

One afternoon, Steve showed up at rehearsals unannounced. He came down and sat next to me as we worked. He didn't tell me that the producers had asked him to check in, but it wasn't hard to surmise. At one point, he nudged me and whispered that I was indulging Mandy, and that I should move the proceedings along. I found it a bit humiliating, but it wasn't worth making a big deal of it. And to some degree, the producers may well have been right to have Steve come by. At Playwrights, Mandy had been upset that he didn't have enough to do. On Broadway, he was frustrated that the second act wasn't finished. He was not communicative with me, and he was eating up rehearsal time. Maybe his insecurity about his performance manifested itself in the fact that he wanted to rehearse every moment over and over. Steve stayed for about a half hour, then got up and left.

KATHRYN GRODY

LAPINE: One rehearsal day, Mandy was just mumbling through the scenes. Nobody could hear him. He said something about saving his voice, and I said, "Fine, I'm putting a mic on you." I started getting much more pushy as a director, which I think was probably a good thing for both of us.

GRODY: I think it was a relief—

LAPINE: That somebody was in charge?

GRODY: Exactly.

LAPINE: When I was directing *A Midsummer Night's Dream* in Central Park, Joe Papp wanted me to use a megaphone instead of shouting to everyone onstage. I said I didn't want it. He shoved it in my hands and said, "You're the director and you're using a megaphone." It was so against my nature, taking this position of authority. On some level I guess I didn't want to be the "boss." Another difficulty I had with Mandy came when giving performance notes. Maybe it was my inability or inexperience, but I guess I was overly critical. Because that's where I live.

GRODY: It's healthy to be critical, because you're trying to make the performance better. One of the first things Mandy said to me after we'd been going out for a week was, "I grew up with a very critical mother; I don't know if I can handle your criticism." I said, "If you mean my critical judgment about politics and theater, I like that about myself. If you mean my judgment, I'm aware of it. I've been working on it all my life, so take your chances."

LAPINE: When I decided to type out my notes and send them up to your apartment instead of trying to give them in person to Mandy, I think you read them first and told Mandy to read them.

PATINKIN: Sending me written notes gave me time to digest your thoughts. I still have those notes. Kathryn kept them all because she thought they documented the most extraordinary relationship between an actor and a director.

LAPINE: Well, I learned that taking our personalities out of the discussion really helped us turn a corner. I could articulate what I was trying to impart better in writing than I had in conversation. And this allowed you to read the notes when you wanted to read them, when you were in the right frame of mind.

PATINKIN: I can't absorb a note right at the moment, because then I'll only play that one color. I need some time to sleep on it and digest it.

LAPINE: Actually, I learned from that. After our experience, I have asked producers I'm working with to send me notes rather than come up to me after a preview to share their thoughts. It's much better all the way around.

PATINKIN: I remember something else you said to Kathryn that meant the world to me. "When Mandy misbehaves, it's not because he is a megalomaniac. He's misbehaving because he's frustrated about the work." She passed that remark on to me, and it was one of the kindest things anyone ever gave me. I know that people get afraid of my nature. My children get afraid of my nature. I've had to learn that. Let's face it, it just was a very stressful time for all of us.

LAPINE: I guess we were both putting it together by ourselves instead of putting it together *together*. I was doing my thing and you were doing your thing and it took us a long time to work in tandem.

PATINKIN: But we couldn't have done it without Steve. We couldn't have done it without those final songs. As our opening loomed, Steve came to my dressing room and I grabbed him by the shoulders and said, "Write me anything. Anything! Even if it's a piece of shit. We don't care. Give us something!" I might have freaked him out a little. My children always used to say, "Daddy, you don't know your intensity." And I don't.

LAPINE: What did Steve say?

GEORGE

Three major notes:

1. At the top of "Putting It Together", can we go back to the
old lyrics..."All right, George -- as long as it's your night,
George..." etc. (We can keep the placement as it was yesterday.)

2. The end of "Color and Light" was so rushed! Please, take your
time here. And, take a beat before you resume painting. Last night
you were out of tempo with the music, as well. Be especially careful
at "too green...".

3. Chromolume breakdown -- new speech: review it so that it's more
fluid (it feels a bit tentative to me). The speech is not of any
great interest -- it's merely to show George's enthusiasm and to
establish that he takes what he does very seriously. (If you don't
feel comfortable about this area -- we can cut it -- but try to work
on it today.)

First Sunday: enunciate "bustle high". I also think you dropped the
work "yes" after Jules says, "I am pleased there was an independent
exhibition."

Color and Light: I always liked it when you said with irony, "Your
hat so black. So Black to you, so red to me."

Second Sunday (with Boatman): I liked it when you recoiled after the
Boatman slapped your pad.

Dogs' Song: don't look in the direction of Fifi on the line "There's
a dripping from the looney with the palette." At top of song -- I've
asked Charlie to bring down spot on the "bum-bum-bums" and to bring up
the opposite spot on the page flip.

At top of Nurse's song: it's not a good idea to point to the daisy
and the clover as it confuses the audience. You are the observer
here (there's no interaction).

In the park: "Jules" still sounds as if you're saying "jewels".

Quartet scene: I really thing you have to take a beat before you reply,
"It will be finished soon." (This has to be an awkward moment for
George. After singing, "I thought you were a part of..." with Dot, you
do not have to close the door as you go to the other side of the canvas.

Finishing the Hat: please keep your eyes on the pad through the line
"...where there never was a hat" and then, look up.

Final Sunday: I couldn't hear "Connect, George. Connect." Also
if you could try and stop on the final chord that ends the chaos --
it will clean up that moment if everything on stage stops.

ACT TWO

Take your time when you say "My grandmother, Marie" then indicate
to her to start reading. We need a beat before you say "Marie"
just to allow us to make the connection with the First Act.

On the card, it reads: "My latest machine." It should read:
"My latest invention."

I loved the little exchange about the little red book last night.
(You kept looking at the cards as if trying to find your place
and it was funny and worked well.)

Make a stronger transition with the ad libs about the family connection
to the prepared and formal "I now invite you into my Sunday island
of light."

Marie's new song: be back down to her by the time she's ready to
sing: "You would have liked her -- no, you would have loved her."

It's important in "Putting It Together" to hold center stage for
"Put yourself on exhibition -- put your work on exhibition." -- then,
move over to Marie.

In the scene with Dennis on the island: it might be worth trying not
being quite so angry on the line, "I have to do something I care about."
(It seems to me that George is frustrated by this and sometimes you
make this come out as if George is simply angry at Dennis. Because
of that -- we unfortunately lose the meaning of the line.)

Lesson #8: Try to look around when singing, "George looks around,
he sees the park."

I think the fake move when the Old Lady leaves and you look from the
Old Lady to Dot back to the Old Lady and back to Dot doesn't really
work -- because the audience still sees the Old Lady (so she hasn't
disappeared for us). There may be something else we can find to do
here.

Dot and George should be cross stage a little faster starting on
"On an island in the river..." so that Dot can be crossing upstage
on the final chords of the song and we can then bring in the white
canvas in this pause. (I will give this note to Bernadette, also.)

I'd like to put in the new lyrics for "Move On", tomorrow.

Thank you. See you at half hour if you need me.

PATINKIN: Nothing. He just stuttered, "I am."

LAPINE: Once when I was trying to get a song out of him, Steve said to me, "Do you want it Tuesday, or do you want it good?" I have to admit, since then, I have used that same line myself. There is no timetable for ideas and inspiration to strike.

PATINKIN: Yeah.

LAPINE: I think the other turning point for us was when you and Kathryn went off to the Mohonk Mountain House one week, on our days off.

PATINKIN: As our opening approached.

LAPINE: Yeah. I called the hotel and had them send you—

PATINKIN: Champagne.

LAPINE: I think I put a note in that said, "Think about anything but the show this weekend."

PATINKIN: Right, you did. "Take a break."

Daily notes sent to Mandy

LAPINE: And when you came back, you were *renewed*. We had found common ground. I think what maybe neither of us realized was, when you are the star of the show you're kind of like Dad. And if Dad's unhappy, everybody's unhappy.

KATHRYN GRODY

LAPINE: When you guys went off to Mohonk and Mandy came back transformed, what was going on there? You must have had great sex.
GRODY: Oh, God, I wish, James. I will tell you what happened. I can't believe that that weekend had a positive impact on the work. He was in a state about the show and about being a father and about me. Isaac was twenty-one months old. We'd never been away together without the baby. I picked Mandy up at the theater and we drove up to the Mohonk Mountain House barely speaking. It was so fogged in that it took us an hour and a half to make the twenty-minute drive up the road to the top of the mountain. The next morning, he was sobbing. I said, "I can't do this anymore. You need to get some help." He couldn't do it anymore, either. He wanted to be a good husband and a good father and a good performer, and he wasn't sure how to do it all. I'd been carrying around the names of three shrinks in my pocket, and when he called the first one, the guy said, "Do you have any Valium with you?" He was worried about the way Mandy sounded. Next, he reached an extraordinary person named Mary, who he went to see as soon as we got back. He felt really great about her. So, it was an extremely intense weekend up there—not at all what you assumed.

The Last Two Songs

As we began the third week of previews, there was still no sign of the last two songs: "Children and Art," which is sung by Marie to George as she looks at Seurat's painting in the museum; and "Lesson #8," which is sung by George on the island as he looks at Dot's red lesson book. To this day, I am baffled about why it took Steve so long to deliver them.

STEPHEN SONDHEIM

SONDHEIM: I don't remember why they took so long. I do remember thinking that the key number in the show was going to be "Lesson #8" and I didn't quite know what to write.

LAPINE: Going through your papers now, I see that you actually wrote something longer and more elaborate, and then cut it down.

SONDHEIM: Yeah.

LAPINE: Were you seeing your shrink then?

SONDHEIM: Oh, sure, but I rarely discussed writing with him, if ever.

LAPINE: I'm just wondering what your anxiety level was during that time, when we were experiencing such poor word of mouth and the second act was still unfinished.

SONDHEIM: I think the anxiety was my thought that it now devolved on me to, quote, "save the show." Seriously. Obviously, the songs were needed, and the actors were complaining. Mandy was saying, "I don't know what my arc is, what my journey is." I thought, Everybody's depending on me. And I also had a feeling of letting you down.

LAPINE: So do you think that slowed the process? Do you think you became too precious about it?

SONDHEIM: No, I don't think so; I think I'm a slow writer.

LAPINE: It's funny . . . you say that, but—

SONDHEIM: Occasionally I write fast.

LAPINE: When we did the workshop, you wrote a shitload in a short amount of time.

SONDHEIM: I am best when there's a real deadline. It has to be a practical deadline, like, "What are we going to perform tomorrow night, Steve?"

LAPINE: Maybe because it was a workshop, that took the pressure off you. It wasn't being reviewed. No one was expecting the show to be finished.

But we were previewing on Broadway, having postponed our opening once. That deadline was as real as it gets.

SONDHEIM: The funny thing is, I don't remember having a lot of trouble writing either of those last numbers once I knew what to write. "Children and Art" was like a two-day job, and—

LAPINE: Then how did it happen that it came so late?

SONDHEIM: I think it was about getting to it. You know, the problem with songwriting is to figure out what you're going to do.

LAPINE: Once you literally work everything out, then you can write it quickly?

SONDHEIM: Yes. And sometimes, it's not even working things out, it's knowing what the song is about. I saw your line, "There are only two worthwhile things to leave behind when you depart this world: children and art." And I thought, That's something to sing about.

LAPINE: That had been mapped out early on. We knew both of those final songs were going to be in the second act before we even started rehearsing. You did have a huge amount of time to develop those songs.

SONDHEIM: I can't tell you why they took so long.

LAPINE: I think what you're saying makes sense, that you didn't know *what* you were writing. That I understand. Maybe it was just the nature of those songs, or because they were the last songs in the show, that gave them additional weight, perhaps greater importance?

SONDHEIM: Before I wrote "Lesson #8," what was George doing to get into the past?

LAPINE: I had written a short monologue. I think it was underscored.

GEORGE: (*Sitting with the red book. To the audience*): Sunday was the day when I had to stay at home. The day the family spent together. Just Dad, Mom, and George. No brother or sister. I hated the stillness of that house. When I could, I would just stay in my room, usually looking at photographs or paintings of far-off places populated by people who seemed far more interesting than the ones that I knew. My imagination would be off and running—escaping to those places—searching for connections. (DOT *appears.*)

LAPINE: Your song was intended to summon Dot back to the present.

SONDHEIM: Yes. That was the idea.

LAPINE: I always thought of it this way: "Children and Art" explained the show and "Lesson #8" explained George.

SONDHEIM: Oh, that's nice.

LAPINE: I'm not sure I could have defined it so simply when we were mapping out the show. But looking at those songs, I think, between the two, they made our most important points in the second act—and consequently made the show complete. As you remember, many people thought there shouldn't even *be* a second act.

SONDHEIM: Of course.

LAPINE: I'm really curious about your anxiety level at this time.

SONDHEIM: I'm always anxious during writing in the sense that I wonder, Can I make this work? Aren't you anxious when you're writing a play?

LAPINE: Not when I'm writing it. I'm anxious when there's an audience.

SONDHEIM: Okay.

LAPINE: I'm anxious the night before I know I've got to fix some scene that's not working.

SONDHEIM: It seems to me it would be abnormal for a playwright or songwriter not to be anxious when an audience is there. For me, the first preview is always terrifying. But no, I don't remember any extraordinary anxiety during the writing.

LAPINE: No writer's block?

SONDHEIM: No. No.

LAPINE: You know, researching this book, going through news clippings and such, reminded me that you had a heart attack two months after we opened.

SONDHEIM: Probably not a coincidence.

LAPINE: That's what I was going to say.

SONDHEIM: My heart attacks did not come from anxiety, they came from physical problems. I would remember that kind of anxiety. No, no.

LAPINE: I bring it up because my stomach was in a knot every single day.

SONDHEIM: Well, hello? It's your professional life on the line. You know, as a joke on opening nights, I used to send people a telegram that read, "Don't be nervous. Your entire career depends on tonight."

LAPINE: But you know what? That was so *not* in my head. My anxiety came from having to walk into that room every day. The hard part was not *being* in the room, it was *getting into* the room. It was about getting up every morning and going there and facing all the issues that came with that. It was about dealing with people I didn't want to face. Once I was there, I just put my head down and pushed what I could forward.

SONDHEIM: Got it.

LAPINE: On the other hand, my time working with you was the complete opposite experience. It was always so comfortable and enjoyable and stimulating.

SONDHEIM: There's nothing better than writing before the writing gets out there and people read it or perform it.

LAPINE: I asked you once why you didn't write librettos or plays. One of the things you said was that you didn't want to be alone in the bunker.

SONDHEIM: If you're a director, at least you can blame the writer. You know? And by blame, I just mean, "Okay, he'll fix that." But when it's "*I'll* have to fix that," it's another matter.

LAPINE: Toward the end of our preview period, I felt I had pretty much done all I could. Did I nag you for the last two songs?

SONDHEIM: Nope. You certainly let me know that it would really be helpful if the second act had the two songs that would provide the show with its climax.

LAPINE: Okay, enough of this discussion. Back to a very basic question: Did you have a methodology when you wrote this score? Or was every song approached differently?

SONDHEIM: No, it's a methodology. It begins by talking to the playwright, deciding what should be sung. It's about saying, "This moment probably should be musical." Quite often, as in the case of "Children and Art," a line will pop out and I think, That's got to be the core of the song. And then I'll try to find an overriding, so-called refrain line or title, and that will suggest music, because I often write tunes from the inflection of something.

LAPINE: So the dialogue line "children and art" had a rhythm to it?

SONDHEIM: Exactly. And the inflection of those words helped me find a tune. I'll often put the script on the easel of the piano and just look at it, sometimes sort of sing it in my head. Sometimes my fingers play idly over the keys and something comes out that is either harmonic or melodic. I'm able to get a harmonic or melodic idea by just looking at the dialogue. In this case, it was the phrase "children and art." Also, as you know, I sometimes ask my collaborator to give me a monologue.

LAPINE: And monologues are musical in a way.

SONDHEIM: Yes, they are.

LAPINE: They have a rhythm.

SONDHEIM: But so does dialogue. I will always take a cue from the dialogue. So, in that sense, the words come first. The other thing that's interesting about "Children and Art"—which Marie sings—is that the scene is really about George.

LAPINE: Yes. She is trying to reach him. It's not unlike the way Dot tries to reach George in the first act with "We Do Not Belong Together."

SONDHEIM: Exactly. So it's got to be seductive. In every score I write, there's a Harold Arlen song. "Children and Art" is the Harold Arlen song.

LAPINE: And how do you characterize a Harold Arlen song?

SONDHEIM: It's about seduction and warmth and yearning.

LAPINE: "Yearning" definitely speaks to those two characters' states of mind.

SONDHEIM: Arlen kills me. He's as inventive a composer as there ever was.

LAPINE: You were able to accomplish so much in "Children and Art." It speaks to the theme of the show, but in a way that feels light and offhanded when Marie sings it to George. The music is simple and haunting all at once.

SONDHEIM: What I love about Arlen's work is that his heart is always breaking. This just kills me.

Looking at Sondheim's notes, it's easy to see the great amount of time he put into thinking through these last two songs. He took pages and pages of notes: first on ideas for the song, then breaking the ideas down and discovering the structure of the song.

As for the song "Lesson #8," it turned out to be only fifty-eight bars long and the shortest in the show. Steve and I looked at his lyric and music sketches together.

SONDHEIM: As always, we discussed the song before I began writing it. I asked, "What is George feeling at this moment?" Here, I jotted down my thoughts about this. "He has no center. He has no vision. He's not connecting. He's feeling empty." That's an example of the librettist saying something and then my starting to put it into rhythm in response to his thoughts. You see what I mean? This is the core of what this song's going to be about.

LAPINE: So, you kind of start with the general: What's the song have to accomplish? What does it need to say?

SONDHEIM: Exactly. I always tell young writers, "The important thing is to make sure that you and your collaborator are on the same page. Make sure you're writing the same show." I once had an experience where I wrote an entire score and somebody wrote an entire book, and they were both good but they didn't go together. So, it's important to always make sure that you're both talking about the same show. It's very tricky.

LAPINE: You originally thought this song might be called "Primer"?

SONDHEIM: Yes, because the red primer book became so important to the show and George was reading from it. I thought: Primer. Ooh. That's also primer—what an artist uses to prepare a canvas. So I thought I'd call it "Primer." Then I decided that's very good as a program note, but completely useless in a song. Primer is a terrible word to sing. It's no fun; it doesn't sing. Since the song was coming as George tries to decipher the writing in the red book, I thought, Start the song with George reading from the exact place as Dot does in Act One.

LAPINE: That's what's great about "Lesson #8." It's so simple and in the voice of Dot.

SONDHEIM: And it comes right out of the scene. That's the Rodgers and Hammerstein principle for carrying forward a dramatic moment. In this case, George is announcing that he has turned down a commission and that he doesn't know what to do next.

General thoughts about "Children and Art," breaking down the ideas into specific subjects

LAPINE: So then you begin your lists.

SONDHEIM: Oh, I'm a list-maker, sure. Generally, that's what I do.

LAPINE: Assemble your building blocks.

SONDHEIM: Yeah, I suppose so. This is the way I write. I get a rhythm or a tune or something like that and then start trying different lyric phrases on it. I make a list of different lyric phrases, all of which are singable to the tune. I knew George's Act Two song was going to be a kind of a recital because I wanted it to echo Dot from Act One: "Marie wants Charles's ball. Marie wants h-i-s ball." So, naturally, I thought, Now George is going to do that about himself. The rhythm for the song came from what you had written for the primer. I thought, That would be really nice. He reads/sings an exercise from the book. He doesn't quite understand what's going on and it blends into his mind. So, then he begins to sing about himself: "George gets the ball. George feels this. George is alone," etc. It seems like an obvious idea now, to use the rhythm of the primer as the rhythm of what George sings about himself, but it took me time to come up with that idea.

LAPINE: And then you made your lists?

SONDHEIM: Yes, once I have the idea, from my general lists dealing with the subject of the song, I then make lists of rhymes.

LAPINE: Would you have used a rhyming dictionary for this?

SONDHEIM: Oh, yes. Clement Wood's rhyming dictionary. That's the only one to use. It's unlike all others because the rhymes are listed vertically as opposed to horizontally. This means that as you're looking for a rhyme, your eyes move downward. If you're reading horizontally, you tend to go faster.

LAPINE: How old is that rhyming dictionary?

SONDHEIM: I would say the Clement Wood probably goes back to about 1938.

LAPINE: So, what you want to say suggests keywords, and then you go on to find rhyming words.

SONDHEIM: In this case, I wanted to make the point that the island was not what George expected. So I began to look for "-ected" rhymes: "isn't connected." Or "as I expected, nothing's reflected." So he's talking about the emptiness he's feeling. Rhymes suggest other thoughts, too.

LAPINE: Then you make lists of quatrains?

SONDHEIM: Yes, groups that represent a quatrain—a possible section of the song.

LAPINE: This is all the prep that went into writing the song?

SONDHEIM: Yes, exactly right. "George misses the ball, George misses Marie." I'm trying out that whole notion of George speaking of himself in the third person, which is an important part of the song, of course. Then I make a list of thoughts. "George wanted more, wouldn't we all?" "George has his doubts." "So little time, so much to do."

LAPINE: So these are like free associations?

SONDHEIM: Free associations but within the rhythm I'd established: *Ba-diddy-dum, ba-diddy-dum, ba-diddy-dum.* I knew the song was going to be rhythmically monotonous. Once I have the rhythm, I write a group of thoughts and then I build them into either a quatrain or sometimes a couplet. It takes a long time to write a lyric.

LAPINE: When you look at your notes, it's one, two, three, four, five, six pages to get one—

SONDHEIM: One quatrain, yes. It's endless work, but doing it releases or suggests other thoughts that become useful later.

LAPINE: And how do you organize your notes?

SONDHEIM: The left-hand margin is almost always rhymes. Sometimes synonyms. Here are the choices you've got. Okay, make a choice. But that's what's useful about these yellow pads. They have this marginal section where you can make lists. There are lyric pages and then there are music ideas.

LAPINE: At what point do you then put these jottings up on the piano?

SONDHEIM: First I type the lyric sketches and then I put them on the piano and maybe sing to them. I'll have a rhythmic idea and maybe even some of the music. These were just all experiments, and I probably tried them out by playing the piano and singing them in my head. Then I can say, "Okay, that's no good, that's no good, that doesn't work, that's a useful idea."

On this sheet of music, you can see the chords I used for the opening of the show. They became the theme of the show, and the first time they reoccur is in the first song, "Sunday in the Park with George." The point is, you can have chordal motifs as well as melodic motifs. I often have chordal motifs in my shows, because that's something that hits the audience's unconscious. A chord or chord progression will make them remember something that happened earlier. These chords at the beginning of "Lesson #8" happen throughout the show; they become the theme. One of the things about motifs: you've written something that you can then use later, as opposed to having to start all over again. I can build from those chords that have become associated with George; same thing with the tune. Usually, I keep lists of the various chords I am thinking about using on the outside of the folders where I keep my musical notations. These are musical ideas for the structure of the song that I can come back and reference when I am composing.

LAPINE: The music that begins "Lesson #8" feels very much like Marie. It ties Marie and Dot together.

SONDHEIM: Well, that's the idea.

LAPINE: Were you thinking of a southern feel for her because she came from South Carolina?

SONDHEIM: Yeah. By then, I'd heard Bernadette speak the role, and the accent suggested to me Harold Arlen. He was a Buffalo boy who kept writing southern-inflected music, and I thought, southern inflection . . . hey, there's my favorite composer. And I was off and running. It just took a lot of time. Sometimes I will write out in prose what a song is about or what I want to remember about the song, to remind myself of what the song needs to accomplish. And often, I keep the speech the writer has written either for the song or that precedes it. I write notes on it, and that's the birth of the song.

LAPINE: Going through the paperwork, I also saw that "Lesson #8" was at one point a much longer song.

SONDHEIM: I think the challenge in a song like this was to be succinct. It had a very specific purpose to accomplish in the storytelling.

LAPINE: Did the fact that they were the last two songs going into the show put an extra weight on you in writing them?

SONDHEIM: I didn't think of them as the last songs going into the show. I just thought about the particular moments in which these characters were singing.

LAPINE: I remember you once said, "Let me state the themes of the show in the songs."

SONDHEIM: Yes, because if you do it in the dialogue, it can be preachy. Oscar Hammerstein made a career out of preaching in music.

LAPINE: So when we finally got those last two songs in the show, Mandy said it best: it was like a magic trick.

SONDHEIM: That's the miracle. Maybe that's also true in playwriting, when an important scene goes into a show. When music is used correctly, then everything coalesces.

"Move On"

LAPINE: We were going to open in less than a week, and finally "Children and Art" came in on a Wednesday and the next day, "Lesson #8."

STAROBIN: I got them on a Friday. You put them into the show for the weekend with just the piano accompaniment, and I had the weekend to orchestrate them.

GEMIGNANI: It was nuts how fast we threw them in—without orchestration. By the time we got midway through the weekend, half the band was playing along anyway.

LAPINE: They just joined in?

GEMIGNANI: That's right. Les Scott added a saxophone part to Mandy's song before Michael had even written it. I didn't even know he was going to play it. There was no score, just the piano copy. And everybody—I don't mean just the musicians, but Bernadette and Mandy—just jumped right in. It was thrilling.

STAROBIN: By Monday, the day off, both songs were orchestrated and copied. Tuesday, they went into the show the day before critics arrived.

LAPINE: That was pretty crazy.

STAROBIN: And pretty exciting.

CHARLES KIMBROUGH

KIMBROUGH: "Children and Art" and "Lesson #8" were slender songs, but they were very important. Before they were in the show, we were in the wings every night for the last scene. As Dot made her entrance, we braced ourselves, because it was really rough some nights. There'd be little groans and things from the audience. "What? She changed back to her nineteenth-century clothes? Is this a curtain call? What are we doing here now?" But the addition of these songs laid that carpet of feeling under the moment. When Dot entered to the music of "Lesson #8," it was clear that this George had summoned her. It was pure gold. And then they sang "Move On" and that just killed. And then when the "Sunday" reprise came around, *bam!*

LAPINE: It was a pretty remarkable experience after having sat so often with an audience that wasn't buying the second act.

KIMBROUGH: Now, when you think back, is all that a painful memory?

LAPINE: No. Not at all. It's not painful. In fact, I'm actually somewhat in awe of my younger self. At the time, I was just trying to keep my head above water. But when I look back now, I think: Boy, I had some chutzpah!

WILLIAM PARRY

PARRY: When it came to our curtain calls, we were used to seeing what I call "walking ovations": people applauding as they are filing up the aisles to go home. Not every single one of them, but a lot of them. They're clapping on their way out. That's them telling us, the actors, "It's not your fault." When "Children and Art" and "Lesson #8" went into the show for the first time, we came out for our curtain call and there were some people actually standing and applauding. You could feel the difference immediately. And I kind of looked over at Nancy Opel and she was looking at me with those blue eyes, and she said, "Remember this." It was just fantastic. The connection had been made. The thing that these men, the two of you, had worked so hard to find—to bring these worlds together—it had happened. And that was something. Whenever a cast goes through a difficult time with a show, a time of turmoil, and then it gets better, that's extraordinary. And it links the cast.

CHARLES KIMBROUGH

KIMBROUGH: The way Stephen works, it's like the Roman arch. Until you put that last stone in, it doesn't hold up. It's not an arch. It's just a bunch of rocks.

LAPINE: Did *Company* have songs coming in at the last minute?

KIMBROUGH: "Being Alive" came in last—the number that pulls everything together. They tried using big statement songs in that spot first.

LAPINE: Oh, right. There were different songs in the "eleven-o'clock number" slot. "Marry Me a Little"—

KIMBROUGH: And "Happily Ever After." Very angry songs. Both George Furth and Steve were thinking of a considerably darker version of people trying to make a life together.

LAPINE: Marriage.

KIMBROUGH: Marriage. Neither of them was married. So Hal said no, this final number should have some lift to it. The number came in around our third week in Boston and it just clicked. Before that, it was a very chilly show. But audiences there didn't go crazy for it. They were just like, What the fuck is going on? "Being Alive"? They didn't get it. But they got it in New York.

MANDY PATINKIN

PATINKIN: We hadn't had the complete second act, and we knew as performers it was having a domino effect. When we finally got the last two songs, it changed the energy right out of the gate in the second act, because we knew where the finish line was. "Lesson #8" is, I think, an unbelievable piece of genius. For me, more so than "Finishing the Hat."

LAPINE: The last two songs were worth waiting for, and made "Move On" pay off as an eleven-o'clock number. It was like George applying the final dabs of paint that made his picture whole. The pressure of a deadline can sometimes be a good thing because at that point you can't overthink what you're doing. Uncensored thoughts emerge. We had written a kind of cerebral show. Those two songs come straight from the heart.

PATINKIN: Well, it was foreign territory to me. I'd never worked that way before.

LAPINE: Don't underestimate your own stress of having to get out every night and perform a show that wasn't finished. In retrospect, I realize how unfair that is to performers—and the audience. If I had understood that, I might have had the wisdom to not go to Broadway so quickly.

One of the unexpected downsides of postponing an opening is that you have already sold tickets to the performances that critics will now be attending. This made it impossible for our press agents to do what they usually do: give away tickets ("paper the house") in the hope of having a friendly audience. We had to rely on ticket buyers, and, unfortunately, though we had begun to attract a more engaged audience, some were still baffled or just plain didn't like it. The critics were going to experience walkouts and empty seats for the second act.

MANDY PATINKIN

PATINKIN: We had finally gotten our last two songs in and the critics were coming. To this day, I find that situation hard to deal with. I'm self-conscious. It's not a true performance. But, because of your unemotional nature, you made that night different. You were quiet. You were internal, whereas I was overemotional. You were very controlled and contained, and you were very insistent on your ideas and your vision. Like a dog with a bone, you would never let go of something you had, and that strength was hard. There was no arguing with it. I didn't see many holes in it, either. It wasn't like I thought you were really *off.* It seemed appropriate.

At the end of rehearsal that last day, you gathered us together to have a talk.

WILLIAM PARRY

PARRY: What I thought I was seeing after our final rehearsal was that you kind of opened yourself up for the first time. You were very vulnerable and you told us that you believed in the show. We knew you and

Steve were under a lot of pressure from various parties to take the show here, to take the show there, to do this with it, to do that with it. There was a lot of scuttlebutt within the company. Cast members would say, "Maybe they should do this . . ." or "It would be better if they rewrote that . . ." There's always that crap on a new show. Always. And the way you talked about what you believed in that afternoon, it seemed to me you were asking, Are you with me? And I remember sitting there thinking, I couldn't be more with you.

MANDY PATINKIN

PATINKIN: You got choked up, which took us all by surprise. You choked the words out, "Trust this show. Please believe in what we've made." Your plea, coming from this unemotional person now unable to control his emotions, was so powerful. You were asking the people you had worked with to respect what we'd made and be proud of it. Be proud of ourselves. Go out there and live it. You can't imagine how it ignited all of us. It was a powerful plea.

LAPINE: Well, I don't remember exactly what I said, but I do remember the feeling you're talking about. I felt such a struggle to try and connect with everyone at that moment. I think I said something like, "We've been through a war, and no matter what happens, we have to take pride in what we've made. Because we did something remarkable, and if somebody else thinks it's remarkable, great, and if they don't, they don't, but they're not going to take this experience away from us."

PATINKIN: A lot of us were young. We were nervous. We were focused on our "careers," as silly as that seems now. But we all understood at that moment that we had to come together as one that night.

LAPINE: I probably didn't show how much *I* cared until that moment. That was the moment my work was finished. I had to let go of the show and turn it over to all of you.

PATINKIN: And you did, in a way that was a cumulative watershed event. That was unforgettable, and it was incredibly moving.

LAPINE: While I was directing the show, there were times when I thought to myself, I'm never going to do this again. I'm going to go back to graphic design. I'm going to be a photographer. This isn't for me. I loved the writing process with Steve. It was exhilarating. But the directing part—working with the actors—that really wore me down. So I was not worrying about my "career," but I was proving something to myself. I so wanted the show to succeed for Steve. It wasn't that I wasn't totally invested in it or hadn't given it everything I had, but . . . well, we all cope with these stressful situations in our own way. Mine—and I think you and I might be a little similar, though we manifest it differently—is to have one foot out the door emotionally. And what you're talking about is that at the end, when I opened myself up to the company, I was finally "all in."

PATINKIN: I had been so terrified because of the weight on my shoulders—and you took it off my shoulders by your passion for the effort and your desire to get us to respect our journey.

LAPINE: I think I took a weight off my own shoulders, too. I don't think I could have done that any earlier in the process. Part of the struggle of doing this show was for us to connect. We both grew up a lot during the experience.

PATINKIN: You had a vision and you didn't give up on it. Even the nature of the games you had us play—you know, the touchy-feely games and exercises—you had some sense of the characters and how you wanted them to move, and wanted to connect people to that possibility. And now, you're the guy who did *Sunday in the Park with George*. Now, you don't have to prove yourself anymore.

LAPINE: Well, I could give you a list of people I've worked with since *Sunday* who couldn't seem to have cared less that I did that show. To some degree, we're always proving ourselves on every outing. If not to someone else, then certainly to ourselves.

Michiko Kakutani wrote a piece on the show for The New York Times *in which I was quoted as saying, "Our process ended up being not unlike Seurat's. We had to wait until all the dots filled the canvas . . . before we could step back and look at what we made. You go through the process of doing what you do, and then finally, you just have to put it up there and hope others respond. The irony is, you want it to look effortless, and to get that, it's such hard work."*

Opening Night: May 2, 1984

Bernie and Gerry came up to me backstage a couple of hours before the show and told me they had just gotten a call from the press agent. The New York Post *and* Daily News *reviews were not good. It was not exactly what you want to hear before your opening-night performance. There was nothing to do but pin our hopes on Frank Rich from* The New York Times *and Linda Winer from* Newsday. *My family had never been to a Broadway opening, let alone one of mine. Come to think of it, neither had I. They were having drinks across the street and I went to meet them and share the bad news. I insisted that we were going to have a good time one way or the other. I was genuinely relieved that the project had finally come to fruition, and that it was what Steve and I hoped it would be. That in and of itself was reason to celebrate— regardless of the reviews.*

It was a wonderful performance that night. Afterward, as we were walking over to the opening-night party at Sardi's, my father said sweetly, "You didn't tell me that you put your grandfather in the show." I had never met his father, who passed away long before I was born and about whom I really knew nothing. "What are you talking about, Dad?" I said. "My father, Louis. He was a baker." That stopped me dead in my tracks. I had unknowingly conjured my grandfather while writing a show about a contemporary artist conjuring his great-grandfather!

The party was sort of what you would imagine a Broadway opening-night party to be, complete with caricatures of Broadway luminaries of the past and present staring down at us from the walls of Sardi's.

John Breglio, Bernie Jacobs, Flora Roberts

Victoria Clark, Ted Sperling, and his parents

With my mom and dad, David and Lillian

With my sibs, Mark, Phyllis, and Larry

In the middle of the celebration, a couple of people suddenly appeared and be-gan dropping copies of The New York Times *on all the tables. My brother Mark, always the joker, picked up the paper and immediately went to the sports page to report the latest baseball scores. Eventually we got him to turn to the theater section.*

STEPHEN SONDHEIM

LAPINE: We were lucky to get that great review from Frank Rich.

SONDHEIM: Although, when you reread that review, it's enthusiastic, but not what you call a "money review." It's very respectful, maybe a little

Tony Straiges and Sarah Kernochan

My dad with Bill Parry and Bob Westenberg

hotter than respectful. But read it again. It's not the kind of review that makes you want to run to see the show. It was his follow-up pieces that really gave us our life.

LAPINE: I think he came back to see the show again the night after we opened.

SONDHEIM: Yes, he did. And it's the kind of show that, if you like it, it gets better the more times you see it.

LAPINE: Yes. There are things in the show you might not get right off the bat. I remember you asking me something about what I had written, six months after we opened: When you wrote this, did you mean that? It was funny. I did the same thing with your lyrics. I heard things that—

SONDHEIM: That you hadn't heard before. Sure, sometimes that happens.

LAPINE: That's what I meant about sitting there at the recent revival on Broadway and thinking: "Who wrote this?" Somehow we were writing—I don't know how you'd put it—*unconsciously* to our future selves, too.

SONDHEIM: Well, this show is about our attitude toward art and artists and the difficulty of living.

Finale

Postscript

Less than a week after we opened, the Tony Award nominations were announced. Sunday in the Park received the most recognition of any show, with ten nominations. That came as a surprise, as La Cage aux Folles *had been the big hit of the season. Prior to the Tony ceremony,* Sunday *won both the New York Drama Critics' Circle Award and the Drama Desk Award for Best Musical.*

On Tony night, I actually thought I had a good chance of winning. My naïve thinking was that I had written an original musical; isn't that more difficult than adapting someone else's movie and play? Of course, I lost, as did Steve, Mandy, Bernadette, Dana Ivey, Pat Zipprodt, and Ann Hould-Ward. Tony Straiges and Richard Nelson won for their designs, but La Cage *swept up the other awards that night. Jerry Herman won for best score, and upon receiving his Tony he said: "This award forever shatters a myth about the musical theater. There's been a rumor around for a couple of years that the simple, hummable show tune was no longer welcome on Broadway. Well, it's alive and well at the Palace!" So much for congeniality in the theater. Steve, who was sitting in front of me, turned to me and gave me a wry smile that said, "Welcome to my world."*

I don't think I'd ever watched the Tony Awards, so I was fascinated by the event, even if I was disappointed by the results and appalled by Jerry Herman's remarks. The best thing about the experience was that it put the whole "award" thing in perspective for the rest of my career in the theater.

(opposite) Tony Awards

André Bishop and Wendy Wasserstein at our first Tony Awards, 1984

LORETTA ROBERTSON

ROBERTSON: I saw Gerry Schoenfeld a few days after the Tonys and told him how disappointed I was that we had lost. He said, "Loretta, your show could never have won. We can't tell Middle America that this is what they should be going to see, because they won't get it." I thought, Well, that's depressing. I said, "Are you telling me this isn't strictly about talent?" "Loretta," he said, "you are so naïve I can't believe it."

LAPINE: Well, I think the Shuberts were very proud of the show at the end of the day.

ROBERTSON: They were.

LAPINE: We all were.

In April of 1985, Sunday in the Park with George was awarded the Pulitzer Prize for Drama. At the time, it was only the sixth musical to win the award in the prize's fifty-seven-year history. It was almost a year since the show opened and this news came as a most pleasant surprise. When we got the news, Steve and I were in a meeting with the projection designer Wendall Harrington for an upcoming revival of Merrily We Roll Along, which I was to direct. We ran over to the theater to congratulate the cast at the end of their matinee. Bernadette, who had since left the show, surprised us outside the theater.

Sometimes I would wonder what Georges Seurat would have made of our show. Would he be amused or appalled? Maybe a little of both. All indications were that he

The day the Pulitzer Prize
was announced

was a very serious dude. The one thing I am pretty confident about is that he would have loved that his painting was being widely seen and appreciated because of our efforts. It pains me to think of his having never sold a major painting in his short lifetime and dying without the recognition he deserved. Or maybe he knew his work would one day be embraced. That he trusted that his work would inspire others to think about art in a new way long after he was gone.

I don't think Sunday in the Park with George could be done today as we did it in 1984. Today, you would have to have umpteen workshops and readings. We were actually able to write a show in front of an audience at Playwrights Horizons. Then we got to Broadway, and for all the pain we went through, we continued that process. Today, even if we were opening first out of town, The New York Times would come and review it. And if the reviews weren't strong, the show would probably be stopped in its tracks before reaching Broadway. The cost of Sunday in 1984 was $2.1 million (currently roughly $5 million). Today, the cost to do this show would be at least $13 million. We certainly wouldn't be able to present it in the Booth Theatre—the math could never be made to work.

Sunday ran for 604 performances, including previews, just shy of a year and a half. I happened to be at the theater one night after the show and the doorman told me that there was a group outside that would be thrilled to meet me. I walked out and was greeted by the St. Peter's Girl Scout Troop No. 156 from Mansfield, Ohio. I visited with them and signed autographs. Shortly afterward, I got a clipping in the mail from The Mansfield News Journal that included a photograph of the girls sitting on the front lawn of my childhood home holding their Playbills.

ter hometown celebrity

The St. Peter's students who met Pulitzer Prize-winning playwright James Lapine clutch their autographs and pictures taken with him on Broadway last summer. The girls are sitting on the lawn of his former home at 255 Cline Ave., now the residence of Mr. and Mrs. Myron Kalish. Seated in the foreground is Joan Rathburn; second row from left, Mary Zimmerman, Anne Quitter and Jeannette Sgambellone; back row, Amy Kozlowski, Kim Snyder, Ann Dannhoff and Kristin Wehrle. (Photo by Jeff Sprang)

A couple of nights before we opened, a director I knew, a contemporary of mine, rushed up to me as I was leaving my seat at the end of the show. She gave me a big hug and whispered in my ear: "It's so wonderful! You never have to do anything again." I probably thanked her, but I wasn't quite sure what to make of that remark. And a few weeks after we opened, a downtown artist friend of mine came to the show. He was older than me and had had quite a mercurial rise in the art world at *a young age, but now, a decade later, his notoriety had faded a bit. After seeing the show, he said ominously: "Well, now everything you do next will be compared to this." Both of these remarks have stayed with me and taken on different meanings throughout the last thirty-five years.*

Sunday, of course, to this day has its fans and its detractors. Perhaps each of the two groups is a bit more enthusiastic in their opinions of the show than is warranted. Maybe not. After this recent revival, many people told me that the second act meant more to them than it had on their first viewing—in fact, many admitted they hadn't liked the second act at first. Could it have been that the simplicity of this production helped them to hear the material in a way they hadn't before? Or maybe the times have caught up to some of its themes? Or is it the obvious point that any work of art can speak to us differently as time carries us forward to a new or more mature perspective?

Many years ago, on a Sunday, I was home writing a new project and the work felt labored and forced. I was not having a good workday. The phone rang and it was Steve, who was in a similar state of mind with a project he was working on. We chatted for a while—always a treat—and then I hung up and decided to take a break. I went and turned on the TV and began to channel surf. By some incredible act of the divine, the PBS telecast of Sunday in the Park *was being broadcast at that very moment, and George and Dot were singing "Move On." They came to the final phrase:*

Anything you do,
Let it come from you.
Then it will be new.
Give us more to see . . .

I immediately called Steve back and told him of this bizarre coincidence. We had written ourselves a message in a bottle, though perhaps this poetic advice proves easier said than done the older you get.

Endings are difficult. Putting the last dot on the canvas, the final note on the sheet music, the last period on the page. There are mixed feelings when you are facing the finality of an effort—on the one hand, relief, and on the other, trepidation as you send it into the world. Georges Seurat never had the good fortune of being able to look back on his work, though I would like to believe that on some level he knew his art would eventually be embraced and his ambitious painting style understood. He was that certain of his artistic vision. Sharing memories of making this show with Sondheim and many of the people who were there in the trenches with us has completed the circle for me. How often, if ever, does one get to go back thirty-five years and revisit an experience? At the time, none of us could have been aware that Sunday in the Park with George *would be a watershed event in our lives. We were too absorbed, inside our painting, putting it together.*

Sunday in the Park with George

Music and Lyrics by
Stephen Sondheim
Book by James Lapine

Cast of Characters

ACT I

George, *an artist*

Dot, *his mistress*

Old Lady

Her Nurse

Jules, *another artist*

Yvonne, *his wife*

Louise, *the daughter of Jules and Yvonne*

A Boatman

Franz, *servant to Jules and Yvonne*

Frieda, *cook for Jules and Yvonne, wife to Franz*

A Soldier

Mr. and Mrs., *an American couple*

Louis, *a baker*

A Woman *with baby carriage*

A Man *with bicycle*

A Little Girl

Celeste #1, *a shopgirl*

Celeste #2, *another shopgirl*

A Boy *bathing in the river*

A Young Man *sitting on the bank*

A Man *lying on the bank*

ACT II

George, *an artist*

Marie, *his grandmother*

Dennis, *a technician*

Bob Greenberg, *the museum director*

Naomi Eisen, *a composer*

Harriet Pawling, *a patron of the arts*

Billy Webster, *her friend*

A Photographer

A Museum Assistant

Charles Redmond, *a visiting curator*

Alex, *an artist*

Betty, *an artist*

Lee Randolph, *the museum's publicist*

Blair Daniels, *an art critic*

A Waitress

Elaine, *George's former wife*

Musical Numbers

"Move On" .... George, Dot
"Sunday" .... Company

Act I takes place on a series of Sundays from 1884 to 1886 and alternates between a park on an island in the Seine just outside Paris and George's studio.

Act II takes place in 1984 at an American art museum and on the island.

Act I

A white stage. White floor, slightly raked and extended in perspective. Four white portals define the space. The proscenium arch continues across the bottom as well, creating a complete frame around the stage.

GEORGE enters downstage. He is an artist. Tall, with a dark beard, wearing a soft felt hat with a very narrow brim crushed down at the neck, and a short jacket. He looks rather intense. He sits downstage on the apron at an easel with a large drawing pad and a box of chalk. He stares momentarily at the pad before turning to the audience.

GEORGE: White. A blank page or canvas. The challenge: bring order to the whole.

(Arpeggiated chord. A tree flies in stage right.)

Through design.

(Four arpeggiated chords. The white portals fly out and the white ground cloth comes off, revealing a grassy-green expanse and portals depicting the park scene.)

Composition.

(Two arpeggiated chords. A tree tracks on from stage left.)

Balance.

(Two arpeggiated chords. Two trees descend.)

Light.

(Arpeggiated chord. The lighting bumps, giving the impression of an early morning sunrise on the island of La Grande Jatte—harsh shadows and streaming golden light through the trees.)

And harmony.

(The music coalesces into a theme, "Sunday," as a cutout of a couple rises at the back of the stage. GEORGE begins to draw, then stops suddenly and goes to the wings and brings on a young woman, DOT. She wears a traditional nineteenth-century outfit: full-length dress with bustle, etc. When he gets her downstage right, he turns her profile, then returns downstage to his easel. He begins to draw. She turns to him. Music continues under. Annoyed.)

No. Now I want you to look out at the water.

DOT: I feel foolish.

GEORGE: Why?

DOT *(Indicating bustle)*: I hate this thing.

GEORGE: Then why wear it?

DOT: Why wear it? Everyone is wearing them!

GEORGE *(Begins sketching)*: Everyone . . .

DOT: You know they are.

(She begins to move.)

GEORGE: Stand still, please.

(Music stops.)

DOT *(Sighs)*: I read they're even wearing them in America.

GEORGE: They are fighting Indians in America—and you cannot read.

DOT *(Defensive)*: I can read . . . a little.

(Pause.)

Why did we have to get up so early?

GEORGE: The light.

DOT: Oh.

(GEORGE lets out a moan.)

What's the matter?

GEORGE *(Erasing feverishly)*: I hate this tree.

(Arpeggio. A tree rises back into the fly space.)

DOT (*Hurt*): I thought you were drawing me.

GEORGE (*Muttering*): I am. I am. Just stand still.

(DOT *is oblivious to the moved tree. Through the course of the scene the landscape can continue to change. At this point a sailboat begins to slide into view.*)

DOT: I wish we could go sailing. I wouldn't go this early in the day, though.

GEORGE: Could you drop your head a little, please.

(*She drops her head completely.*)

   Dot!

(*She looks up, giggling.*)

   If you wish to be a good model you must learn to concentrate. Hold the pose. Look out to the water.

(*She obliges.*)

   Thank you.

(OLD LADY *enters.*)

OLD LADY: Where is that tree? (*Pause.*) Nurse! NURSE!

DOT (*Startled*): My God!

(*Sees* OLD LADY.)

   She is everywhere.

(NURSE *enters. She wears an enormous headdress.*)

OLD LADY: NURSE!

NURSE: What is it, Madame?

OLD LADY: The tree. The tree. Where is our tree?

NURSE: What tree?

OLD LADY: The tree we always sit near. Someone has moved it.

NURSE: No one has moved it, Madame. It is right over there. Now come along—

(NURSE *attempts to help the* OLD LADY *along.*)

OLD LADY: Do not push me!

NURSE: I am not pushing. I am helping.

OLD LADY: You are pushing and I do not need any help.

NURSE (*Crossing the stage*): Yes, Madame.

OLD LADY: And this is not our tree!

(*She continues her shuffle.*)

NURSE: Yes, Madame.

(*She helps* OLD LADY *sit in front of tree.*)

DOT: I do not envy the nurse.

GEORGE (*Under his breath*): She can read . . .

DOT (*Retaliating*): They were talking about you at La Coupole.

GEORGE: Oh.

DOT: Saying strange things . . .

GEORGE: They have so little to speak of, they must speak of me?

DOT: Were you at the zoo, George?

(*No response.*)

    Drawing the monkey cage?

GEORGE: Not the monkey cage.

DOT: They said they saw you.

GEORGE: The monkeys, Dot. Not the cage.

DOT (*Giggling*): It is true? Why draw monkeys?

OLD LADY: Nurse, what is that?

NURSE: What, Madame?

OLD LADY (*Points out front*): That! Off in the distance.

NURSE: They are making way for the exposition.

OLD LADY: What exposition?

NURSE: The International Exposition. They are going to build a tower.

OLD LADY: Another exposition . . .

NURSE: They say it is going to be the tallest structure in the world.

OLD LADY: More foreigners. I am sick of foreigners.

GEORGE: More boats.

(*An arpeggiated chord. A tugboat appears.*)

More trees.

(*Two chords. More trees track on.*)

DOT: George.

(*Chord.*)

Why is it you always get to sit in the shade while I have to stand in the sun?

(*Chord. No response.*)

George?

(*Still no response.*)

Hello, George?

(*Chord.*)

There is someone in this dress!

(*Twitches slightly, sings to herself.*)

A trickle of sweat.

(*Twitch.*)

The back of the—

(*Twitch.*)

—head.
He always does this.

(*Hiss.*)

> Now the foot is dead.
> Sunday in the park with George.
> One more Su—

(*Twitch.*)

> The collar is damp,
> Beginning to pinch.
> The bustle's slipping—

(*Hiss and twitch.*)

> I won't budge one inch.

(*Undulating with some pleasure, mixed with tiny twitches of vexation.*)

> Who was at the zoo, George?
> Who was at the zoo?
> The monkeys and who, George?
> The monkeys and who?

GEORGE: Don't move!

> **DOT** (*Still*):
> Artists are bizarre. Fixed. Cold.
> That's you, George, you're bizarre. Fixed. Cold.
> I like that in a man. Fixed. Cold.
> God, it's hot out here.
>
> Well, there are worse things
> Than staring at the water on a Sunday.
> There are worse things
> Than staring at the water
> As you're posing for a picture
> Being painted by your lover
> In the middle of the summer
> On an island in the river on a Sunday.

(GEORGE *races over to* DOT *and rearranges her a bit, as if she were an object, then returns to his easel and resumes sketching.* DOT *hisses, twitching again.*)

> The petticoat's wet,
> Which adds to the weight.

The sun is blinding.

(*Closing her eyes.*)

All right, concentrate . . .

GEORGE: Eyes open, please.

DOT:
Sunday in the park with George . . .

GEORGE: Look out at the water. Not at me.

DOT:
Sunday in the park with George . . .
Concentrate . . . concentrate . . .

(*The dress opens and* DOT *walks out of it. The dress closes behind her, remaining upright;* GEORGE *continues sketching it as if she were still inside. During the following,* DOT *moves around the stage, continuing to undulate, taking representative poses as punctuation to the music, which is heavily rhythmic.*)

Well, if you want bread
And respect
And attention,
Not to say connection,
Modeling's no profession.

(*Does mock poses.*)

If you want instead,
When you're dead,
Some more public
And more permanent
Expression

(*Poses.*)

Of affection,

(*Poses.*)

You want a painter,

(*Brief, sharp poses throughout the following.*)

Poet,
Sculptor, preferably:
Marble, granite, bronze.
Durable.
Something nice with swans
That's durable
Forever.
All it has to be is good.

(*Looking over* GEORGE's *shoulder at his work, then at* GEORGE.)

And George, you're good.
You're really good.

George's stroke is tender,
George's touch is pure.

(*Sits or stands nearby and watches him intently.*)

Your eyes, George.
I love your eyes, George.
I love your beard, George.
I love your size, George.
But most, George,
Of all,
But most of all,
I love your painting . . .

(*Looking up at the sun.*)

I think I'm fainting . . .

(*The dress opens and she steps back into it, resumes pose, gives a twitch and a wince, then sings sotto voce again.*)

The tip of a stay.

(*Wince.*)

Right under the tit.
No, don't give in, just

(*Shifts.*)

Lift the arm a bit . . .

GEORGE: Don't lift the arm, please.

DOT:
Sunday in the park with George . . .

GEORGE: The bustle high, please.

DOT:
Not even a nod.
As if I were trees.
The ground could open,
He would still say "please."

Never know with you, George,
Who could know with you?
The others I knew, George.
Before we get through,
I'll get to you, too.

God, I am so hot!

Well, there are worse things
Than staring at the water on a Sunday.
There are worse things
Than staring at the water
As you're posing for a picture
After sleeping on the ferry
After getting up at seven
To come over to an island
In the middle of a river
Half an hour from the city
On a Sunday.
On a Sunday in the park with—

GEORGE (*The music stopping*): Don't move the mouth!!

DOT
(*Holds absolutely still for a very long beat. As music resumes,
she pours all her extremely mixed emotions into one word*):
—George!

(*Speaks.*)

I am getting tired. The sun is too strong today.

GEORGE: Almost finished.

DOT (*Sexy*): I'd rather be in the studio, George.

GEORGE (*Wryly*): I know.

OLD LADY (*Looking across the water*): They are out early today.

NURSE: It is Sunday, Madame.

OLD LADY: That is what I mean, Nurse! Young boys out swimming so early on a Sunday?

NURSE: Well, it is very warm.

OLD LADY: Hand me my parasol.

NURSE: I am, Madame.

(NURSE *stands up and opens the parasol for the* OLD LADY. FRANZ, *a coachman, enters, stares at the two women for a moment, then moves downstage. He sees* GEORGE, *and affects a pose as he sits.*)

DOT: Oh, no.

GEORGE: What?

DOT: Look. Look who is over there.

GEORGE: So?

DOT: When he is around, you know who is likely to follow.

GEORGE: You have moved your arm.

DOT: I think they are spying on you, George. I really do.

GEORGE: Are you going to hold your head still?

(*The* NURSE *has wandered over in the vicinity of* FRANZ.)

NURSE: You are here awfully early today.

FRANZ (*Speaks with a German accent*): *Ja.* So are you.

NURSE: And working on a Sunday.

FRANZ: *Ja . . .*

NURSE: It is a beautiful day.

FRANZ (*Sexy*): It is too hot.

NURSE: Do you think?

OLD LADY: Where is my fan!

NURSE: I have to go back.

OLD LADY: Nurse, my fan!

NURSE: You did not bring it today, Madame.

OLD LADY: Of course I brought it!

FRANZ: Perhaps we will see each other later.

NURSE: Perhaps . . .

OLD LADY: There it is. Over there.

(OLD LADY *picks up the fan.*)

NURSE: That is my fan—

OLD LADY: Well, I can use it. Can I not? It was just lying there . . . What is all that commotion?

(*Music. Laughter from off right. A wagon tracks on bearing a tableau vivant of Seurat's* Bathing at Asnières.)

FRANZ: *Jungen! Nicht so laut! Ruhe, bitte!*

(*The following is heard simultaneously from the characters in the tableau.*)

BOY: Yoo-hoo! Dumb and fat!

YOUNG MAN: Hey! Who you staring at?

MAN: Look at the lady with the rear!

(*The* YOUNG MAN *gives a loud Bronx cheer.*)

BOY: Yoo-hoo—kinky beard!

YOUNG MAN: Kinky beard.

YOUNG MAN *and* BOY: Kinky beard!

(GEORGE *gestures, as when an artist raises and extends his right arm to frame an image before him—all freeze. Silence. A frame comes in around them.* JULES and YVONNE, *a well-to-do middle-aged couple, stroll on and pause before the painting.*)

JULES: Ahh . . .

YVONNE: Ooh . . .

JULES: Mmm . . .

YVONNE: Oh, dear.

JULES: Oh, my.

YVONNE: Oh, my dear.

> JULES (*Sings*):
> It has no presence.

> YVONNE (*Sings*):
> No passion.

> JULES:
> No life.

(*They laugh.*)

> It's neither pastoral
> Nor lyrical.

> YVONNE (*Giggling*):
> You don't suppose that it's satirical?

(*They laugh heartily.*)

> JULES:
> Just density
> Without intensity—

> YVONNE:
> No life.

(*Speaks.*)

Boys with their clothes off—

JULES (*Mocking*): *I must paint a factory next!*

YVONNE:

It's so mechanical.

JULES:

Methodical.

YVONNE:

It might be in some dreary
Socialistic periodical.

JULES (*Approvingly*): Good.

YVONNE:

So drab, so cold.

JULES:

And so controlled.

BOTH:

No life.

JULES: His touch is too deliberate, somehow.

YVONNE: The dog.

(*They shriek with laughter.*)

JULES:

These things get hung—

YVONNE: Hmm.

JULES:

And then they're gone.

YVONNE: Ahhh . . .

Of course he's young—

(JULES *shoots her a look. Hastily.*)

But getting on.

JULES: Oh . . .

All mind, no heart.

No life in his art.

> **YVONNE:**
> No life in his *life*—

(JULES *nods in approval.*)

> **BOTH:**
> No—

(*They giggle and chortle.*)

> Life.

(*Arpeggio. The BOYS in the picture give a loud Bronx cheer. The wagon with the picture tracks off. JULES and YVONNE turn and slowly stroll upstage.*)

NURSE (*Seeing* JULES): There is that famous artist—what is his name . . .

OLD LADY: What *is* his name?

NURSE: I can never remember their names.

(JULES *tips his hat to the ladies. The couple continues toward* GEORGE.)

JULES: George! Out very early today.

(GEORGE *nods as he continues sketching.* DOT *turns her back on them.*)

GEORGE: Hello, Jules.

YVONNE: A lovely day . . .

JULES: I couldn't be out sketching today—it is too sunny!

(YVONNE *laughs.*)

GEORGE: Have you seen the painting?

JULES: Yes. I was just going to say! Boys bathing—what a curious subject.

(YVONNE *stops him.*)

> We must speak.

YVONNE (*Sincere*): I loved the dog.

(*Beat.*)

JULES: I *am* pleased there was an independent exhibition.

GEORGE: Yes . . .

JULES: We *must* speak. Really.

(*Beat.*)

YVONNE: Enjoy the weather.

JULES: Good day.

(*As they exit,* YVONNE *stops* JULES *and points to* DOT.)

YVONNE: That dress!

(*They laugh and exit.*)

DOT: I hate them!

GEORGE: Jules is a fine painter.

DOT: I do not care. I hate them.

(JULES *and* YVONNE *return.*)

JULES: Franz!

YVONNE: We are waiting!

(*They exit.*)

FRANZ: *Ja*, Madame, Monsieur. At your service.

(FRANZ, *who has been hiding behind a tree, eyeing the* NURSE, *quickly dashes offstage after* JULES *and* YVONNE. GEORGE *closes his pad.* DOT *remains frozen.*)

GEORGE: Thank you.

(*Beat.*)

DOT (*Moving*): I began to do it.

GEORGE: What?

DOT: Concentrate. Like you said.

GEORGE (*Patronizing*): You did very well.

DOT: Did I really?

GEORGE (*Gathering his belongings*): Yes. I'll meet you back at the studio.

DOT (*Annoyed*): You are not coming?

GEORGE: Not now.

(*Angry,* DOT *begins to exit.*)

Dot. We'll go to the Follies tonight.

(*She stops, looks at him, then walks off.* GEORGE *walks to the* NURSE *and* OLD LADY.)

Bonjour.

NURSE: Bonjour, Monsieur.

GEORGE: Lovely morning, ladies.

NURSE: Yes.

GEORGE: I have my pad and crayons today.

NURSE: Oh, that would—

OLD LADY: Not today!

GEORGE (*Disappointed*): Why not today?

OLD LADY: Too warm.

GEORGE: It *is* warm, but it will not take long. You can go—

OLD LADY (*Continues to look out across the water*): Some other day, Monsieur.

(*Beat.*)

GEORGE (*Kneeling*): It's George, Mother.

OLD LADY (*As if it is to be a secret*): Sssh . . .

GEORGE (*Getting up*): Yes. I guess we will all be back.

(*He exits as lights fade to black.*)

(GEORGE's *studio. Downstage,* DOT [*in a likeness of Seurat's* La Poudreuse] *is at her vanity, powdering her face. Steadily, unhurried, persistent rhythmic figure underneath.*)

DOT (*As she powders rhythmically*): George taught me all about concentration. "The art of being still," he said.

(*Checks herself, then resumes powdering.*)

I guess I did not learn it soon enough.

(*Dips puff in powder.*)

Sometimes he will work all night long painting. We fought about that. I need sleep. I love to dream.

(*Upstage, GEORGE on a scaffold, behind a large canvas, which is a scrim, comes into view. He is painting. It is an in-progress version of the painting* A Sunday Afternoon on the Island of La Grande Jatte.)

George doesn't need as much sleep as everyone else.

(*Dips puff, starts powdering neck.*)

And he never tells me his dreams. George has many secrets.

(*Lights down on DOT, up on GEORGE. A number of brushes in his hand, he is covering a section of the canvas—the face of the woman in the foreground—with tiny specks of paint, in the same rhythm as DOT's powdering.*)

GEORGE (*Pauses, checks*): Order.

(*Dabs with another color, pauses, checks, dabs palette.*)

Design.

(*Dabs with another brush.*)

Composition.

Tone.

Form.

Symmetry.

Balance.

(*Sings.*)

> More red . . .

SUNDAY IN THE PARK WITH GEORGE

(Dabs with more intensity.)

And a little more red . . .

(Switches brushes.)

Blue blue blue blue
Blue blue blue blue
Even even . . .

(Switches quickly.)

Good . . .

(Humming.)

Bumbum bum bumbumbum
Bumbum bum . . .

(Paints silently for a moment.)

More red . . .

(Switches brushes again.)

More blue . . .

(Again.)

More beer . . .

(Takes a swig from a nearby bottle, always eyeing the canvas, puts the bottle down.)

More light!

(He dabs assiduously, delicately attacking the area he is painting.)

Color and light.
There's only color and light.
Yellow and white.
Just blue and yellow and white.

(Addressing the woman he is painting.)

Look at the air, Miss—

(Dabs at the space in front of her.)

See what I mean?
No, look over there, Miss—

(*Dabs at her eye, pauses, checks it.*)

That's done with green . . .

(*Swirling a brush in the orange cup.*)

Conjoined with orange . . .

(*Lights down on GEORGE, up on DOT, now powdering her breasts and armpits. Rhythmic figure persists underneath.*)

DOT: Nothing seems to fit me right.

(*Giggles.*)

The less I wear, the more comfortable I feel.

(*Sings, checking herself.*)

More rouge . . .

(*Puts puff down, gets rouge, starts applying it in small rhythmic circles, speaks.*)

George is very special. Maybe I'm just not special enough for him.

(*Puts rouge down, picks up eyebrow tweezers, sings.*)

If my legs were longer.

(*Plucks at her eyebrow.*)

If my bust was smaller.

(*Plucks.*)

If my hands were graceful.

(*Plucks.*)

If my waist was thinner.

(*Checks herself.*)

If my hips were flatter.

(*Plucks again.*)

If my voice was warm.

(*Plucks.*)

If I could concentrate—

(*Abruptly, her feet start to cancan under the table.*)

I'd be in the Follies.
I'd be in a cabaret.
Gentlemen in tall silk hats
And linen spats
Would wait with flowers.
I could make them wait for hours.
Giddy young aristocrats
With fancy flats
Who'd drink my health,
And I would be as
Hard as nails . . .

(*Looks at her nails, reaches for the buffer.*)

And they'd only want me more . . .

(*Starts buffing nails rhythmically.*)

If I was a Folly girl . . .
Nah, I wouldn't like it much.
Married men and stupid boys
And too much smoke and all that noise
And all that color and light . . .

(*Lights up on* GEORGE, *talking to the woman in the painting. Rhythmic figure continues underneath.*)

GEORGE: Aren't you proper today, Miss? Your parasol so properly cocked, your bustle so perfectly upright. No doubt your chin rests at exactly the proper angle from your chest.

(*Addressing the figure of the man next to her.*)

And you, Sir. Your hat so black. So black to you, perhaps. So red to me.

DOT (*Spraying herself with perfume*):
None of the others worked at night . . .

GEORGE: So composed for a Sunday.

DOT:
How do you work without the right

(*Sprays.*)

Bright

(*Sprays.*)

White

(*Sprays.*)

Light?

(*Sprays.*)

How do you fathom George?

GEORGE (*Sings in a mutter, trancelike, as he paints*):
Red red red red
Red red orange
Red red orange
Orange pick up blue
Pick up red
Pick up orange
From the blue-green blue-green
Blue-green circle
On the violet diagonal
Di-ag-ag-ag-ag-ag-o-nal-nal
Yellow comma yellow comma

(*Humming, massaging his numb wrist.*)

Numnum num numnumnum
Numnum num . . .

(*Sniffs, smelling DOT's perfume.*)

Blue blue blue blue
Blue still sitting
Red that perfume
Blue all night

Blue-green the window shut
Dut dut dut
Dot Dot sitting
Dot Dot waiting
Dot Dot getting fat fat fat
More yellow
Dot Dot waiting to go
Out out out but
No no no George
Finish the hat finish the hat
Have to finish the hat first
Hat hat hat hat
Hot hot hot it's hot in here . . .

(*Whistles a bit, then joyfully.*)

Sunday!
Color and light!

DOT (*Pinning up her hair*): But how George looks. He could look forever.

GEORGE:
There's only color and light.

DOT: As if he sees you and he doesn't all at once.

GEORGE:
Purple and white . . .

DOT: What is he thinking when he looks like that?

GEORGE:
. . . And red and purple and white.

DOT: What does he see? Sometimes, not even blinking.

GEORGE (*To the young girls in the painting*):
Look at this glade, girls,
Your cool blue spot.

DOT: His eyes. So dark and shiny.

GEORGE:
No, stay in the shade, girls.
It's getting hot . . .

DOT: Some think cold and black.

GEORGE:
It's getting orange . . .

DOT (*Sings*):
But it's warm inside his eyes . . .

GEORGE (*Dabbing more intensely*):
Hotter . . .

DOT:
And it's soft inside his eyes . . .

(GEORGE *steps around the canvas to get paint or a clean brush. He glances at* DOT. *Their eyes meet for a second, then* DOT *turns back to her mirror.*)

And he burns you with his eyes . . .

GEORGE: Look at her looking.

DOT:
And you're studied like the light.

GEORGE: Forever with that mirror. What does she see? The round face, the tiny pout, the soft mouth, the creamy skin . . .

DOT:
And you look inside the eyes.

GEORGE: The pink lips, the red cheeks . . .

DOT:
And you catch him here and there.

GEORGE: The wide eyes. Studying the round face, the tiny pout . . .

DOT:
But he's never really there.

GEORGE: Seeing all the parts and none of the whole.

DOT:
So you want him even more.

GEORGE (*Sings*):
But the way she catches light . . .

DOT:
And you drown inside his eyes . . .

GEORGE:
And the color of her hair . . .

DOT:	GEORGE:
I could look at him	I could look at her
Forever . . .	Forever . . .

(*A long beat. Music holds under, gradually fading.*)

GEORGE (*At his work table*): It's going well . . .

DOT: Should I wear my red dress or blue?

GEORGE: Red.

(*Beat.*)

DOT: Aren't you going to clean up?

GEORGE: Why?

DOT: The Follies, George!

(*Beat.*)

GEORGE: I have to finish the hat.

(*He returns to his work.* DOT *slams down her brush and stares at the back of the canvas. She exits. Lights fade downstage as the rhythmic figure resumes. As he paints.*)

Damn. The Follies. Will she yell or stay silent? Go without me or sulk in the corner? Will she be in the bed when the hat and the grass and the parasol have finally found their way? . . .

(*Sings.*)

> Too green . . .
> Do I care? . . .
> Too blue . . .
> Yes . . .
> Too soft . . .
> What shall I do?

(*Thinks for a moment.*)

> Well . . .
> Red.

(*Continues painting; music swells as he is consumed by light.*)

(*Afternoon. Another Sunday on the island. Downstage right* GEORGE *sketches a* BOATMAN; *a cutout of a black dog stands close by;* NURSE *and* OLD LADY *sit near their tree.* CELESTE #1 *and* CELESTE #2, *young shopgirls, sit on a bench stage left.*)

BOATMAN: The water looks different on Sunday.

GEORGE: It is the same water you boat on all week.

BOATMAN (*Contentious*): It looks different from the park.

GEORGE: You prefer watching the boats to the people promenading?

BOATMAN (*Laughing*): People all dressed up in their Sunday best pretending? Sunday is just another day.

(DOT *and* LOUIS *enter arm in arm. They look out at the water.*)

I wear what I always wear—then I don't have to worry.

GEORGE: Worry?

BOATMAN: They leave me alone dressed like this. No one comes near.

(*Music under.*)

CELESTE #1: Look who's over there.

CELESTE #2: Dot! Who is she with?

CELESTE #1: Looks like Louis the baker.

CELESTE #2: How did Dot get to be with Louis?

CELESTE #1: She knows how to make dough rise!

(*They laugh.*)

NURSE (*Noticing* DOT): There is that woman.

OLD LADY: Who is she with?

NURSE (*Squinting*): Looks like the baker.

OLD LADY: Moving up, I suppose.

NURSE: The artist is more handsome.

(DOT *and* LOUIS *exit.*)

OLD LADY: You cannot eat paintings, my dear—not when there's bread in
the oven.

(JULES, YVONNE, *and their child* LOUISE *appear. They stand to one side and
strike a pose. Music continues under, slow and stately.*)

JULES: They say he is working on an enormous canvas.

YVONNE: I heard somewhere he's painting little specks.

JULES: You heard it from me! A large canvas of specks. Really . . .

YVONNE: Look at him. Drawing a slovenly boatman.

JULES: I think he is trying to play with light.

YVONNE: What next?

JULES: A monkey cage, they say.

(*They laugh.*)

BOATMAN: Sunday hypocrites. That's what they are. Muttering and
murmuring about this one and that one. I'll take my old dog for
company any day. A dog knows his place. Respects your privacy.
Makes no demands.

(*To the dog.*)

Right, Spot?

SPOT (GEORGE): Right.

> **CELESTE #1** (*Sings*):
> They say that George has another woman.

> **CELESTE #2** (*Sings*):
> I'm not surprised.

> **CELESTE #1**:
> They say that George only lives with tramps.

> **CELESTE #2**:
> I'm not surprised.

> **CELESTE #1**:
> They say he prowls through the streets
> In his top hat after midnight—

> **CELESTE #2**:
> No!

> **CELESTE #1**:
> —and stands there staring up at the lamps.

> **CELESTE #2**:
> I'm not surprised.

> **BOTH**:
> Artists are so crazy . . .

> **OLD LADY** (*Sings*):
> Those girls are noisy.

NURSE: Yes, Madame.

> **OLD LADY** (*Referring to* JULES):
> That man is famous.

NURSE: Yes, Madame.

> **OLD LADY** (*Referring to* BOATMAN):
> That man is filthy.

NURSE: Your son seems to find him interesting.

OLD LADY:

That man's deluded.

(NURSE *thinks, nods.*)

THE CELESTES:

Artists are so crazy.

OLD LADY *and* **NURSE** (*Sing*):

Artists are so peculiar.

YVONNE: Monkeys!

BOATMAN (*Sings*):

Overprivileged women
Complaining,
Silly little simpering
Shopgirls,
Condescending artists
"Observing,"
"Perceiving" . . .
Well, screw them!

ALL:

Artists are so—

CELESTE #2:

Crazy.

CELESTE #1:

Secretive.

BOATMAN:

High and mighty.

NURSE:

Interesting.

OLD LADY:

Unfeeling.

BOATMAN: What do you do with those drawings, anyway?

(DOT *and* LOUIS *reenter.*)

DOT (*To* LOUIS): That's George.

(*All heads turn, first to* DOT, *then to* GEORGE.)

JULES: There's a move on to include his work in the next group show.

YVONNE: Never!

JULES: I agree.

(*Pause.*)

I agree.

(*They exit. Music stops.*)

CELESTE #1: He draws anyone.

CELESTE #2: Old boatman!

CELESTE #1: Peculiar man.

CELESTE #2: Like his father, I said.

CELESTE #1: I said so first.

(LOUIS *escorts* DOT *to a park bench stage left and exits. She sits with a small red lesson book in hand.*)

DOT (*Very slowly, she reads aloud*): "Lesson number eight. Pro-nouns."

(*Proudly, she repeats the word, looking toward* GEORGE.)

Pronouns.

(*She reads.*)

"What is a pronoun? A pronoun is the word used in the place of a noun. Do you recall what a noun is?"

(*Looks up.*)

Certainly, I recall.

(*She pauses, then quickly flips back in the book to an earlier lesson on nouns. She nods her head knowingly, then flips back to the present lesson. She reads.*)

"Example: Charles has a book. Marie wants Charles's book."

(*To herself.*)

Not Marie again . . .

(*Reads.*)

"Marie wants *his* book. Fill in the blanks. Charles ran with Marie's ball. Charles ran with . . ."

(*She writes as she spells aloud.*)

h-e-r ball.

(*To herself.*)

Get the ball back, Marie.

(LOUISE *dashes in upstage.*)

OLD LADY: Children should not go unattended.

NURSE: She is very young to be alone.

OLD LADY: I do not like what I see today, Nurse.

NURSE (*Confused*): What do you see?

OLD LADY: Lack of discipline.

NURSE: Oh.

OLD LADY: Not the right direction at all.

BOATMAN: Fools rowing. Call that recreation!

GEORGE: Almost finished.

(LOUISE *has come up to pet the dog.* BOATMAN *turns on her in a fury.*)

BOATMAN: Get away from that dog!

(*All eyes turn toward the* BOATMAN. LOUISE *screams and goes running offstage crying.*)

GEORGE: That was hardly necessary!

BOATMAN: How do you know what's necessary? Who are you, with your fancy pad and crayons? You call that work? You smug goddamn holier-than-thou shitty little men in your fancy clothes—born with pens and pencils, not pricks! You don't know . . .

(BOATMAN *storms off.* GEORGE, *stunned, begins to draw the dog.*)

CELESTE #1 (*To* GEORGE): Well, what are you going to do—now that you have no one to draw?

CELESTE #2: Sshh. Don't talk to him.

GEORGE: I am drawing this dog.

CELESTE #2: His dog!

CELESTE #1: Honestly . . .

GEORGE: I have already sketched you ladies.

CELESTE #1: What?

CELESTE #2: You have?

(*The* CELESTES *approach* GEORGE.)

CELESTE #1: I do not believe you.

CELESTE #2: When?

(*During the above, the* OLD LADY *and* NURSE *have exited.*)

GEORGE: A few Sundays ago.

CELESTE #1: But we never sat for you.

GEORGE: I studied you from afar.

CELESTE #2: No!

CELESTE #1: Where were you?

CELESTE #2: I want to see.

GEORGE: Some day you shall.

THE CELESTES: When?

GEORGE: Good day.

(GEORGE *moves upstage.*)

CELESTE #1: He did not so much as ask.

CELESTE #2: No respect for a person's privacy.

CELESTE #1: I would not sit for him anyway.

CELESTE #2: Probably that's why he did not ask.

(*They exit.*)

GEORGE (*From across the stage to* DOT): Good afternoon.

DOT (*Surprised*): Hello.

GEORGE: Lesson number eight?

DOT: Yes. Pronouns. My writing is improving. I even keep notes in the back of the book.

GEORGE: Good for you.

DOT: How is your painting coming along?

GEORGE: Slowly.

DOT: Are you getting more work done now that you have fewer distractions in the studio?

GEORGE (*Beat; he moves closer*): It has been quiet there.

(LOUIS *bounds onstage with a pastry tin.*)

LOUIS: Dot. I made your favorite—

(*He stops when he sees* GEORGE.)

GEORGE: Good day.

(*He retreats across the stage.* DOT *watches him, then turns to* LOUIS.)

LOUIS (*Opens the tin*): Cream puffs!

(*The bench on which they are sitting tracks offstage as* DOT *continues to look at* GEORGE. GEORGE, *who has been staring at his sketch of* SPOT, *looks over and sees they have left. Music. He begins to lose himself in his work. Lights change, leaving the dog onstage.* GEORGE *sketches the dog.*)

GEORGE (*Sings*):
If the head were smaller.
If the tail were longer.
If he faced the water.

If the paws were hidden.
If the neck was darker.
If the back was curved.
More like the parasol.
Bumbum bum bumbumbum
Bumbum bum . . .
More shade.
More tail.
More grass . . .
Would you like some more grass?
Mmmm . . .

> SPOT (GEORGE) (*Barks*):
> Ruff! Ruff!
> Thanks, the week has been

(*Barks.*)

> Rough!
> When you're stuck for life on a garbage scow—

(*Sniffs around.*)

> Only forty feet long from stern to prow,
> And a crackpot in the bow—wow, rough!

(*Sniffs.*)

> The planks are rough
> And the wind is rough
> And the master's drunk and mean and—

(*Sniffs.*)

> Grrrruff! Gruff!
> With the fish and scum
> And planks and ballast,

(*Sniffs.*)

> The nose gets numb
> And the paws get callused.
> And with splinters in your ass,
> You look forward to the grass

On Sunday.
The day off.

(Barks.)

Off! Off! Off!
Off!
The grass needs to be thicker. Perhaps a few weeds. With
    some ants, if you would. I love fresh ants.
Roaming around on Sunday,
Poking among the roots and rocks.
Nose to the ground on Sunday,
Studying all the shoes and socks.
Everything's worth it Sunday,
The day off.

(Sniffs.)

Bits of pastry.

(Sniffs.)

Piece of chicken.

(Sniffs.)

Here's a handkerchief
That somebody was sick in.

(Sniffs.)

There's a thistle.

(Sniffs.)

That's a shallot.

(Sniffs.)

That's a dripping
From the loony with the palette.

(*A cutout of a pug dog,* FIFI, *appears.*)

                FIFI (GEORGE):
Yap! Yap!

(Pants.)

Yap!

(High voice.)

Out for the day on Sunday,
Off of my lady's lap at last.
Yapping away on Sunday
Helps you forget the week just past—

(Yelps.)

Yep! Yep!
Everything's worth it Sunday,
The day off.
Yep!
Stuck all week on a lady's lap,
Nothing to do but yawn and nap,
Can you blame me if I yap?

SPOT:
Nope.

FIFI: There's just so much attention a dog can take.

(Sings.)

Being alone on Sunday,
Rolling around in mud and dirt—

SPOT:
Begging a bone on Sunday,
Settling for a spoiled dessert—

FIFI:
Everything's worth it

SPOT:
Sunday—

FIFI:
The day off.

SPOT *(Sniffs)*:
Something fuzzy.

FIFI (*Sniffs*):

Something furry.

SPOT (*Sniffs*):

Something pink
That someone tore off in a hurry.

FIFI:

What's the muddle
In the middle?

SPOT:

That's the puddle
Where the poodle did the piddle.

(*Cutout of* HORN PLAYER *rises from the stage. Two horn calls. Music continues under. Enter* FRANZ; FRIEDA, *his wife; the* CELESTES, *with fishing poles; and* NURSE.)

GEORGE (*Sings*):

Taking the day on Sunday,
Now that the dreary week is dead.
Getting away on Sunday
Brightens the dreary week ahead.
Everyone's on display on Sunday—

ALL:

The day off!

(GEORGE *flips open a page of his sketchbook and starts to sketch the* NURSE *as she clucks at the ducks.*)

GEORGE:

Bonnet flapping,
Bustle sliding,
Like a rocking horse that nobody's been riding.
There's a daisy—
And some clover—
And that interesting fellow looking over . . .

OLD LADY (*Offstage*): Nurse!

NURSE *and* GEORGE (*Sing*):

One day is much like any other,
Listening to her snap and drone.

NURSE:
Still, Sunday with someone's dotty mother
Is better than Sunday with your own.
Mothers may drone, mothers may whine—
Tending to his, though, is perfectly fine.
It pays for the nurse that is tending to mine
On Sunday,
My day off.

(*The* CELESTES, *fishing. Music continues under.*)

CELESTE #2: This is just ridiculous.

CELESTE #1: Why shouldn't we fish?

CELESTE #2: No one will notice us anyway.

(SOLDIER *enters, attached to a life-size cutout of another soldier,* *his* COMPANION.)

CELESTE #1: Look.

CELESTE #2: Where?

CELESTE #1: Soldiers.

CELESTE #2: Alone.

CELESTE #1: What did I tell you?

CELESTE #2: They'll never talk to us if we fish. Why don't we—

CELESTE #1: It's a beautiful day for fishing.

(*She smiles in the direction of the* SOLDIERS.)

SOLDIER (*Looking at his* COMPANION): What do you think?

(*Beat.*)

   I like the one in the light hat.

(LOUISE *enters, notices* FRIEDA *and* FRANZ, *and dashes over to them.*)

LOUISE: Frieda, Frieda—

FRANZ: Oh, no.

FRIEDA (*Speaks with a German accent*): Not now, Louise.

LOUISE: I want to play.

FRANZ: Go away, Louise. We are not working today.

LOUISE: Let's go throw stones at the ducks.

FRIEDA: Louise! Do not throw stones at the ducks!

LOUISE: Why not?

FRANZ: You know why not, and you know this is our day off, so go find
your mother and throw some stones at her, why don't you.

(*He begins to choke* LOUISE; FRIEDA *releases his grip.*)

FRIEDA: Franz!

LOUISE: I'm telling.

FRANZ: Good. Go!

(LOUISE *exits.*)

FRIEDA: Franzel—relax.

FRANZ: *Ja* . . . relax.

(*He opens a bottle of wine.* GEORGE *flips a page and starts to sketch* FRANZ
and FRIEDA.)

GEORGE *and* FRIEDA (*Sing*):
Second bottle . . .

GEORGE *and* FRANZ (*As* FRANZ *looks off at* NURSE):
Ah, she looks for me . . .

FRIEDA:
He is bursting to go . . .

FRANZ:
Near the fountain . . .

FRIEDA:
I could let him . . .

FRANZ:

How to manage it—?

FRIEDA:

No.

(*Speaks.*)

You know, Franz—I believe that artist is drawing us.

FRANZ: Who?

FRIEDA: Monsieur's friend.

FRANZ (*Sees* GEORGE. *They pose*): Monsieur would never think to draw us! We are only people he looks down upon.

(*Pause.*)

I should have been an artist. I was never intended for work.

FRIEDA: Artists work, Franz. I believe they work very hard.

FRANZ: Work! . . . *We* work.

(*Sings*)

> We serve their food,
> We carve their meat,
> We tend to their house,
> We polish their
> Silverware.

FRIEDA (*Sings*):
> The food we serve
> We also eat.

FRANZ:
> For them we rush,
> Wash and brush,
> Wipe and wax—

FRIEDA:
> Franz, relax.

While he "creates,"
We scrape their plates
And dust their knickknacks,
Hundreds to the shelf.
Work is what you do for others,
Liebchen,
Art is what you do for yourself.

(JULES *enters, as if looking for someone. Notices* GEORGE *instead.*)

JULES: Working on Sunday again? You should give yourself a day off.

GEORGE: Why?

JULES: You must need time to replenish—or does your well never run dry?

(*Laughs; notices* FRIEDA *and* FRANZ.)

Drawing my servants? Certainly, George, you could find more colorful subjects.

GEORGE: Who should I be sketching?

JULES: How about that pretty friend of yours? Now why did I see her arm in arm with the baker today?

(GEORGE *looks up.*)

She is a pretty subject.

GEORGE: Yes . . .

(BOATMAN *enters.*)

JULES: Your life needs spice, George. Go to some parties. That is where you'll meet prospective buyers. Have some fun. The work is bound to reflect—

GEORGE: You don't like my work, do you?

JULES: I did once.

GEORGE: You find it too tight.

JULES: People are talking about your work. You have your admirers, but you—

GEORGE: I am using a different brushstroke.

JULES (*Getting angry*): Always changing! Why keep changing?

GEORGE: Because I do not paint for your approval.

(*Beat.*)

JULES: And I suppose that is why I like you.

(*Begins to walk away.*)

   Good to see you, George.

(*JULES crosses as if to exit.*)

GEORGE (*Calling after him*): Jules! I would like you to come to the studio
   sometime. See the new work . . .

JULES: For my approval?

GEORGE: No! For your opinion.

JULES (*Considers the offer*): Very well.

(*He exits.* GEORGE *flips a page over and starts sketching the* BOATMAN.)

GEORGE *and* BOATMAN (*Sing*):
You and me, pal,
We're the loonies.
Did you know that?
Bet you didn't know that.

BOATMAN:
'Cause we tell them the truth!
Who you drawing?
Who the hell you think you're drawing?
Me?
You don't know me!
Go on drawing,
Since you're drawing only what you want to see,
Anyway!

(*Points to his eyepatch.*)

One eye, no illusion—
That you get with two:

(Points to GEORGE's eye.)

One for what is true.

(Points to the other.)

One for what suits you.
Draw your wrong conclusion,
All you artists do.
I see what is true . . .

(Music continues under.)

Sitting there, looking everyone up and down. Studying every move like
you see something different, like your eyes know more—

(Sings.)

You and me, pal,
We're society's fault.

(YVONNE, LOUISE, OLD LADY enter. GEORGE packs up his belongings.)

ALL *(Sing)*:
Taking the day on Sunday
After another week is dead.

OLD LADY: Nurse!

ALL:
Getting away on Sunday
Brightens the dreary week ahead.

OLD LADY: Nurse!

(GEORGE begins to exit, crossing paths with DOT and LOUIS, who enter. He gives DOT a hasty tip of the hat and makes a speedy exit.)

ALL:
Leaving the city pressure

Behind you,
Off where the air is fresher,
Where green, blue,
Blind you—

(LOUIS *leaves* DOT *to offer some pastries to his friends in the park. Throughout the song, he divides his time between* DOT *and the others.*)

DOT (*Looking offstage in the direction of* GEORGE's *exit, sings*):
Hello, George . . .
Where did you go, George?
I know you're near, George.
I caught your eyes, George.
I want your ear, George.
I've a surprise, George . . .
Everybody loves Louis,
Louis's simple and kind.
Everybody loves Louis,
Louis's lovable.

FRANZ (*Greeting* LOUIS): Louis!

DOT:
Seems we never know, do we,
Who we're going to find?

(*Tenderly.*)

And Louis the baker—
Is not what I had in mind.
But . . .
Louis's really an artist:
Louis's cakes are an art.
Louis isn't the smartest—
Louis's popular.
Everybody loves Louis:
Louis bakes from the heart . . .

The bread, George.
I mean the bread, George.
And then in bed, George . . .
I mean he kneads me—

I mean like dough, George . . .
Hello, George . . .

Louis's always so pleasant,
Louis's always so fair.
Louis makes you feel present,
Louis's generous.
That's the thing about Louis:
Louis always is "there."
Louis's thoughts are not hard to follow,
Louis's art is not hard to swallow.

Not that Louis's perfection—
That's what makes him ideal.
Hardly anything worth objection:
Louis drinks a bit,
Louis blinks a bit.
Louis makes a connection,
That's the thing that you feel . . .

We lose things.
And then we choose things.
And there are Louis's
And there are Georges—
Well, Louis's
And George.

But George has George
And I need—
Someone—
Louis—!

(LOUIS *gives her a pastry and exits.*)

Everybody loves Louis,
Him as well as his cakes.
Everybody loves Louis,
Me included, George.
Not afraid to be gooey,
Louis sells what he makes.
Everybody gets along with him.
That's the trouble, nothing's wrong with him.

Louis has to bake his way,
George can only bake his . . .

(*Licks a pastry.*)

Louis it is!

(*She throws pastry away and exits. Enter an American southern couple, MR. and MRS., followed by GEORGE, who sketches them. They are overdressed, eating French pastries and studying the people in the park.*)

MR.: Paris looks nothin' like the paintings.

MRS.: I know.

MR. (*Looking about*): I don't see any passion, do you?

MRS.: None.

MR.: The French are so placid.

MRS.: I don't think they have much style, either.

MR.: What's all the carryin' on back home? Delicious pastries, though.

MRS.: Excellent.

MR.: Lookin' at those boats over there makes me think of our return voyage.

MRS.: I long to be back home.

MR.: You do?

MRS.: How soon could we leave?

MR.: You're that anxious to leave? But, Peaches, we just arrived!

MRS.: I know!

MR. (*Gives it a moment's thought*): I don't like it here, either! We'll go right back to the hotel and I'll book passage for the end of the week. We'll go to the galleries this afternoon and then we'll be on our way home!

MRS.: I am so relieved.

(*As they exit.*)

I *will* miss these pastries, though.

MR.: We'll take a baker with us, too.

MRS.: Wonderful!

(*They exit.*)

CELESTE #1: You really should try using that pole.

CELESTE #2: It won't make any difference.

CELESTE #1 (*Starts yelping as if she had caught a fish*): Oh! Oh!

CELESTE #2: What is wrong?

CELESTE #1: Just sit there.

(*She carries on some more, looking in the direction of the* SOLDIER *and his* COMPANION, *who converse for a moment, then come over.*)

SOLDIER: May we be of some service, Madame?

CELESTE #1: Mademoiselle.

CELESTE #2: She has a fish.

CELESTE #1: He knows.

SOLDIER: Allow me.

(SOLDIER *takes the pole from her and pulls the line and hook. There is nothing on the end.*)

CELESTE #1: Oh. It tugged so . . .

SOLDIER: There's no sign of a fish here.

CELESTE #1: Oh me. My name is Celeste. This is my friend.

CELESTE #2: Celeste.

(SOLDIER *fools with the fishing pole.*)

CELESTE #1: Do you have a name?

SOLDIER: I beg your pardon. Napoleon. Some people feel I should change it.

(*The* CELESTES *shake their heads no.*)

CELESTE #2: And your friend?

SOLDIER: Yes. He is my friend.

CELESTE #1 (*Giggling, to* SOLDIER): He's very quiet.

SOLDIER: Yes. Actually he is. He lost his hearing during combat exercises.

CELESTE #1: What a shame.

SOLDIER: He can't speak, either.

CELESTE #2: Oh. How dreadful.

SOLDIER: We have become very close, though.

CELESTE #1 (*Nervous*): So I see.

(*Music.*)

> **SOLDIER** *and* **GEORGE** (*Sudden and loud, sing*):
> Mademoiselles,
> I and my friend,
> We are but soldiers!

(*Rumble from the* COMPANION: SOLDIER *raises hand to quiet him.*)

> **SOLDIER**:
> Passing the time
> In between wars
> For weeks at an end.

> **CELESTE #1** (*Aside*):
> Both of them are perfect.

> **CELESTE #2**:
> You can have the other.

> **CELESTE #1**:
> I don't want the other.

> **CELESTE #2**:
> I don't want the other, either.

> **SOLDIER**:
> And after a week

Spent mostly indoors
With nothing but soldiers,
Ladies, I and my friend
Trust we will not offend,
Which we'd never intend.
By suggesting we spend—

THE CELESTES (*Excited*):
Oh, spend—

SOLDIER:
—this magnificent Sunday—

THE CELESTES (*A bit deflated*):
Oh, Sunday—

SOLDIER:
—with you and your friend.

(SOLDIER *offers his arm. Both* CELESTES *rush to take it;* CELESTE #1 *gets there first.* CELESTE #2 *tries to get in between the* SOLDIERS, *can't, and rather than join the* COMPANION, *takes the arm of* CELESTE #1. *They all start to promenade.*)

CELESTE #2 (*To* CELESTE #1):
The one on the right's an awful bore . . .

CELESTE #1:
He's been in a war.

SOLDIER (*To* COMPANION):
We may get a meal and we might get more . . .

(CELESTE #1 *shakes free of* CELESTE #2, *grabs the arm of the* SOLDIER, *freeing him from his* COMPANION.)

CELESTE #1 *and* SOLDIER (*To themselves, as they exit*):
It's certainly fine for Sunday . . .
It's certainly fine for Sunday . . .

(*Dejected,* CELESTE #2 *grabs the* COMPANION.)

CELESTE #2 (*As she exits, carrying* COMPANION):
It's certainly fine for Sunday . . .

(GEORGE *is alone. He moves downstage as* FIFI *rises. He sits.*)

GEORGE (*Leafing back through his sketches. Sings*):
　　Mademoiselles . . .

(*Flips a page.*)

　　You and me, pal . . .

(*Flips.*)

　　Second bottle . . .
　　Ah, she looks for me . . .

(*Flips.*)

　　Bonnet flapping . . .

(*Flips.*)

　　Yapping . . .

(*Flips.*)

　　Ruff! . . .
　　Chicken . . .
　　Pastry . . .

(*Licks lips; looks offstage to where* DOT *has exited.*)

　　Yes, she looks for me—good.
　　Let her look for me to tell me why she left me—
　　As I always knew she would.
　　I had thought she understood.
　　They have never understood.
　　And no reason that they should.
　　But if anybody could . . .
　　Finishing the hat,
　　How you have to finish the hat.
　　How you watch the rest of the world
　　From a window
　　While you finish the hat.

　　Mapping out a sky,
　　What you feel like, planning a sky,
　　What you feel when voices that come

Through the window
Go
Until they distance and die,
Until there's nothing but sky.

And how you're always turning back too late
From the grass or the stick
Or the dog or the light,
How the kind of woman willing to wait's
Not the kind that you want to find waiting
To return you to the night,
Dizzy from the height,
Coming from the hat,
Studying the hat,
Entering the world of the hat,
Reaching through the world of the hat
Like a window,
Back to this one from that.

Studying a face,
Stepping back to look at a face
Leaves a little space in the way like a window,
But to see—
It's the only way to see.

And when the woman that you wanted goes,
You can say to yourself, "Well, I give what I give."
But the woman who won't wait for you knows
That, however you live,
There's a part of you always standing by,
Mapping out the sky,
Finishing a hat . . .
Starting on a hat . . .
Finishing a hat . . .

(*Showing sketch to* FIFI.)

Look, I made a hat . . .
Where there never was a hat . . .

(MR. *and* MRS. *enter stage right. They are lost. The* BOATMAN *crosses near them and they stop in his path.*)

SUNDAY IN THE PARK WITH GEORGE

MR.: Excusez, Masseur. We are lost.

BOATMAN: Huh?

MRS.: Let me try, Daddy.

(*Slowly and wildly gesticulating with her every word.*)

　　We are alien here. Unable to find passage off island.

BOATMAN (*Pointing to the water*): Why don't you just walk into the water until your lungs fill up and you die.

(BOATMAN *crosses away from them, laughing.*)

MRS.: I detest these people.

MR. (*Spotting* LOUIS, *who has entered in search of* DOT): Isn't that the baker?

MRS.: Why, yes, it is!

(*They cross to* LOUIS. GEORGE *brings on the* HORN PLAYER *cutout.* OLD LADY *enters.*)

OLD LADY: Where is that tree? Nurse? NURSE!

(*Horn call.* DOT *enters, and suddenly she and* GEORGE *are still, staring at one another. Everyone onstage turns slowly to them. People begin to sing fragments of songs.* DOT *and* GEORGE *move closer to one another, circling each other like gun duelers. The others close in around them until* DOT *and* GEORGE *stop, opposite each other. Silence.* DOT *takes her bustle and defiantly turns it around, creating a pregnant stance. There is an audible gasp from the onlookers. Blackout.*)

(*Music. Lights slowly come up on* GEORGE *in his studio, painting.* DOT *enters and joins* GEORGE *behind the painting. He continues painting as she watches. He stops for a moment when he sees her, then continues working.*)

DOT: You are almost finished.

GEORGE: If I do not change my mind again. And you?

DOT: Two more months.

GEORGE: You cannot change your mind.

DOT: Nor do I want to.

(*Beat.*)

Is it going to be exhibited?

GEORGE: I am not sure. Jules is coming over to look at it. Any minute, in fact.

DOT: Oh, I hope you don't mind my coming.

GEORGE: What is it that you want, Dot?

DOT: George. I would like my painting.

GEORGE: Your painting?

DOT: The one of me powdering.

GEORGE: I did not know that it was yours.

DOT: You said once that I could have it.

GEORGE: In my sleep?

DOT: I want something to remember you by.

GEORGE: You don't have enough now?

DOT: I want the painting, too.

(GEORGE *stops painting.*)

GEORGE: I understand you and Louis are getting married.

DOT: Yes.

GEORGE: He must love you very much to take you in that condition.

DOT: He does.

GEORGE: I didn't think you would go through with it. I did not think that was what you really wanted.

DOT: I don't think I can have what I really want. Louis is what I think I need.

GEORGE: Yes. Louis will take you to the Follies! Correct?

DOT: George, I didn't come here to argue.

(JULES *and* YVONNE *enter.*)

JULES: George?

GEORGE: Back here, Jules.

DOT: I will go.

GEORGE: Don't leave! It will only be a minute—

JULES (*Crossing behind canvas to* GEORGE): There you are. I brought
Yvonne along.

YVONNE: May I take a peek?

DOT: I will wait in the other room.

YVONNE (*Sees* DOT): I hope we are not interrupting you.

(*She and* JULES *step back and study the painting.* GEORGE *looks at* DOT *as she exits to the front room.*)

JULES: It is so large. How can you get any perspective? And this light . . .

(GEORGE *pulls a lantern close to the canvas.*)

GEORGE: Stand here.

YVONNE: Extraordinary! Excuse me.

(YVONNE *exits to the other room.* DOT *is sitting at her vanity, which is now cleared of her belongings.* YVONNE *and* DOT *look at each other for a moment.*)

Talk of painting bores me. It is hard to escape it when you are with an artist.

(*Beat.*)

I do not know how you can walk up all those steps in your condition.
I remember when I had Louise. I could never be on my feet for long
periods of time. Certainly could never navigate steps.

DOT: Did someone carry you around?

YVONNE: Why are you so cool to me?

DOT: Maybe I don't like you.

YVONNE: Whatever have I done to make you feel that way?

DOT: "Whatever have I done . . . ?" Maybe it is the way you speak. What
are you really doing here?

YVONNE: You know why we are here. So Jules can look at George's work.

DOT: I do not understand why George invites you. He knows you do not like his painting.

YVONNE: That is not entirely true. Jules has great respect for George. And he has encouraged him since they were in school.

DOT: That is not what I hear. Jules is jealous of George now.

YVONNE (*Beat*): Well . . . jealousy is a form of flattery, is it not? I have been jealous of you on occasion.

(DOT *looks surprised.*)

When I have seen George drawing you in the park. Jules has rarely sketched me.

DOT: You are his wife.

YVONNE (*Uncomfortable*): Too flat. Too angular.

DOT: Modeling is hard work. You wouldn't like it anyway.

YVONNE: It is worth it, don't you think?

DOT: Sometimes . . .

YVONNE: Has your life changed much now that you are with the baker?

DOT: I suppose. He enjoys caring for me.

YVONNE: You are very lucky. Oh, I suppose Jules cares—but there are times when he just does not know Louise and I are there. George always seems so oblivious to everyone.

(*Lowers her voice.*)

Jules says that is what is wrong with his painting. Too obsessive. You have to have a life! Don't you agree?

(DOT *nods.*)

JULES: George . . . I do not know what to say. What *is* this?

GEORGE: What is the dominant color? The flower on the hat?

JULES: Is this a school exam, George?

GEORGE: What is that color?

JULES (*Bored*): Violet.

(GEORGE *takes him by the hand and moves him closer to the canvas.*)

GEORGE: See? Red and blue. Your eye made the violet.

JULES: So?

GEORGE: So, your eye is perceiving both red and blue *and* violet. Only eleven colors—no black—divided, not mixed on the palette, mixed by the eye. Can't you see the shimmering?

JULES: George . . .

GEORGE: Science, Jules. Fixed laws for color, like music.

JULES: You are a painter, not a scientist! You cannot even see these faces!

GEORGE: I am not painting faces! I am—

JULES: George! I have touted your work in the past, and now you are embarrassing me! People are talking—

GEORGE: Why should I paint like you or anybody else? I am trying to get through to something new. Something that is my own.

JULES: And I am trying to understand.

GEORGE: And I want you to understand. Look at the canvas, Jules. Really look at it.

JULES: George! Let us get to the point. You have invited me here because you want me to try to get this included in the next group show.

GEORGE (*Beat—embarrassed*): It will be finished soon. I want it to be seen.

(YVONNE, *who has been eavesdropping at the studio door, leans into the room.*)

YVONNE: Jules, I am sorry to interrupt, but we really must be going. You know we have an engagement.

JULES: Yes.

YVONNE: Thank you, George.

JULES: Yes. Thank you.

GEORGE: Yes. Thank you for coming.

JULES: I will give the matter some thought.

(*They exit.* GEORGE *stands motionless for a moment staring at the canvas, then dives into his work, painting the girls.*)

GEORGE: He does not like you. He does not understand or appreciate you. He can only see you as everyone else does. Afraid to take you apart and put you back together again for himself. But we will not let anyone deter us, will we?

(*Hums.*)

Bumbum bum bumbumbum bumbum—

DOT (*Calling to him*): George!

(GEORGE, *embarrassed, crosses in front of canvas. He begins to speak.* DOT *tries to interrupt him.*)

GEORGE: Excuse me—speaking with Jules about the painting— well, I just picked up my brushes—I do not believe he even looked at the painting, though—	DOT: You asked me to stay, George, and then you forget that I am even here. George!

DOT: I have something to tell you.

GEORGE: Yes. Now, about "your" painting—

DOT: I may be going away.

(*Beat.*)

To America.

GEORGE: Alone.

DOT: Of course not! With Louis. He has work.

GEORGE: When?

DOT: After the baby arrives.

GEORGE: You will not like it there.

DOT: How do you know?

GEORGE (*Getting angry*): I have read about America. Why are you telling me this? First, you ask for a painting that is *not* yours—then you tell me this.

(*Beginning to return to the studio.*)

I have work to do.

(*Chord; music continues under.*)

DOT: Yes, George, run to your work. Hide behind your painting. I have come to tell you I am leaving because I thought you might *care* to know—foolish of me, because you care about nothing—

GEORGE: I care about many things—

DOT: Things—not people.

GEORGE: People, too. I cannot divide my feelings up as neatly as you, and I am not hiding behind my canvas—I am living in it.

> DOT (*Sings*):
> What you care for is yourself.

GEORGE: I care about this painting. *You* will be in this painting.

> DOT:
> I am something you can use.

> GEORGE (*Sings*):
> I had thought you understood.

> DOT:
> It's because I understand that I left,
> That I am leaving.

> GEORGE:
> Then there's nothing I can say,
> Is there?

> DOT:
> Yes, George, there is!

> You could tell me not to go.
> Say it to me,

Tell me not to go.
Tell me that you're hurt,
Tell me you're relieved,
Tell me that you're bored—
Anything, but don't assume I know.
Tell me what you feel!

GEORGE:

What I feel?
You know exactly how I feel.
Why do you insist
You must hear the words,
When you know I cannot give you words?
Not the ones you need.

There's nothing to say.
I cannot be what you want.

DOT:

What do *you* want, George?

GEORGE:

I needed you and you left.

DOT:

There was no room for me—

GEORGE (*Overriding her*):

You will not accept who I am.
I am what I do—
Which you knew,
Which you always knew,
Which I thought you were a part of!

(*He goes behind the canvas.*)

DOT:

No,
You are complete, George,
You are your own.
We do not belong together.
You are complete, George,
You are alone.

I am unfinished,
I am diminished
With or without you.

We do not belong together,
And we should have belonged together.
What made it so right together
Is what made it all wrong.
No one is you, George,
There we agree,
But others will do, George.

No one is you and
No one can be,
But no one is me, George,
No one is me.
We do not belong together.
And we'll never belong—!

You have a mission,
A mission to see.
Now I have one, too, George.
And we should have belonged together.

I have to move on.

(DOT *leaves.* GEORGE *stops painting and comes from around the canvas. He is left standing alone onstage. The lights fade.*)

(*The set changes back to the park scene around him. When the change is complete, he moves downstage right with the* OLD LADY, *and begins to draw her. They are alone, except for the cutout of the* COMPANION, *which stands toward the rear of the stage. There is a change of tone in both* GEORGE *and the* OLD LADY. *She has assumed a kind of loving attitude, soft and dreamlike.* GEORGE *is rather sullen in her presence.*)

OLD LADY (*Staring across the water*): I remember when you were a little boy. You would rise up early on a Sunday morning and go for a swim . . .

GEORGE: I do not know how to swim.

OLD LADY: The boys would come by the house to get you . . .

GEORGE: I have always been petrified of the water.

OLD LADY: And your father would walk you all to the banks of the Seine . . .

GEORGE: Father was never faithful to us.

OLD LADY: And he would give you boys careful instruction, telling you just how far to swim out . . .

GEORGE: And he certainly never instructed.

OLD LADY: And now, look across there—in the distance—all those beautiful trees cut down for a foolish tower.

(Music under.)

GEORGE: I do not think there were ever trees there.

OLD LADY: How I loved the view from here . . .

(Sings.)

Changing . . .

GEORGE: I am quite certain that was an open field . . .

OLD LADY:
It keeps changing.

GEORGE: I used to play there as a child.

OLD LADY:
I see towers
Where there were trees.

Going,
All the stillness,
The solitude,
Georgie.

Sundays,
Disappearing
All the time,
When things were beautiful . . .

GEORGE (*Sings*):
All things are beautiful,
Mother.
All trees, all towers,
Beautiful.
That tower—
Beautiful, Mother,
See?

(*Gestures.*)

A perfect tree.

Pretty isn't beautiful, Mother,
Pretty is what changes.
What the eye arranges
Is what is beautiful.

OLD LADY:
Fading . . .

GEORGE:
I'm changing.
You're changing.

OLD LADY:
It keeps fading . . .

GEORGE:
I'll draw us now before we fade, Mother.

OLD LADY:
It keeps melting
Before our eyes.

GEORGE:
You watch
While I revise the world.

OLD LADY:
Changing,
As we sit here—
Quick, draw it all,
Georgie!

OLD LADY *and* **GEORGE**:

Sundays—

OLD LADY:

Disappearing,
As we look—

GEORGE: Look! . . . Look! . . .

OLD LADY (*Not listening, fondly*):
You make it beautiful.

(*Music continues.*)

Oh, Georgie, how I long for the old view.

(*Music stops. The* SOLDIER *and* CELESTE #2 *enter arm in arm and promenade.*)

SOLDIER (*Noticing his* COMPANION): I am glad to be free of him.

CELESTE #2: Friends can be confining.

SOLDIER: He never understood my moods.

CELESTE #2: She only thought of herself.

(MR. *and* MRS. *enter. He is carrying a big steamer trunk. She is carrying a number of famous paintings, framed, under her arm. They are followed by* DOT, *who is carrying her baby bundled in white, and* LOUIS.)

SOLDIER: It felt as if I had this burden at my side.

CELESTE #2: She never really cared about me.

SOLDIER: We had very different tastes.

CELESTE #2: She had no taste.

SOLDIER: She did seem rather pushy.

MR.: This damned island again! I do not understand why we are not goin' straight to our boat.

MRS.: They wanted to come here first.

MR.: That much I figured out—but why? Didn't you ask them?

MRS.: I don't know.

CELESTE #2: Very! And he was so odd.

(MR. *and* MRS. *are stopped by the* SOLDIER*'s line, "He is not odd."*)

SOLDIER (*Angry*): HE IS NOT ODD!

CELESTE #2: No. No, I didn't really mean odd . . .

(*They exit.* LOUISE *runs onstage.* BOATMAN *rushes after her.*)

BOATMAN (*Mutters as he chases after* LOUISE): . . . you better not let me get my hands on you, you little toad.

(LOUISE *puts her hand over her eye and stiffens her leg in imitation of the* BOATMAN. *As he chases her offstage.*)

Now stop that!

MR.: Are we ever going to get home?!

(MR. *and* MRS. *exit.* DOT *crosses downstage to* GEORGE.)

GEORGE (*Not looking up*): You are blocking my light.

DOT: Marie and I came to watch.

GEORGE (*Turning toward* DOT): Marie . . .

(*Back to his sketch pad.*)

You know I do not like anyone standing over my shoulder.

DOT: Yes, I know.

(*She moves to another position.*)

George, we are about to leave for America. I have come to ask for the painting of me powdering again. I would like to take it with me.

GEORGE (*He stops for a moment*): Oh? I have repainted it.

(*He draws.*)

DOT: What?

GEORGE: Another model.

DOT: You knew I wanted it.

GEORGE: Perhaps if you had remained still—

DOT: Perhaps if you would look up from your pad! What is wrong with you, George? Can you not even look at your own child?

GEORGE: She is not my child. Louis is her father.

DOT: Louis is not her father.

GEORGE: Louis is her father now. Louis will be a loving and attentive father. I cannot because I cannot look up from my pad.

(*She stands speechless for a moment, then begins to walk away;* GEORGE *turns to her.*)

Dot.

(*She stops.*)

I *am* sorry.

(DOT *and* LOUIS *exit.* GEORGE *drawing* OLD LADY.)

OLD LADY: I worry about you, George.

GEORGE: Could you turn slightly toward me, please.

(*She does so.*)

OLD LADY: No future in dreaming.

GEORGE: Drop the head a little, please.

(*She does so.* CELESTE #1 *enters and goes to the* COMPANION.)

OLD LADY: I worry about you and that woman, too.

GEORGE: I have another woman in my life now.

OLD LADY: They are all the same woman.

GEORGE (*Chuckles*): Variations on a theme.

OLD LADY: Ah, you always drifted as a child.

GEORGE (*Muttering*): Shadows are too heavy.

OLD LADY: You were always in some other place—seeing something no one else could see.

GEORGE: Softer light.

(*Lights dim slowly.*)

OLD LADY: We tried to get through to you, George. Really we did.

(GEORGE *stops drawing. He looks at her. Looks at the page.*)

GEORGE (*Laments*): Connect, George.

(*Trails off.*)

Connect . . .

(FRIEDA *and* JULES *enter. They seem to be hiding.*)

FRIEDA: Are you certain you wish to do this?

JULES (*Uncertain*): Of course. We just have to find a quiet spot. I've wanted
to do it outside for a long time.

FRIEDA: Franz would kill you—

JULES (*Panics*): Is he in the park?

FRIEDA: I am not certain.

JULES: Oh. Well. Perhaps some other day would be better.

FRIEDA: Some other day? Always some other day. Perhaps you do not
really wish to—

JULES (*Subservient*): I do. I do! I love tall grass.

FRIEDA: *Ja.* Tall grass. You wouldn't toy with my affections, would you?

JULES: No. No. Of course not.

FRIEDA: I see a quiet spot over there.

JULES (*Pointing where she did, nervous*): Over there. There are people in that
grove—

(FRIEDA *places his hand on her breast. They are interrupted by the
entrance of* CELESTE #2 *and the* SOLDIER. FRIEDA, *then* JULES,
exits; as he leaves.)

Bonjour.

SOLDIER: Do you suppose there is a violation being perpetrated by that man?

CELESTE #2: What?

SOLDIER: There is something in the air today . . .

CELESTE #1 (*To the* COMPANION): Being alone is nothing new for me.

SOLDIER (*Noticing* CELESTE #1): Look who is watching us.

CELESTE #1: Sundays are such a bore. I'd almost rather be in the shop. Do you like your work? I hate mine!

CELESTE #2: I do not care if she never speaks to me again.

SOLDIER: She won't.

(*Chord.* FRANZ *and the* NURSE *enter as if to rendezvous.*)

YVONNE (*Entering*): FRANZ!

(NURSE *exits.* YVONNE *goes to* FRANZ.)

Franz, have you seen Louise?

FRANZ (*Angry*): *Nein*, Madame.

YVONNE: I thought Frieda was going to care for her today.

FRANZ: But it's Sunday.

YVONNE: What of it?

FRANZ: Our day off!

YVONNE: Oh. But I have just lost my little girl!

(FRANZ *shrugs his shoulders and begins looking for* LOUISE.)

SOLDIER: Let's say hello to Celeste.

YVONNE (*Calling*): Louise?

CELESTE #2 (*Indignant*): I do not wish to speak with her!

SOLDIER: Come. It will be fun!

(SOLDIER *takes* CELESTE #2 *toward* CELESTE #1. LOUISE *comes running in, breathless. She immediately goes to* YVONNE'*s side.*)

YVONNE: Louise! Where have you been, young lady?!

LOUISE: With Frieda.

YVONNE (*To* FRANZ): There, you see.

FRANZ: Frieda?

LOUISE: And with Father.

YVONNE: Your father is in the studio.

LOUISE: No, he's not. He's with Frieda. I saw them.

FRANZ: Where?

LOUISE: Over there. Tonguing.

(FRANZ *exits. Music under, agitated.*)

OLD LADY: Manners. Grace. Respect.

YVONNE (*Beginning to spank* LOUISE): How dare you, young lady!

LOUISE: It's true. It's true!

(JULES *enters, somewhat sheepishly.*)

YVONNE: Where the hell have you been? What are you doing here?

JULES: Darling, I came out here looking for Louise.

LOUISE (*Crying*): You came to tongue.

(SOLDIER *and* CELESTE #2 *reach* CELESTE #1.)

CELESTE #1: What do you want?

SOLDIER: We've come for a visit.

CELESTE #1: I don't want to say hello to her. Cheap Christmas wrapping.

CELESTE #2: Cheap! Look who is talking. You have the worst reputation of anyone in Paris.

CELESTE #1: At least I have a reputation. You could not draw a fly to flypaper!

(BOATMAN *enters and begins chasing* LOUISE *around the stage.* MR. *and* MRS. *enter and are caught up in the frenzy. All hell breaks loose, everyone speaking at once, the stage erupting into total chaos.*)

YVONNE: How dare you, Jules!

(*She goes to him and begins striking him.*)

JULES: Nothing, I swear.

YVONNE: Nothing. Look.

(FRANZ *drags in* FRIEDA.)

Have you been with my husband?

FRIEDA: Madame, he gave me no choice.

FRANZ: What do you mean he gave you no choice?

JULES (*Letting go of* LOUISE, *who drifts off to the side*): That is not so. Your wife lured me.

FRIEDA: Lured you! You all but forced me—

JULES: You are both fired!

FRANZ: FIRED! You think we would continue to work in your house?

YVONNE: Jules, you cannot change the subject. What were you doing?

SOLDIER: Ladies, you mustn't fight.

CELESTE #2: I seem to be doing just fine.

CELESTE #1: Hah. With a diseased soldier!

SOLDIER: Wait just a minute.

CELESTE #1: Disgusting sores everywhere.

CELESTE #2: Don't say that about him.

SOLDIER: Yes, don't say that—

CELESTE #1: I'll say whatever I like. You are both ungrateful, cheap, ugly, diseased, disgusting garbage . . .

SOLDIER: Listen here, lady, if in fact there is anything ladylike about you. You should be glad to take what you can get, any way you can get it, and I—

CELESTE #2: You think you know everything. You are not so special, and far from as pretty as you think, and everyone that comes into the shop knows exactly what you are and what—

(*Everyone has slowly fought their way to the middle of the stage, creating one big fight.* GEORGE *and the* OLD LADY *have been watching the chaos.* GEORGE *begins to cross stage to exit. Arpeggiated chord, as at the beginning of the play. Everybody suddenly freezes in place.*)

OLD LADY: Remember, George.

(*Another chord.* GEORGE *turns to the group.*)

GEORGE: Order.

(*Another chord. Everyone turns simultaneously to* GEORGE. *As chords continue under, he nods to them, and they each take up a position onstage.*)

Design.

(*Chord.* GEORGE *nods to* FRIEDA *and* FRANZ, *and they cross downstage right onto the apron. Chord.* GEORGE *nods to* MR. *and* MRS., *and they cross upstage.*)

Tension.

(*Chord.* GEORGE *nods to* CELESTE #1 *and* CELESTE #2, *and they cross downstage. Another chord.* JULES *and* YVONNE *cross upstage.*)

Balance.

(*Chord.* OLD LADY *crosses right as* DOT *and* LOUIS *cross center.* GEORGE *signals* LOUIS *away from* DOT. *Another chord.* SOLDIER *crosses upstage left;* LOUISE, *upstage right. Chord.* GEORGE *gestures to the* BOATMAN, *who crosses downstage right.*)

Harmony.

(*The music becomes calm, stately, triumphant.* GEORGE *turns front. The promenade begins. Throughout the song,* GEORGE *is moving about, setting trees, cutouts, and figures—making a perfect picture.*)

ALL (*Sing*):
Sunday,
By the blue
Purple yellow red water
On the green
Purple yellow red grass,
Let us pass
Through our perfect park,
Pausing on a Sunday
By the cool
Blue triangular water
On the soft

Green elliptical grass
As we pass
Through arrangements of shadows
Toward the verticals of trees
Forever . . .

(The horn sounds.)

By the blue
Purple yellow red water
On the green
Orange violet mass
Of the grass
In our perfect park,

GEORGE *(To* DOT):
Made of flecks of light
And dark,
And parasols:
Bumbum bum bumbumbum
Bumbum bum . . .

ALL:
People strolling through the trees
Of a small suburban park
On an island in the river
On an ordinary Sunday . . .

(The horn sounds. Chimes. They all reach their positions.)

Sunday . . .

(The horn again. Everyone assumes the final pose of the painting. GEORGE *comes out to the apron.)*

Sunday . . .

(At the last moment, GEORGE *rushes back and removes* LOUISE's *eyeglasses. He dashes back onto the apron and freezes the picture. Final chord. The completed canvas flies in. Very slow fade, as the image of the characters fades behind the painting with* GEORGE *in front. Blackout.)*

Act II

Lights fade up slowly, and we see everyone in the tableau. There is a very long pause before we begin. The audience should feel the tension. Finally, music begins. One by one, they sing.

DOT:

It's hot up here.

YVONNE:

It's hot and it's monotonous.

LOUISE:

I want my glasses.

FRANZ:

This is not my good profile.

NURSE: Nobody can even *see* my profile.

CELESTE #1:

I hate this dress.

CELESTE #2:

The soldiers have forgotten us.

FRIEDA:

The boatman *schwitzes*.

JULES: I am completely out of proportion.

SOLDIER:

These helmets weigh a lot on us.

OLD LADY:

This tree is blocking my view.

LOUISE:
I can't see anything.

BOATMAN:
Why are they complaining?
It could have been raining.

DOT:
I hate these people.

ALL:
It's hot up here
A lot up here.
It's hot up here
Forever.

A lot of fun
It's not up here.
It's hot up here,
No matter what.

There's not a breath
Of air up here,
And they're up here
Forever.

It's not my fault
I got up here.
I'll rot up here,
I am so hot up here.

YVONNE (*To* LOUISE): Darling, don't clutch mother's hand quite so tightly.
   Thank you.

CELESTE #1:
It's hot up here.

FRIEDA:
At least you have a parasol.

SOLDIER, NURSE, YVONNE, *and* **LOUISE:**
Well, look who's talking,
Sitting in the shade.

JULES (*To* DOT): I trust my cigar is not bothering you—unfortunately, it
   never goes out.

(*She pays him no attention.*)

You have excellent concentration.

> **SOLDIER** (*To* COMPANION):
> It's good to be together again.

> **CELESTE #2** (*To* CELESTE #1):
> See, I told you they were odd.

> **CELESTE #1**:
> Don't slouch.

> **LOUISE**:
> He took my glasses!

> **YVONNE**:
> You've been eating something sticky.

> **NURSE**:
> I put on rouge today, too . . .

> **FRIEDA** (*To* BOATMAN):
> Don't you ever take a bath?

> **OLD LADY**:
> Nurse! Hand me my fan.

> **NURSE**:
> I can't.

> **FRANZ**:
> At least the brat is with her mother.

> **LOUISE**:
> I heard that!

> **JULES** (*To* DOT):
> Do you like tall grass?

> **FRIEDA**:
> Ha!

YVONNE:

Jules!

BOATMAN:

Bunch of animals . . .

DOT:

I hate these people.

ALL:

It's hot up here
And strange up here,
No change up here
Forever.

How still it is,
How odd it is,
And God, it is
So hot!

SOLDIER: I like the one in the light hat.

DOT:

Hello, George.
I do not wish to be remembered
Like this, George,
With them, George.
My hem, George:
Three inches off the ground
And then this monkey
And these people, George—

They'll argue till they fade
And whisper things and grunt.
But thank you for the shade,
And putting me in front.
Yes, thank you, George, for that . . .
And for the hat . . .

CELESTE #1:

It's hot up here.

YVONNE:

It's hot and it's monotonous.

LOUISE:

I want my glasses!

FRANZ:

This is not my good profile.

CELESTE #1:

I hate this dress.

(Overlapping.)

CELESTE #2:

The soldiers have forgotten us.

CELESTE #1:

Don't slouch!

BOATMAN:

Animals . . .

JULES:

Are you sure you don't like tall grass?

NURSE:

I put on rouge today, too . . .

FRIEDA:

Don't you ever take a bath?

SOLDIER:

It's good to be together again.

OLD LADY:

Nurse, hand me my fan.

DOT:

It's hot up here.

YVONNE:

It's hot and it's monotonous.

LOUISE:

He took my glasses, I want my glasses!

FRANZ:
This is not my good profile.

ALL:
And furthermore,
Finding you're
Fading
Is very degrading
And God, I am so hot!

Well, there are worse things than sweating
By a river on a Sunday.
There are worse things than sweating by a river

BOATMAN:
When you're sweating in a picture
That was painted by a genius

FRANZ:
And you know that you're immortal

FRIEDA:
And you'll always be remembered

NURSE:
Even if they never see you

OLD LADY:
And you're listening to drivel

SOLDIER:
And you're part of your companion

LOUISE:
And your glasses have been stolen

YVONNE:
And you're bored beyond endurance

LOUIS:
And the baby has no diapers

CELESTE #1 (*To* CELESTE #2):
And you're slouching

CELESTE #2:

I am not!

JULES:

And you are out of all proportion!

DOT:

And I hate these people!

ALL:

You never get
A breeze up here,
And she's (he's) up here
Forever.

You cannot run
Amok up here,
You're stuck up here
In this gavotte.
Perspectives don't
Make sense up here.
It's tense up here
Forever.

The outward show
Of bliss up here
Is disappear-
Ing dot by dot.

(*Long pause. Music continues for a long moment.*)

And it's hot!

(*They shake themselves loose from the pose for a brief moment, but at the last beat of the music resume their positions. GEORGE enters downstage and stands on the apron in front of the tableau.*)

GEORGE: A fascination with light. The bedroom where I slept as a child—
it has a window. At night, the reflections of the light—that is, the light
outside the window—created a shadow-show on my wall. So it was,
lying in my bed, looking at the wall, I was able to make out shapes of
night activity from the street. These images were not rich in detail, so
my mind's eye filled in the shapes to bring them to life. Straying from

the point. The point? Light and sleep. I didn't sleep. Well, of course I slept, but always when there was a choice, when I might fight the urge, I would lie awake, eyes fixed on the wall, sometimes until the bright sunlight of the morning washed the image away. Off and running. Off and running. First into the morning light. Last on the gas-lit streets. Energy that had no time for sleep. A mission to see, to record impressions. Seeing . . . recording . . . seeing the record, then feeling the experience. Connect the dots, George. Slowing to a screeching halt— in one week. Fighting to wake up. "Wake up, Georgie." I can still feel her cool hand on my warm cheek. Could darkness be an inviting place? Could sleep surpass off and running? No. Lying still, I can see the boys swimming in the Seine. I can see them all, on a sunny Sunday in the park.

(*He exits. During the following, the characters break from their poses when they speak. Accompanying their exits, pieces of scenery disappear; by the time the* BOATMAN *exits at the end of the sequence, the set is returned to its original white configuration.*)

CELESTE #2: Thirty-one . . .

CELESTE #1: It is hard to believe.

CELESTE #2: Yes.

CELESTE #1: It seems like only yesterday we were posing for him.

CELESTE #2: We never posed for him!

CELESTE #1: Certainly we did! We are in a painting, aren't we?

CELESTE #2: It's not as if he asked us to sit!

CELESTE #1: If you had sat up—

SOLDIER: Will you two just keep QUIET!

(*He steps downstage. The* CELESTES *exit.*)

I hardly knew the man. I would spend my Sundays here, and I would see him sketching, so I was surprised when he stopped showing up. Of course, I did not notice right away. But one day, I realized, something was different—like a flash of light, right through me, the way that man would stare at you when he sketched—I knew, he was no longer.

(SOLDIER *exits.* LOUISE *breaks away from her mother and dashes downstage.*)

LOUISE: I am going to be a painter when I grow up!

BOATMAN: If you live.

(LOUISE *runs off*.)

FRIEDA: Honestly!

BOATMAN: Keep your mouth shut!

FRIEDA: It is my mouth and I shall do as I please!

FRANZ: Quiet! George was a gentleman.

FRIEDA: Soft-spoken.

FRANZ: And he was a far superior artist to Monsieur.

FRIEDA: George had beautiful eyes.

FRANZ: *Ja*, he—beautiful eyes?

FRIEDA: *Ja* . . . well . . . eyes that captured beauty.

FRANZ (*Suspicious*): *Ja* . . . he chose his subjects well.

(*They exit*.)

DOT: I was in Charleston when I heard. At first, I was surprised by the news. Almost relieved, in fact. Perhaps I knew this is how it would end—perhaps we both knew.

(*She exits*.)

OLD LADY: A parent wants to die first. But George was always off and running, and I was never able to keep up with him.

NURSE: No one knew he was ill until the very last days. I offered to care for him, but he would let no one near. Not even her.

(OLD LADY *and* NURSE *exit*.)

JULES (*Too sincere*): George had great promise as a painter. It really is a shame his career was ended so abruptly. He had an unusual flair for color and light, and his work was not as mechanical as some have suggested. I liked George. He was dedicated to his work—seldom did anything but work—and I am proud to have counted him among my friends.

YVONNE: George stopped me once in the park—it was the only time I had spoken to him outside the company of Jules. He stared at my jacket for an instant, then muttered something about beautiful colors and just walked on. I rather fancied George.

(JULES *looks at her.*)

Well, most of the women did!

(JULES *and* YVONNE *exit.*)

BOATMAN: They all wanted him and hated him at the same time. They wanted to be painted—splashed on some fancy salon wall. But they hated him, too. Hated him because he only spoke when he absolutely had to. Most of all, they hated him because they knew he would always be around.

(BOATMAN *exits. The stage is bare.*)

(*Lights change. Electronic music. It is 1984. We are in the auditorium of the museum where the painting now hangs. Enter* GEORGE. *He wheels in his grandmother,* MARIE *[played by* DOT*], who is ninety-eight and confined to a wheelchair.* DENNIS, GEORGE's *technical assistant, rolls on a control console and places it stage right. An immense white machine rolls on and comes to rest center stage. Our contemporary* GEORGE *is an inventor-sculptor, and this is his latest invention, Chromolume #7. The machine is postmodern in design and is dominated by a four-foot-in-diameter sphere at the top. It glows a range of cool colored light.* MARIE *sits on one side of the machine, and* GEORGE *stands at the console on the other. Behind them is a full-stage projection screen.*)

GEORGE: Ladies and gentlemen, in 1983 I was commissioned by this museum to create an art piece commemorating Georges Seurat's painting *A Sunday Afternoon on the Island of La Grande Jatte.* My latest Chromolume stands before you now, the seventh in a continuing series. Because I have a special association with this painting, the museum director, Robert Greenberg, suggested I assemble a short presentation to precede the activation of my latest invention. I have brought my grandmother along to give me a hand.

(*Introducing her.*)

My grandmother, Marie.

(What follows is a coordinated performance of music, text [read from index cards by GEORGE and MARIE], film projections of the images referred to, and light emissions from the machine. The first section is accompanied by film projections.)

MARIE: I was born in Paris, France, ninety-eight years ago. My grandson, George.

GEORGE: I was born in Lodi, New Jersey, thirty-two years ago.

MARIE: My mother was married to Louis, a baker. They left France when I was an infant to travel to Charleston, South Carolina.

GEORGE: Georges Seurat.

MARIE: Born: December 2, 1859.

GEORGE: It was through his mother that the future artist was introduced to the lower-class Parisian parks. Seurat received a classical training at the Beaux-Arts.

MARIE: Like his father, he was not an easy man to know.

GEORGE: He lived in an age when science was gaining influence over Romantic principles.

MARIE: He worked very hard.

GEORGE: His first painting, at the age of twenty-four, *Bathing at Asnières*, was rejected by the Salon, but was shown by the Group of Independent Artists.

MARIE: They hung it over the refreshment stand.

(Ad-libbing.)

Wasn't that awful?

GEORGE: On Ascension Day 1884, he began work on his second painting, *A Sunday Afternoon on the Island of La Grande Jatte*. He was to work two years on this painting.

MARIE: He always knew where he was going before he picked up a paintbrush.

GEORGE: He denied conventional perspective and conventional space.

MARIE: He was unconventional in his lifestyle as well.

(Ad-libbing again.)

So was I! You know I was a Florodora Girl for a short time—when I left Charleston and before I was married to my first husband—

GEORGE (*Interrupting her*): Marie. Marie!

(She looks over to him.)

The film is running.

MARIE: Excuse me.

(She reads.)

They hung it over the refreshment stand.

GEORGE: Marie!

(He reads.)

Having studied scientific findings on color, he developed a new style of painting. He found by painting tiny particles, color next to color, that at a certain distance the eye would fuse the specks optically, giving them greater intensity than any mixed pigments.

MARIE: He wanted to paint with colored lights.

GEORGE: Beams of colored light, he hoped.

MARIE: It was shown at the eighth and last Impressionist Exhibition.

GEORGE: Monet, Renoir, and Sisley withdrew their submissions because of his painting.

MARIE: They placed it in a small room off to the side of the main hall, too dark for the painting to truly be seen.

GEORGE: The painting was ridiculed by most. But there were also a handful of believers in his work.

MARIE: He went on to paint six more major paintings before his sudden death at the age of thirty-one. He never sold a painting in his lifetime.

GEORGE: On this occasion, I present my latest Chromolume—

MARIE: Number Seven—

GEORGE: —which pays homage to *La Grande Jatte* and to my grandmother,

Marie. The score for this presentation has been composed by Naomi Eisen.

(NAOMI *enters, bows, and exits.*)

MARIE (*She reads a stage direction by mistake*): George begins to activate the Chromolume machine as . . .

GEORGE: Don't read that part, Grandmother.

MARIE: Oh . . . don't read this . . .

(*Music begins to increase in volume and intensity. Strobe lights begin emitting from the machine along with shafts of brilliant light. Colors begin to fill the stage and audience, creating a pointillist look. Just as the sphere begins to illuminate, producing various images from the painting, there is a sudden explosion of sparks and smoke. The lighting system flickers on and off until everything dies, including music. There is a moment of silence in the darkness.*)

GEORGE (*Under his breath*): Shit.

(*Calling out.*)

   Robert Greenberg?

GREENBERG (*From the back of the house.*): Just a minute, George!

(*Some light returns to the smoke-filled stage.*)

DENNIS (*Offstage*): It's the regulator, George.

(*Lights come up on GEORGE, who is looking inside the machine. He steps downstage toward the audience.*)

GEORGE: My apologies, ladies and gentlemen. For precise synchronization of all the visual elements, I've installed a new state-of-the-art Japanese microcomputer which controls the voltage regulator. I think that the surge from the musical equipment has created an electrical short.

(*Beat.*)

   Unfortunately, no electricity, no art. Give us a moment and we'll be able to bypass the regulator and be back in business.

(*After "no electricity, no art," GREENBERG has entered and stands to the side of the apron. DENNIS enters and joins GEORGE at the Chromolume.*)

GREENBERG: I am very sorry, ladies and gentlemen. We seem to be having a little electrical difficulty.

(NAOMI *has entered and rushed to the machine.*)

NAOMI: There's no juice!

GREENBERG: You must realize this is the first time we have had a collaboration like this at the museum and it has offered some extraordinary challenges to us here.

(NAOMI *and* DENNIS *exit arguing.*)

Now, I hope to see all of you at the reception and dinner which will follow the presentation. It's right down the hall in the main gallery, where the painting hangs. And we have a very special treat for you. As I am sure you have noticed, in order to raise additional funds we have chosen to sell the air rights to the museum—and some of the twenty-seven flights of condominiums that stand above us now will be open for your inspection after dinner. You may even wish to become one of our permanent neighbors!

GEORGE: We're ready, Bob.

GREENBERG: Well . . . proceed. Proceed!

(*He exits.*)

GEORGE (*Into his headset*): Dennis! Lights.

(*Lights dim and the presentation continues. Music gathers momentum. The Chromolume begins several seconds before the speaking resumes, with images from the painting projected on its sphere, illustrating the lecture.*)

MARIE: When I was young, Mother loved telling me tales of her life in France, and of her work as an artist's model.

GEORGE: Her mother showed her this great painting and pointed to this woman and said that it was she.

MARIE: And she pointed to a couple in the back—they were holding an infant child—and she said that was me!

GEORGE: Shortly before my great-grandmother's death, she spoke of her association with the artist of this painting. She told Marie that Seurat was her real father.

MARIE: I was shocked!

GEORGE: My parents never believed this story. After all, there was no proof. I do not—

MARIE (*Produces a red book, unbeknownst to* GEORGE): My mother gave me this small red book.

GEORGE: Marie!

MARIE: Oh, George, I wanted to bring the book and show it.

(*To audience.*)

In the back are notes about his great-grandfather, the artist.

GEORGE: Actually, this book is really just a grammar book in the handwriting of a child, and though there *are* notes in the back which mention a Georges—they could be referring to anyone.

MARIE: But they do not.

GEORGE: I do not know that there is any validity to this story.

MARIE: Of course there is validity!

(*To audience.*)

He has to have everything spelled out for him!

GEORGE: The facts are sketchy. The tales are many. I would like to invite you into my *Sunday: Island of Light.* It will be on exhibition here in the upstairs gallery for three weeks.

(*Music crescendos, as laser beams burst over the audience. When they complete their course, the sphere begins to turn, sending out a blinding burst of light. The painting flies in.*)

(*We are now in the gallery where the painting hangs and in front of which the reception is beginning.* HARRIET *and* BILLY *enter, closely followed by* REDMOND, GREENBERG, ALEX, BETTY, *and* NAOMI. *Cocktail music under.*)

BILLY: Well, I can't say that *I* understand what that light machine has to do with this painting.

HARRIET: Darling, it's a theme and variation.

BILLY: Oh. Theme and variation.

GREENBERG (*To* REDMOND): Times change so quickly.

REDMOND: Lord knows.

GREENBERG: That's the challenge of our work. You never know what movement is going to hit next. Which artist to embrace.

(*Rhumba music.*)

NAOMI: I thought it went very well, except for that electrical screw-up. What did you guys think?

ALEX: Terrible.   BETTY: Terrific.

(*Short embarrassed pause.*)

> HARRIET (*Sings*):
> I mean, I don't understand completely—

> BILLY (*Sings*):
> I'm not surprised.

> HARRIET:
> But he combines all these different trends.

> BILLY:
> I'm not surprised.

> HARRIET:
> You can't divide art today
> Into categories neatly—

> BILLY:
> Oh.

> HARRIET:
> What matters is the means, not the ends.

> BILLY:
> I'm not surprised.

HARRIET *and* **BILLY**:
That is the state of the art, my dear,
That is the state of the art.

GREENBERG (*Sings*):
It's not enough knowing good from rotten—

REDMOND (*Sings*):
You're telling me—

GREENBERG:
When something new pops up every day.

REDMOND:
You're telling me—

GREENBERG:
It's only new, though, for now—

REDMOND:
Nouveau.

GREENBERG:
But yesterday's forgotten.

REDMOND (*Nods*):
And tomorrow is already passé.

GREENBERG:
There's no surprise.

REDMOND *and* **GREENBERG**:
That is the state of the art, my friend,
That is the state of the art.

BETTY (*Sings*):
He's an original.

ALEX: Was.

NAOMI:
I like the images.

ALEX: Some.

BETTY:
Come on.
You had your moment,
Now it's George's turn—

ALEX (*Sings*):
It's George's turn?
I wasn't talking turns,
I'm talking art.

BETTY (*To* NAOMI):
Don't you think he's original?

NAOMI:
Well, yes . . .

BETTY (*To* ALEX):
You're talking crap.

ALEX (*Overlapping with* NAOMI):
But is it really new?

NAOMI:
Well, no . . .

ALEX (*To* BETTY):
His own collaborator—!

BETTY (*Overlapping with* NAOMI):
It's more than novelty.

NAOMI:
Well, yes . . .

BETTY (*To* ALEX):
It's just impersonal, but—

ALEX:
It's all promotion, but then—

ALEX *and* BETTY (*To* NAOMI):
That is the state of the art,
Isn't it?

NAOMI (*Caught between them*):
Well . . .

BILLY (*To* HARRIET):
Art isn't easy—

HARRIET (*Nodding*):
Even when you've amassed it—

BETTY:
Fighting for prizes—

GREENBERG:
No one can be an oracle.

REDMOND (*Nodding*):
Art isn't easy.

ALEX:
Suddenly—

(*Snaps fingers.*)

You're past it.

NAOMI:
All compromises—

HARRIET (*To* BILLY):
And then when it's allegorical—!

REDMOND *and* **GREENBERG**:
Art isn't easy—

ALL:
Any way you look at it.

(*Chord, fanfare.* GEORGE *makes a grand entrance with* MARIE *and* ELAINE. *Applause from guests.* GEORGE *and* MARIE *move toward the painting. Lights come down on* GEORGE, *who sings.*)

GEORGE:
All right, George.
As long as it's your night, George . . .
You know what's in the room, George:

Another Chromolume, George.
It's time to get to work . . .

(*Music continues under.*)

MARIE: George, look. All these lovely people in front of our painting.

GREENBERG (*Coming up to* GEORGE): George, I want you to meet one of our board members.

(*He steers* GEORGE *over to* BILLY *and* HARRIET.)

This is Harriet Pawling.

HARRIET: What a pleasure. And this is my friend, Billy Webster.

BILLY: How do you do.

GREENBERG: Well, I'll just leave you three to chat.

(*He exits.*)

BILLY: Harriet was so impressed by your presentation.

HARRIET: This is the third piece of yours I've seen. They are getting so large!

BILLY: What heading does your work fall under?

GEORGE: Most people think of it as sculpture.

BILLY: Sculpture . . .

GEORGE: Actually, I think of myself as an inventor as well as a sculptor.

BILLY: It's so unconventional for sculpture.

(*Lights down on* GEORGE.)

GEORGE
(*To audience and himself, sings*):
Say "cheese," George,
And put them at their ease, George.
You're up on the trapeze, George.
Machines don't grow on trees, George.
Start putting it together . . .

(*Lights up.*)

HARRIET: I bet your great-grandfather would be very proud!

(*They are joined by MARIE and ELAINE, who have been nearby and overheard the conversation.*)

MARIE: Yes. He would have loved this evening.

BILLY: How do you know?

MARIE: I just know. I'm like that.

HARRIET: I'm Harriet Pawling.

BILLY: Billy Webster.

MARIE: How do you do. This is Elaine—George's former wife.

ELAINE (*Embarrassed*): Hello.

MARIE: Elaine is such a darling, I will always think of her as my granddaughter. I am so happy that these children have remained close. Isn't that nice?

BILLY: Yes. Harriet has just gone through a rather messy divorce—

HARRIET: Bill!

(*Awkward pause.*)

What a fascinating family you have!

MARIE: Many people say that. George and I are going back to France next month to visit the island where the painting was made, and George is going to bring the Lomochrome.

(*Music.*)

GEORGE: Chromolume. I've been invited by the government to do a presentation of the machine on the island.

MARIE: George has never been to France.

GEORGE (*Front, sings*):
    Art isn't easy—

(*He raises a cutout of himself in front of BILLY and HARRIET and comes downstage.*)

Even when you're hot.

BILLY (*To cutout*): Are these inventions of yours one of a kind?

GEORGE:
Advancing art is easy—

(*To* BILLY, *but front.*)

Yes.
Financing it is not.

MARIE: They take a year to make.

GEORGE (*Front*):
A vision's just a vision
If it's only in your head.

MARIE: The minute he finishes one, he starts raising money for the next.

GEORGE:
If no one gets to see it,
It's as good as dead.

MARIE: Work. Work. Work.

GEORGE:
It has to come to light!

(*Music continues under.* GEORGE *speaks as if to* BILLY *and* HARRIET, *but away from them, and front.*)

I put the names of my contributors on the side of each machine.

ELAINE: Some very impressive people!

HARRIET: Well, we must speak further. My family has a foundation and we are always looking for new projects.

GEORGE (*Front, sings*):
Bit by bit,
Putting it together . . .

MARIE: Family—it's all you really have.

GEORGE:
Piece by piece—
Only way to make a work of art.
Every moment makes a contribution,
Every little detail plays a part.
Having just the vision's no solution,
Everything depends on execution:
Putting it together—
That's what counts.

HARRIET (*To cutout*): Actually, the board of the foundation is meeting next
week . . .

GEORGE:
Ounce by ounce
Putting it together . . .

HARRIET: You'll come to lunch.

GEORGE:
Small amounts,
Adding up to make a work of art.
First of all, you need a good foundation,
Otherwise it's risky from the start.
Takes a little cocktail conversation,
But without the proper preparation,
Having just the vision's no solution,
Everything depends on execution.

The art of making art
Is putting it together
Bit by bit . . .

(*The cutout remains, as* BILLY *and* HARRIET *talk to it;* GEORGE,
working away, is cornered by CHARLES REDMOND. *Music continues
under.*)

REDMOND: We have been hearing about you for some time. We haven't
met. Charles Redmond. County Museum of Texas.

GEORGE: Nice to meet you.

REDMOND: Your work is just tremendous.

GEORGE: Thank you.

REDMOND: I don't mean to bring business up during a social occasion, but I wanted you to know we're in the process of giving out some very sizable commissions—

GREENBERG: You're not going to steal him away, are you?

(GEORGE *signals and another cutout of himself slides in from the wings. He leaves his drink in its hand, then steps forward.*)

GEORGE:
Link by link,
Making the connections . . .
Drink by drink,
Fixing and perfecting the design.
Adding just a dab of politician
(Always knowing where to draw the line),
Lining up the funds but in addition
Lining up a prominent commission,
Otherwise your perfect composition
Isn't going to get much exhibition.

Art isn't easy.
Every minor detail
Is a major decision.
How to keep things in scale,
Have to hold to your vision—

(*Pauses for a split second.*)

Every time I start to feel defensive,
I remember lasers are expensive.
What's a little cocktail conversation
If it's going to get you your foundation,
Leading to a prominent commission
And an exhibition in addition?

(*The guests promenade briefly, working the room, then sing.*)

ALL (*Except* MARIE):
Art isn't easy—

ALEX *and* **BETTY**:
Trying to make connections—

ALL:
Who understands it—?

HARRIET *and* **BILLY**:
Difficult to evaluate—

ALL:
Art isn't easy—

GREENBERG *and* **REDMOND**:
Trying to form collections—

ALL:
Always in transit—

NAOMI (*To whoever will listen*):
And then when you have to collaborate—!

ALL:
Art isn't easy,
Any way you look at it . . .

(*Chord. Cocktail piano. During the above,* BLAIR DANIELS, *an art critic, has entered.* GEORGE *is approached by* LEE RANDOLPH *with* MARIE.)

MARIE: George, you have to meet Mr. Randolph!

RANDOLPH: Hello! Lee Randolph. I handle the public relations for the museum.

GEORGE: How do you do.

(NAOMI *joins them.*)

NAOMI: There you are, George! Hi, Marie.

(*To* RANDOLPH.)

Naomi Eisen.

RANDOLPH: Delighted. You kids made quite a stir tonight.

NAOMI: You see, George—that electrical foul-up didn't hurt our reception.

RANDOLPH: There's a lot of opportunity for some nice press here.

(GEORGE *gestures; a third cutout of himself rises in front of* NAOMI *and* RANDOLPH. GEORGE *steps forward and sings.*)

GEORGE:
Dot by dot,
Building up the image.

(*Flash.* PHOTOGRAPHER *starts taking pictures of the cutout.*)

Shot by shot,
Keeping at a distance doesn't pay.
Still, if you remember your objective,
Not give all your privacy away—

(*Flash. Beat; he glances at the first cutout.*)

A little bit of hype can be effective,
Long as you can keep it in perspective.
After all, without some recognition
No one's going to give you a commission,

Which will cause a crack in the foundation.
You'll have wasted all that conversation.

(*Music stops suddenly as* DENNIS *comes over, disheveled and apologetic.* DENNIS *is something of a nerd.*)

DENNIS: I am really sorry, George.

(*Cocktail music.*)

I spoke with Naomi in great detail about how much electricity her synthesizer was going to use—I computed the exact voltage—

GEORGE: Dennis! It's okay.

DENNIS: The laser was beautiful, George.

GEORGE: It was, wasn't it? Now go get yourself a drink, Dennis. Mingle.

DENNIS: George. I have one more thing I wanted to talk to you about. I was going to wait—no, I'll wait—

GEORGE: What?

DENNIS: I'm quitting.

(*Music stops suddenly.*)

GEORGE: Quitting?

DENNIS: I'm going back to NASA. There is just too much pressure in this line of work.

GEORGE: Dennis, don't make any rash decisions. Relax, sleep on it, and we'll talk about it tomorrow.

DENNIS: Okay, George.

GEORGE (*Front, sings, music under*):
Art isn't easy . . .

(ALEX *and* BETTY *approach.*)

BETTY: Hey, it's the brains.

GEORGE:
Even if you're smart . . .

ALEX: Little technical screw-up tonight, Dennis?

(DENNIS *exits.*)

GEORGE:
You think it's all together,
And something falls apart . . .

(*Music continues under.*)

BETTY: I love the new machine, George.

GEORGE: Thanks. That means a lot to me.

ALEX: We saw you talking to Redmond from Texas.

GEORGE: Yeah.

BETTY: Did you get one of the commissions?

GEORGE: We talked about it. You guys?

ALEX: Her. My stuff is a little too inaccessible.

GEORGE: I love your work, Alex. I'll put in a good word for you.

ALEX (*Defensive*): He knows my work!

GEORGE (*Uncomfortable*): It's all politics, Alex. Maybe if you just lightened up once in a while.

BETTY (*Mollifying*): Texas would be fun!

(GEORGE *beckons and a fourth cutout slides in and heads toward* BETTY *and* ALEX.)

GEORGE (*Front, sings*):
Art isn't easy.

(*Gesturing toward* ALEX.)

Overnight you're a trend,
You're the right combination—

(*Behind him, cutout #1 begins sinking slowly into the floor.*)

Then the trend's at an end,
You're suddenly last year's sensation . . .

(*Notices the cutout, goes to raise it during the following.*)

So you should support the competition,
Try to set aside your own ambition,
Even while you jockey for position—

(*Cutout #3 has slid in too far, and* BETTY *and* ALEX *have turned away;* GEORGE, *unflustered, spins it back around toward* BETTY *and* ALEX, *who resume talking to it.*)

If you feel a sense of coalition,
Then you never really stand alone.
If you want your work to reach fruition,
What you need's a link with your tradition,
And of course a prominent commission,

(*Cutout #1 starts to sink again;* GEORGE *hastens to fix it.*)

Plus a little formal recognition,
So that you can go on exhibit—

(*Getting flustered.*)

So that your work can go on exhibition—

(*Loud promenade, very brief, during which cutout #1 starts to go again, but stops just as GEORGE reaches it. As he does so, BLAIR DANIELS comes up to him. Chords under.*)

BLAIR: There's the man of the hour.

GEORGE: Blair. Hello. I just read your piece on Neo-Expressionism—

BLAIR: Just what the world needs—another piece on Neo-Expressionism.

GEORGE: Well, I enjoyed it.

(*Chords continue under, irregularly.*)

BLAIR: Good for you! Now, I had no idea you might be related to
      nineteenth-century France.

GEORGE: It's a cloudy ancestral line at best.

BLAIR: I'm dying to meet your grandmother. It was fun seeing the two of
      you onstage with your invention. It added a certain humanity to the
      proceedings.

GEORGE: Humanity?

BLAIR: George. Chromolume Number Seven?

GEORGE (*Sings to himself*):
      Be nice, George . . .

(*Gestures for a cutout; it doesn't rise.*)

BLAIR: I was hoping it would be a series of three—four at the most.

GEORGE:
      You have to pay a price, George . . .

(*Gestures again; nothing.*)

BLAIR: We have been there before, you know.

GEORGE: You never suffer from a shortage of opinions, do you, Blair?

BLAIR: You never minded my opinions when they were in your favor!

BLAIR: I have touted your work from the beginning, you know that. You were really on to something with these light machines—once. Now they're just becoming more and more about less and less.	GEORGE: They like to give Advice, George—

(Gestures offstage; nothing.)

Don't think about it
Twice, George . . .

(Gestures again; nothing.)

GEORGE: I disagree.

(Music. BLAIR turns briefly away from him, rummaging through her purse for a cigarette. GEORGE takes advantage of this to rush offstage and bring on cutout #5, which he sets up in front of her during the following.)

BLAIR: Don't get me wrong. You're a talented guy. If you weren't, I wouldn't waste our time with my opinions. I think you are capable of far more. Not that you couldn't succeed by doing Chromolume after Chromolume—but there are new discoveries to be made, George.

(She holds up her cigarette and waits for a light from the cutout.)

GEORGE
(Increasingly upset):
Be new, George.
They tell you till they're blue, George:
You're new or else you're through, George,
And even if it's true, George—
You do what you can do . . .

(Wandering among cutouts, checking them.)

Bit by bit,
Putting it together.
Piece by piece,
Working out the vision night and day.

All it takes is time and perseverance,
With a little luck along the way,
Putting in a personal appearance.
Gathering supporters and adherents . . .

(*Music stops.* BLAIR, *getting impatient for her light, leaves the cutout to join another group.* GEORGE *notices. Beat.*)

HARRIET (*To* BILLY):
. . . But he combines all these different trends . . .

(*Beat. The cutout with* HARRIET *and* BILLY *falters.*)

GEORGE
(*Moving to it smoothly as music resumes*):
Mapping out the right configuration,

(*Adjusting it.*)

Starting with a suitable foundation . . .

BETTY:
. . . He's an original . . .

ALEX:
. . . Was . . .

(*During the following, all the cutouts falter sporadically, causing* GEORGE *to move more and more rapidly among them.*)

GEORGE:
Lining up a prominent commission—
And an exhibition in addition—
Here a little dab of politician—
There a little touch of publication—
Till you have a balanced composition—
Everything depends on preparation—
Even if you do have the suspicion
That it's taking all your concentration—

(*Simultaneously, with* GEORGE.)

BETTY:
I like those images.

ALEX:

Some.

BETTY:

They're just his personal response.

ALEX:

To what?

BETTY:

The painting!

ALEX:

Bullshit. Anyway the painting's overrated . . .

BETTY:

Overrated? It's a masterpiece!

ALEX:

A masterpiece? Historically important, maybe—

BETTY:

Oh, now you're judging Seurat, are you?

ALEX:

All it is is pleasant, just like George's work.

BETTY:

It's just your jealousy of George's work.

ALEX:

No nuance, no resonance, no relevance—

BETTY:

There's nuance and there's resonance, there's relevance—

ALEX:

There's not much point in arguing.
Besides, it's all promotion, but then—

BETTY:

There's not much point in arguing.
You say it's all promotion, but then—

GREENBERG:

It's only new, though, for now,

And yesterday's forgotten.
Today it's all a matter of promotion,
But then—

REDMOND:

Nouveau.
And yesterday's forgotten
And you can't tell good from rotten
And today it's all a matter of promotion,
But then—

HARRIET:

You can't divide art today.
Go with it!
What will they think of next?

BILLY:

I'm not surprised.
What will they think of next?

OTHERS:

Most art today
Is a matter of promotion, but then—

GEORGE:	**ALL:**
The art of making art	That is the state of the art—
Is putting it together—	And art isn't easy.
Bit by bit—	
Link by link—	
Drink by drink—	
Mink by mink—	
And that	
Is the state	
Of the	

ALL:

Art!

(GEORGE *frames the successfully completed picture of the guests and cutouts with his hands, as at the end of Act I. As soon as he exits, however, the cutouts collapse and disappear.* MARIE *is over at the painting. She is joined by* HARRIET *and* BILLY.)

GREENBERG: Ladies and gentlemen, dinner is served.

(*Most of the party exits.*)

HARRIET (*To* MARIE): Excuse me, could you please tell me: What is that square form up there?

BLAIR (*Who has been standing nearby*): That is a baby carriage.

MARIE: Who told you that?!

BLAIR: I'm sorry to butt in. I'm Blair Daniels and I've been waiting for the opportunity to tell you how much I enjoyed seeing you onstage.

MARIE: Why, thank you. But, my dear, that is not a baby carriage. That is Louis's waffle stove.

BLAIR: Waffle stove? I've read all there is to read about this work, and there's never been any mention of a waffle stove!

MARIE (*Indicating red book*): I have a book, too. My mother's. It is a family legacy, as is this painting. And my mother often spoke of Louis's waffle stove!

BLAIR: Louis. Yes, you mentioned him in your presentation.

(GEORGE *reenters; stays off to one side.*)

MARIE: Family. You know, it is all you really have.

BLAIR: You said that before.

MARIE: I say it often.

HARRIET: Excuse us.

(HARRIET *and* BILLY *exit.*)

MARIE: You know, Miss Daniels, there are only two worthwhile things to leave behind when you depart this world: children and art. Isn't that correct?

BLAIR: I never quite thought of it that way.

(ELAINE *joins them.*)

MARIE: Do you know Elaine?

BLAIR: No. I don't believe we've met. Blair Daniels.

ELAINE: I've heard a lot about you.

BLAIR: Oh, yes.

MARIE: Elaine and George were married once. I was so excited. I thought *they* might have a child. George and I are the only ones left, I'm afraid.

(*Whispers.*)

I want George to have a child—continue the line. You can understand that, can't you, Elaine?

ELAINE: Of course.

MARIE: Are you married, Miss Daniels?

BLAIR: Awfully nice to have met you.

(*She shakes* MARIE's *hand and exits.*)

MARIE: Elaine, fix my chair so I can see Mama.

(*She does.* ELAINE *crosses to* GEORGE.)

ELAINE: George. I think Marie is a little too tired for the party. She seems to be slipping a bit.

GEORGE: I better take her back to the hotel.

ELAINE: I'll take her back. You stay.

GEORGE: Nah, it's a perfect excuse for me to leave early.

ELAINE: George. Don't be silly! You're the toast of the party. You should feel wonderful.

GEORGE (*Edgy*): Well, I don't feel wonderful.

ELAINE: Poor George. Well . . . tonight was a wonderful experience for Marie. I don't remember seeing her so happy. It was very good of you to include her.

GEORGE: She is something, isn't she?

ELAINE: Yes, she is . . .

(ELAINE *begins to leave;* GEORGE *stops her; they embrace. Then she exits. The preceding has been underscored with the chords from Act I.* MARIE *has been staring up at the painting.*)

MARIE (*Sings*):
You would have liked him,
Mama, you would.
Mama, he makes things—
Mama, they're good.
Just as you said from the start:
Children and art . . .

(*Starts nodding off.*)

Children and art . . .

(*Awakens with a start.*)

He should be happy—
Mama, he's blue.
What do I do?

You should have seen it,
It was a sight!
Mama, I mean it—
All color and light—!
I don't understand what it was,
But, Mama, the things that he does:
They twinkle and shimmer and buzz—
You would have liked them . . .

(*Losing her train of thought.*)

It . . .
Him . . .

(*Music continues, speaks.*)

Henry . . . Henry? . . . Henry . . .

GEORGE (*Coming over*): It's George, Grandmother.

MARIE: Of course it is. I thought you were your father for a moment.

(*Indicating painting.*)

Did I tell you who that was?

GEORGE: Of course. That is your mother.

MARIE: That is correct.

(*Sings.*)

> Isn't she beautiful?
> There she is—

(*Pointing to different figures.*)

> There she is, there she is, there she is—
> Mama is everywhere,
> He must have loved her so much . . .

GEORGE: Is she really in all those places, Marie?

> MARIE:
>
> This is our family—
> This is the lot.
> After I go, this is
> All that you've got, honey—

GEORGE: Now, let's not have this discussion—

> MARIE
> (*Before he can protest further*):
> Wasn't she beautiful, though?
>
> You would have liked her.
> Mama did things
> No one had done.
> Mama was funny,
> Mama was fun,
> Mama spent money
> When she had none.
>
> Mama said, "Honey,
> Mustn't be blue.
> It's not so much do what you like
> As it is that you like what you do."
> Mama said, "Darling,
> Don't make such a drama.

A little less thinking,
A little more feeling—"

GEORGE: Please don't start—

MARIE:
I'm just quoting Mama . . .

(*Changing the subject, indicates* LOUISE.)

The child is so sweet . . .

(*Indicating the* CELESTES *at center.*)

And the girls are so rapturous . . .
Isn't it lovely how artists can capture us?

GEORGE: Yes, it is, Marie.

MARIE:
You would have liked her—
Honey, I'm wrong.
You would have loved her.

Mama enjoyed things.
Mama was smart.
See how she shimmers—
I mean from the heart.

(ELAINE *enters and stands off to the side.*)

I know, honey, you don't agree.

(*Indicates painting.*)

But this is our family tree.
Just wait till we're there, and you'll see—
Listen to me . . .

(*Drifting off.*)

Mama was smart . . .
Listen to Mama . . .
Children and art . . .
Children and art . . .

(*She falls asleep and* ELAINE *crosses to her and wheels her off. As they go:*)

Goodbye, Mama.

(GEORGE *looks at the painting for a moment.*)

GEORGE: Connect, George. Connect . . .

(GEORGE *exits; the painting flies out.*)

(*The island is once again revealed, though barely recognizable, as the trees have been replaced by high-rise buildings. The only tree still visible is the one in front of which the* OLD LADY *and* NURSE *sat.* DENNIS *kneels, studying his blueprints.* GEORGE *enters, camera in hand.*)

GEORGE: Are you certain this is the best place for the Chromolume?

DENNIS: George, this is the largest clearing on La Grande Jatte.

GEORGE: Where's the still?

DENNIS: It has been built and should arrive tomorrow morning a few hours before the Chromolume. I wanted it here today, but they don't make deliveries on Sunday.

GEORGE: And fresh water for the cooling system?

DENNIS: We can draw it from the Seine. As for the electricity—

GEORGE: Did you see this tree?

DENNIS: No.

GEORGE: It could be the one in the painting.

DENNIS: Yes. It could.

(GEORGE *hands* DENNIS *the camera and goes to the tree.* DENNIS *takes a picture of him in front of it.*)

GEORGE: At least something is recognizable . . . Now, about the electricity?

DENNIS: The wind generator's over there.

GEORGE: You have been efficient as always.

DENNIS: Thank you.

GEORGE: I will miss working with you, Dennis.

DENNIS: Well, I can recommend some very capable people to help you with the Texas commission.

GEORGE: I turned it down.

DENNIS: What?

GEORGE: Dennis, why are you quitting?

DENNIS: I told you, I want—

GEORGE: I know what you told me! Why are you really leaving?

DENNIS: George. I love the Chromolumes. But I've helped you build the last five, and now I want to do something different.

GEORGE: I wish you had told me that in the first place.

DENNIS: I'm sorry.

GEORGE: Why do you think I turned down the commission? I don't want to do the same things over and over again, either.

DENNIS: There are other things you could do.

GEORGE: I know that. I just want to do something I care about.

(*Beat.* GEORGE *puts camera in pocket and pulls out* DOT's *red book.*)

DENNIS: I see you brought the red book.

GEORGE: Since Marie has died, I thought I would at least bring something of hers along.

DENNIS: Marie really wanted to make this trip.

GEORGE: I know.

DENNIS: I hope you don't mind, but I took a look at the book. It's very interesting.

GEORGE: It's just a grammar book, Dennis.

DENNIS (*Imploring*): Not that part. The notes in the back.

(GEORGE *leafs through it to the back.*)

Well, we just have to wait for it to get dark. I'm not certain about the ambient light.

GEORGE: You go, Dennis. I'd like to be alone, actually.

DENNIS: Are you sure?

GEORGE: Yeah. I'll see you back at the hotel.

(*He sits on the ground.*)

DENNIS (*Begins to exit*): George. I look forward to seeing what you come up with next.

GEORGE (*Smiling*): You're not the only one, Dennis.

(DENNIS *exits. Music.* GEORGE *sings, leafing through the book, reading.*)

"Charles has a book . . ."

(*Turns a page.*)

"Charles shows them his crayons . . ."

(*Turns back a few pages.*)

"Marie has the ball of Charles . . ."

(*Turns the book to read in the margin.*)

"Good for Marie . . ."

(*Smiles at the coincidence of the name, turns a page.*)

"Charles misses his ball . . ."

(*Looks up.*)

George misses Marie . . .
George misses a lot . . .
George is alone.

George looks around.
He sees the park.
It is depressing.
George looks ahead.

George sees the dark.
George is afraid.
Where are the people
Out strolling on Sunday?

George looks within:
George is adrift.
George goes by guessing.
George looks behind:
He had a gift.
When did it fade?
You wanted people out
Strolling on Sunday—
Sorry, Marie . . .

(Looks again at the name in the book.)

See George remember how George used to be,
Stretching his vision in every direction.
See George attempting to see a connection
When all he can see
Is maybe a tree—

(Humorously.)

The family tree—
Sorry, Marie . . .
George is afraid.
George sees the park.
George sees it dying.
George too may fade,
Leaving no mark,
Just passing through.
Just like the people
Out strolling on Sunday . . .

George looks around.
George is alone.
No use denying
George is aground.
George has outgrown
What he can do.

George would have liked to see
People out strolling on Sunday . . .

(DOT *appears.* GEORGE *looks up and discovers her. He stands.*)

DOT: I almost did not recognize you without your beard. You have my
book.

GEORGE: Your book?

DOT: Yes.

GEORGE: It is a little difficult to understand.

DOT: Well, I was teaching myself. My writing got much better. I worked
very hard. I made certain that Marie learned right away.

GEORGE (*Looks at the book*): Marie . . .

DOT: It is good to see you. Not that I ever forgot you, George. You gave me
so much.

GEORGE: What did I give you?

DOT: Oh, many things. You taught me about concentration. At first I
thought that meant just being still, but I was to understand it meant
much more. You meant to tell me to be where I was—not some place in
the past or future. I worried too much about tomorrow. I thought the
world could be perfect. I was wrong.

GEORGE: What else?

DOT: Oh, enough about me. What about you? Are you working on
something new?

GEORGE: No. I am not working on anything new.

(*Music begins.*)

DOT: That is not like you, George.

GEORGE (*Sings*):
I've nothing to say.

DOT: You have many things . . .

GEORGE:
Well, nothing that's not been said.

DOT (*Sings*):
Said by you, though, George . . .

GEORGE:
I do not know where to go.

DOT:
And nor did I.

GEORGE:
I want to make things that count,
Things that will be new . . .

DOT (*Overlapping*):
I did what I had to do:

GEORGE (*Overlapping*):
What am I to do?

DOT:
Move on.

Stop worrying where you're going—
Move on.
If you can know where you're going,
You've gone.
Just keep moving on.

I chose, and my world was shaken—
So what?
The choice may have been mistaken,
The choosing was not.
You have to move on.

Look at what you want.
Not at where you are,
Not at what you'll be.
Look at all the things you've done for me:
Opened up my eyes,
Taught me how to see,
Notice every tree—

GEORGE:

. . . Notice every tree . . .

DOT:

Understand the light—

GEORGE:

. . . Understand the light . . .

DOT:

Concentrate on now—

GEORGE:

I want to move on.
I want to explore the light.
I want to know how to get through,
Through to something new,
Something of my own—

GEORGE *and* **DOT:**

Move on.
Move on.

DOT:

Stop worrying if your vision
Is new.
Let others make that decision—
They usually do.
You keep moving on.

(*Simultaneously.*)

DOT:	**GEORGE**
Look at what you've done,	(*Looking around*):
Then at what you want,	. . . Something in the light,
Not at where you are,	Something in the sky,
What you'll be.	In the grass,
Look at all the things	Up behind the trees . . .
You gave to me.	Things I hadn't looked at
Let me give to you	Till now:
Something in return.	Flower on your hat.
I would be so pleased.	And your smile.

GEORGE:
And the color of your hair.
And the way you catch the light . . .
And the care . . .
And the feeling . . .
And the life
Moving on . . .

DOT:
We've always belonged
Together!

GEORGE *and* **DOT:**
We will always belong
Together!

DOT:
Just keep moving on.

Anything you do,
Let it come from you.
Then it will be new.
Give us more to see . . .

(*Speaks.*)

You never cared what anyone thought. That upset me at the time because I wanted you to care what *I* thought.

GEORGE: I'm sure that I did.

DOT: I am sure that you did, too.

GEORGE: Dot.

(*He takes the book to her.*)

Why did you write these words?

DOT: They are your words, George. The ones you muttered so often when you worked.

GEORGE (*Reads slowly*):

"Order."

(*Chord.* OLD LADY *enters.*)

OLD LADY: George. Is that you?

(GEORGE *turns to her. He looks back to* DOT, *who smiles, then back to the* OLD LADY.)

GEORGE: Yes.

OLD LADY: Tell me! Is this place as you expected it?

GEORGE: What?

OLD LADY: The park, of course.

GEORGE: Somewhat.

OLD LADY: Go on.

GEORGE: Well, the greens are a little darker. The sky a little grayer. Mud tones in the water.

OLD LADY (*Disappointed*): Well, yes, I suppose—

GEORGE: But the air is rich and full of light.

OLD LADY: Good.

(*Chord. As the* OLD LADY *leaves,* GEORGE *reads the next word:*)

GEORGE: "Design."

> (*Music begins: "Sunday." The downstage right building begins to rise. The* CELESTES *appear and begin to cross the stage.*)
>
> "Tension."

(*Two buildings rise stage right and left. More characters from the painting appear and begin to promenade.*)

> "Composition."

(*Building rises.*)

> "Balance."

(*Buildings rise. The stage is filled by the characters from the painting.*)

> "Light."

(*The large building in the back rises.*)

Dot. I cannot read this word.

DOT: "Harmony."

ALL (*Sing*):
Sunday
By the blue
Purple yellow red water
On the green
Purple yellow red grass,
As we pass
Through arrangements of
    shadows
Towards the verticals of trees
Forever

(*All bow to* GEORGE.)

By the blue
Purple yellow red water
On the green
Orange violet mass
Of the grass . . .

GEORGE

(*Reading again, struggling with the
    words*):

"So much love in his words

. . . forever with his colors

. . . how George looks

. . . he can look forever

. . . what does he see?

. . . his eyes so dark and shiny

. . . so careful

. . . so exact . . ."

(DOT *takes* GEORGE *by the arm
    and turns him to the group.*)

DOT:
In our perfect park . . .

GEORGE:
Made of flecks of light
And dark . . .

ALL (*Except* GEORGE *and* DOT):
And parasols . . .
People strolling through the trees
Of a small suburban park
On an island in the river
On an ordinary Sunday . . .

(*The* COMPANY *has settled generally in the area that they occupy in the
painting.*)

Sunday . . .

(*All begin to leave very slowly, except* DOT, *who remains downstage with* GEORGE.)

Sunday . . .

(DOT *leaves* GEORGE, *crossing upstage into the park; she turns toward* GEORGE. *The white canvas drop descends.*)

GEORGE (*Reading from the book*): "White. A blank page or canvas. His favorite. So many possibilities . . ."

(*He looks up and sees* DOT *disappearing behind the white canvas. Lights fade to black.*)

Acknowledgments

Jonathan Galassi thought I had a memoir in me and then guided me along the way with great precision and camaraderie. His very able associates Katharine Liptak and Gretchen Achilles then helped me to put it together.

Stephen Sondheim as always gave me his time, love, and support—without him there would have never been a show, let alone a book about it.

I remain very grateful for Rick Pappas, our wise protector; and Steve Clar and Peter E. Jones, who knew where everything I needed was buried.

I am indebted to all those who so graciously went on the record about their experience birthing the musical *Sunday in the Park with George*.

And thanks to:

Megan Loughran, who kept me organized and generally sane, and Laura Ross, who assured me that it was all worth the effort.

Tiffany Nixon, who led the search for all things "Sunday"; Melissa Barton and Anne Marie Menta, who continued the hunt at the Beinecke Library; and Mark Swartz and Sylvia Wang, who brought me over the finish line at the Shubert Archive.

Those who helped me get my hands on all the beautiful Seurat works that grace this book: Gloria Groom, Jena Carvana, and Devon Lee Pyle-Vowles at the Art Institute of Chicago; and for the invaluable photo and costume archives of the New York Public Library, Tom Lisanti and Patrick Hoffman; and for the additional costume archives, Liz Paris at the McNay Art Museum.

And all the wonderful supporting players who made the lifting ever so lighter:

Josh Brown, Ted Chapin, Douglas Colby, Mariana Cook, Scott Farthing, Hans Kraus, Miles Kreuger, Tim Sanford, Patty Saccente, Ryan Sears, and Ralph Sevrush.

And as always, Sarah Kernochan, champion extraordinaire, and Phoebe Lapine, who wasn't yet around to see this production, but will now know in more detail something about it and me.

JL

Illustration Credits

Page 227   Courtesy of James Lapine

Page 235   Courtesy of Stephen Sondheim

Page 237   Courtesy of Stephen Sondheim

Page 239   Courtesy of Stephen Sondheim

Page 240   Martha Swope / © Billy Rose Theatre Division, The New York Public Library for the Performing Arts

Page 247   Courtesy of James Lapine

Page 249   Courtesy of James Lapine

Page 250   Courtesy of James Lapine

Page 252   Courtesy of James Lapine

Page 254   Courtesy of James Lapine

Page 255   Sara Krulwich / Archive Photos via Getty Images

Page 256   Jeff Sprang / *Mansfield News Journal*